POSTCARD HISTORY SERIES

Washington and Benton Counties

Arkansas

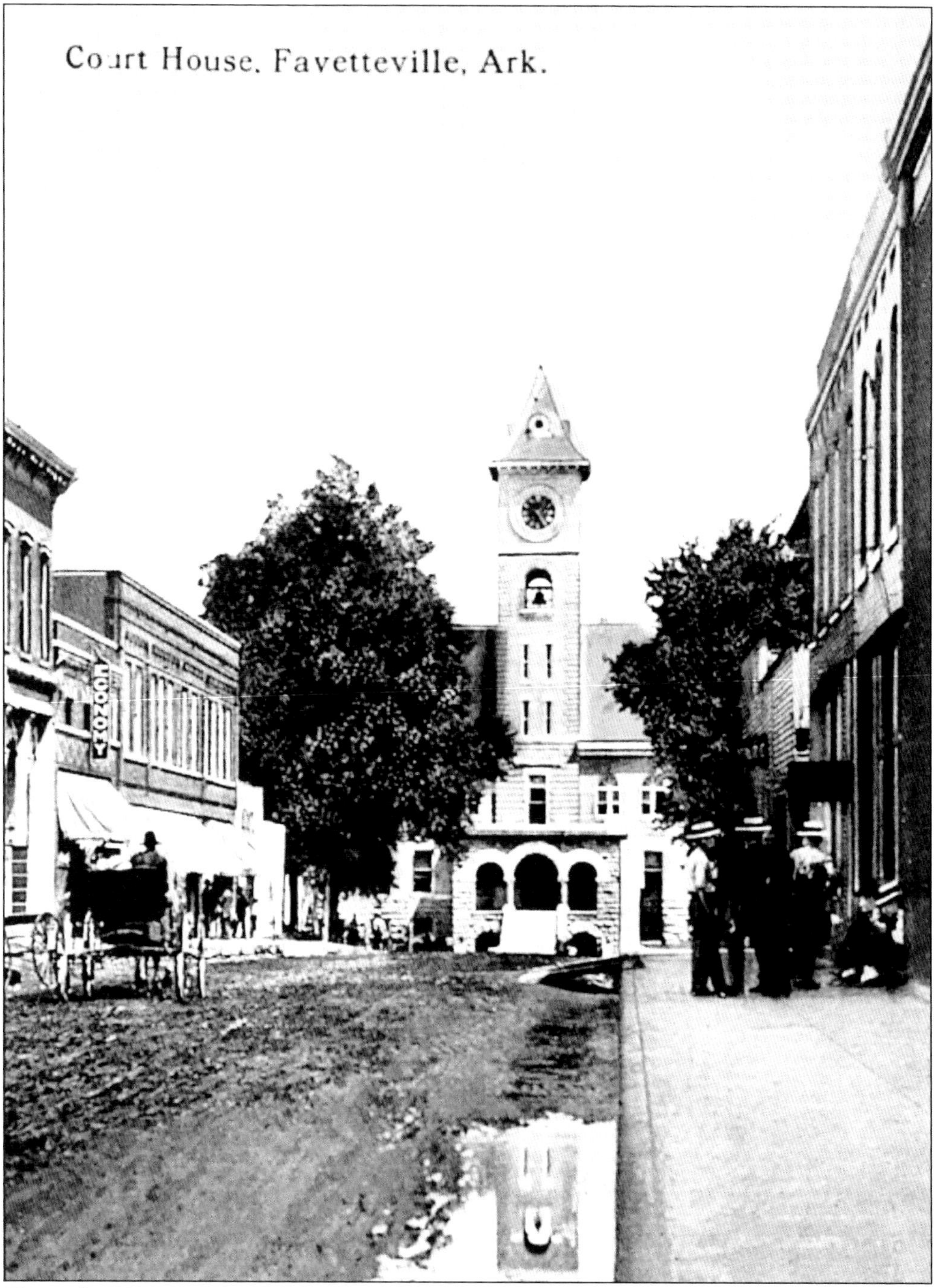

The Italian Renaissance-style Washington County Courthouse, erected in 1904, still serves today and is listed on the National Register of Historic Places. The building was designed by noted architect Charles Thompson, and the contractor was George Donaghey, whose employees erected it at a cost of $125,000. Donaghey would be elected governor in 1908. This postcard view looks down East Center Street in Fayetteville, capturing the courthouse reflection in the puddle of a recent rain. (c. 1907.)

POSTCARD HISTORY SERIES

Washington and Benton Counties
Arkansas

Diane Hanley and Ray Hanley

ARCADIA
PUBLISHING

ISBN 978-0-7385-9705-8

Published by Arcadia Publishing
Charleston, South Carolina

Printed in the United States of America

Library of Congress Catalog Card Number: 98-87776

For all general information contact Arcadia Publishing at:
Telephone 843-853-2070
Fax 843-853-0044
E-mail sales@arcadiapublishing.com
For customer service and orders:
Toll-Free 1-888-313-2665

Visit us on the Internet at www.arcadiapublishing.com

To our daughters Rachel and Emily—whose lives may span much of the new century. May you find there many of the same simple pleasures depicted in the images in this book.

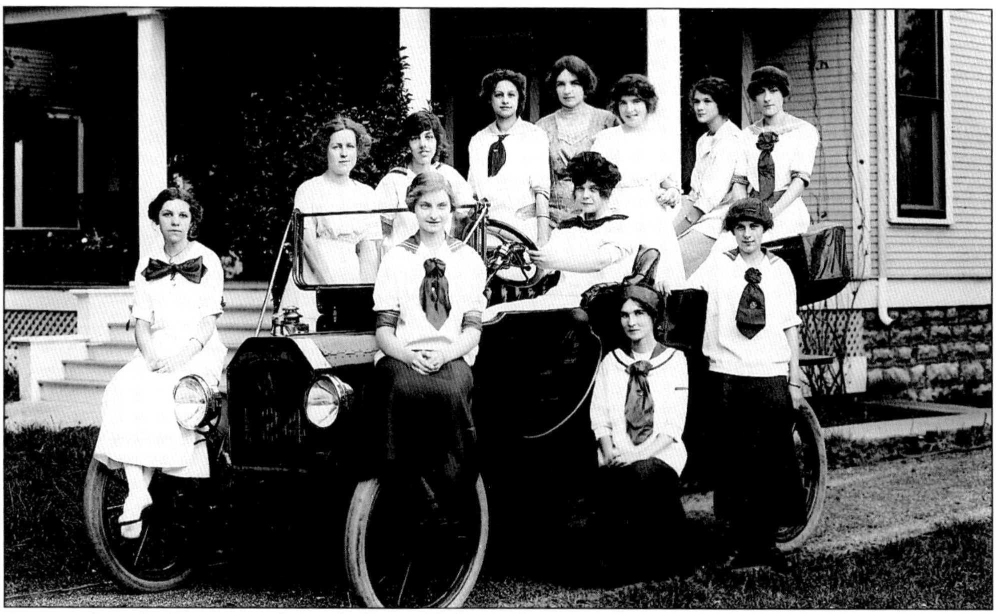

An unidentified group of similarly well-dressed young ladies posed on an automobile in Bentonville around 1915. Consider the world in which these young women came of age—during the World War I era in northwest Arkansas, in a time when this automobile would still have been a novelty.

Contents

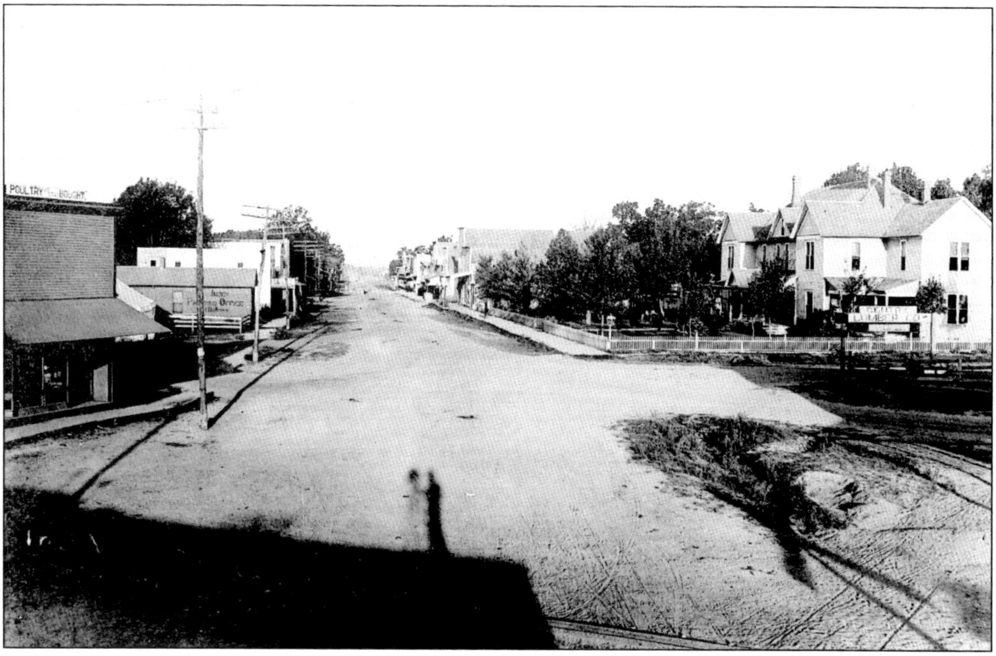

The photographers of northwestern Arkansas traveled to all the towns and backroad villages of the area, leaving the postcard historical legacy found in this book. One such photographer left his shadow on his work in the Benton County town of Gentry around 1905. The photographer stood with his tripod atop a building and focused down Main Street; his image was caught in the dust of the street by the sun at his back.

ACKNOWLEDGMENTS

The photographs in this book are almost all from the author's personal collection, but without the "stories behind the pictures" this book would not contain the history that we hope will be enjoyed by many. For many historical details we owe a debt of thanks to Bob Besom, director of Springdale's Shiloh Museum, and to his staff—Susan Young, Carolyn Reno, and Manon Wilson. Howard Brandes of the University of Arkansas Museum helped us trace the history of Albert Pike's school. From Benton County came the help of Allyn Lord of the Rogers Historical Museum, and Don Warden at the Siloam Springs Museum filled us in on historical details around his town. While we used dozens of books and periodicals to do research for this book, too many to list, we would be remiss if we did not thank J. Dickson Black, author of *History of Benton County*, published in 1975, and *Coin Harvey and His Monte Ne*, published in 1983. Mr. Black has devoted many years to researching and writing about the history of his adopted Benton County, and his books helped us a great deal with researching background on photographs. Lastly, we want to thank Lynn Ewbank at the Arkansas History Commission for tracking down a photo of Coin Harvey for this project.

INTRODUCTION

Tremendous changes have transformed the face of the nation and of Arkansas since the 20th century dawned. Perhaps nowhere in Arkansas is that transformation more evident than in the northwest corner of the state, in Washington and Benton Counties. At the turn of the century the region was remote, with no paved roads and an economy primarily devoted to agriculture. Aside from Fayetteville, with the University of Arkansas and its 600 students, the two counties were a collection of small towns, farms, and emerging resort areas, threaded together by a growing network of railroads that brought in people for business and pleasure.

In 1900, the combined population of Washington and Benton Counties was 65,000 people. Today the two counties comprise one of the nation's most rapidly growing metropolitan areas, with an estimated population of 275,000. The area is home to some of the nation's largest and most profitable corporations, with Wal-Mart's headquarters in Bentonville and Tyson Foods based in Springdale. An interstate highway linkage will reach the area in 1998, and, with the completion of a new airport later that same year, the area will join Little Rock as one of two locations in the state with major jet service. Sometimes visitors and residents fighting traffic along Business Route 71 might assume that the world has turned to a vast sea of fast food and franchised boxes, constituting the same business strip that seems to traverse most American cities today. Yet differences there are, as people continue to pour into the northwest Arkansas area, drawn by the state's lowest unemployment rate and a quality of life perceived as better than in many other regions. Over the past five years large numbers of Hispanic workers and their families have joined the migration into the area, often drawn to work in the huge poultry industry.

Visitors today (and there are thousands a year, for example, who come to call on Wal-Mart alone) will find ever declining reminders of the sleepy villages, quaint streets, farms, dusty rural roads, and winding streams which characterized the area earlier in the century. Fortunately, there is preserved a record of how daily life looked and how it gradually changed as the century advanced. The northwest Arkansas area was very popular with the producers of picture postcards, both on a commercial basis and for residents who often put their photographs onto postcard stock to mail to friends across the state and around the nation. The postcards that illustrate this book will give the reader a look at most of the communities in both counties, including such small villages as Lincoln, Gentry, and Maysville, and the settlements that would grow into the largest towns of Fayetteville, Springdale, Rogers, and Bentonville.

The first privately mailed postcard in the United States was likely published in 1861 by Philadelphia businessmen J.P. Charlton and H.L. Lipman. The cards had blank fronts for a message, and the back side was used only for the address. The cards were marketed as a means of rapid correspondence.

Commercial production of picture postcards in the United States began with the World's Columbian Exposition in Chicago in 1893. Little did the promoters of the great fair realize that they had helped set into motion what would become one of the nation's major hobbies—the collecting of picture postcards. Postcard collecting had become a widespread hobby in Europe by the turn of the century, and visitors returning to the United States from abroad took note, bringing the interest home with them. A reporter for the Hearst newspaper chain, Julian Ralph, came home from Europe in 1901 and did a piece for *Cosmopolitan* entitled, "The Postal-Card

Craze." Such articles helped fuel the nation's passion for collecting the cards, which enticed printers to turn them out by the millions. Thus was preserved an invaluable photographic legacy of the formative years of the 20th century, offering glimpses into daily life across America.

Early in the century most commercial postcards originated in Europe, usually in Germany, where the world's most advanced printing industry was found. Photographs were taken in places like Fayetteville, Arkansas, and then mailed to printers in Germany. The cards would be reproduced, often after being hand-colored, and shipped back to U.S. wholesalers and drugstores, which would then display the cards for sale in prominent racks. In Germany alone an estimated one million people were employed in the printing of postcards, for the demand was great. In 1912, for example, F.W. Woolworth released for sale through its 600-store chain several millions of postcards, to be sold at retail for a price of 10¢ a dozen.

U.S government tariffs were soon imposed on imported postcards, in order to give domestic printers a boost. Postcard production quickly escalated in this country, further fueling Americans' interest in collecting and giving it a more local flavor. *American Magazine* printed a parody in 1906 entitled "Postal Carditis and Some Allied Manias," which said much about the postcard era: "Postal carditis and allied collecting manias are working havoc among the inhabitants of the United States. The germs of these maladies, brought to this country in the baggage of tourists and immigrants, escaped quarantine regulations, and were propagated with amazing rapidity. There is now no hamlet so remote which has not succumbed to the ravages of the microbe postale universelle."

An indication of the passion for the collecting hobby was found in Ohio's *Columbus Dispatch* in 1906: "I wonder what will be the first thing they sight at the North Pole?—Why, Eskimos selling souvenir post cards, of course." The following year the *Woman's Home Companion* magazine depicted a woman asking, "Has this house all the modern improvements?" The answer—"everything . . . here's a special closet for postcards."

In 1906 it was reported by the *Post Card Dealer*, a trade journal, that the annual consumption of postcards in the United States was 770,500,000 cards. By 1913 the United States Postal Service reported handling 968,000,000 postcards, a celebrated event, for the postal service calculated that it was more profitable to handle the 1¢ postage stamped cards than regular letters. The year 1913 was probably the peak of the U.S. postcard era, for WW I soon led to changes in American life. The new interests that came with the post-war "Roaring Twenties" caused the card-collecting hobby to wane, though it never entirely disappeared. Fortunately, enough of the cards from the golden era of postcards have survived to fuel a renewed interest in the hobby as the 20th century draws to a close.

The cards in this book come from a collection of some 10,000 Arkansas cards gathered over the past 25 years. The first Arkansas book for Arcadia, by Steven and Ray Hanley, surveyed the Little Rock area, and has been followed by a collection on the Spa City of Hot Springs. It is our pleasure to present this postcard-based history of the beautiful northwest region of our home state.

One

WASHINGTON COUNTY

FAYETTEVILLE AND SPRINGDALE

Washington County was created in the Arkansas Territory in 1828, six years before statehood, from land that had been purchased under treaty with the Osage Indians in 1818. Because of its central location in the county, the settlement of Fayetteville was selected to be the county seat. Over the years, despite trying events (such as the burning of the town by retreating Confederates during the Civil War), Fayetteville has prospered and remains to this day the largest city in northwest Arkansas. Springdale, just to the north of Fayetteville, would become the second-largest city in a county otherwise comprised of small towns, farms, and the summer resort of Winslow in the southern part of the county.

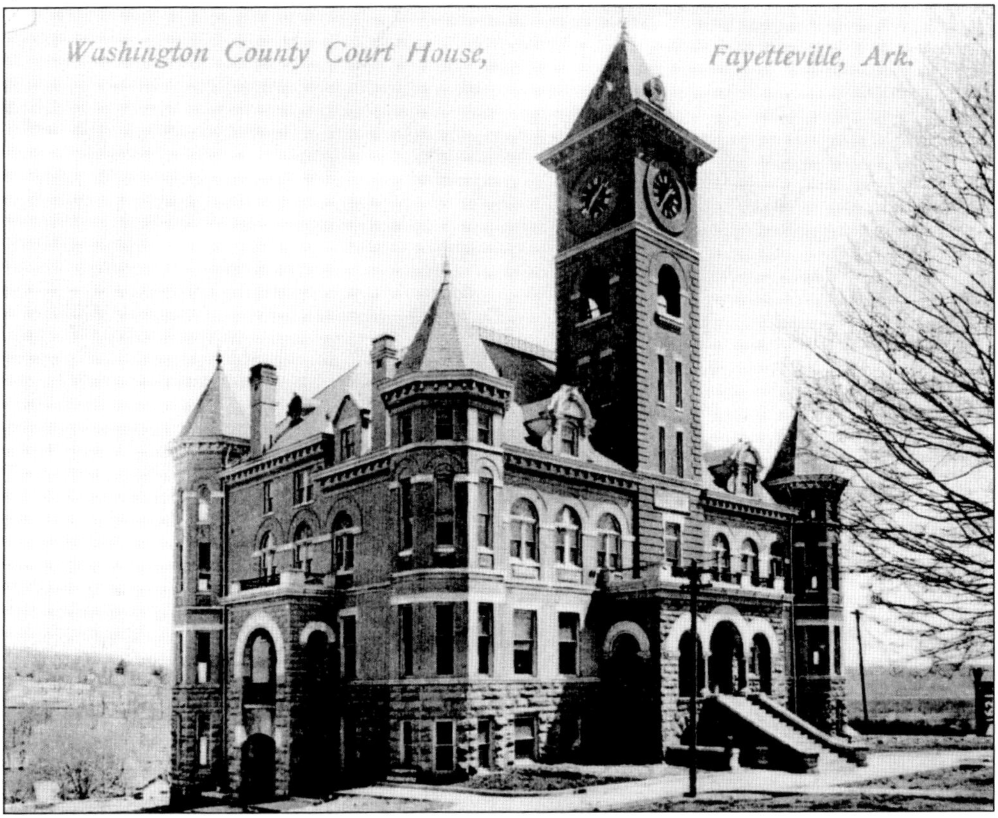

Growing Washington County erected its new courthouse in 1904 on College Avenue. Designed by architect Charles Thompson and built by the firm of George Donaghey, the $125,000 building was dedicated in front of a crowd of 2,000 people. The gathering watched as the World's Fair edition of *Harper's Weekly* and *Cosmopolitan* magazine were encased, along with a 1904 coin, in the cornerstone of the building. The building still serves and is today on the National Register of Historic Places.

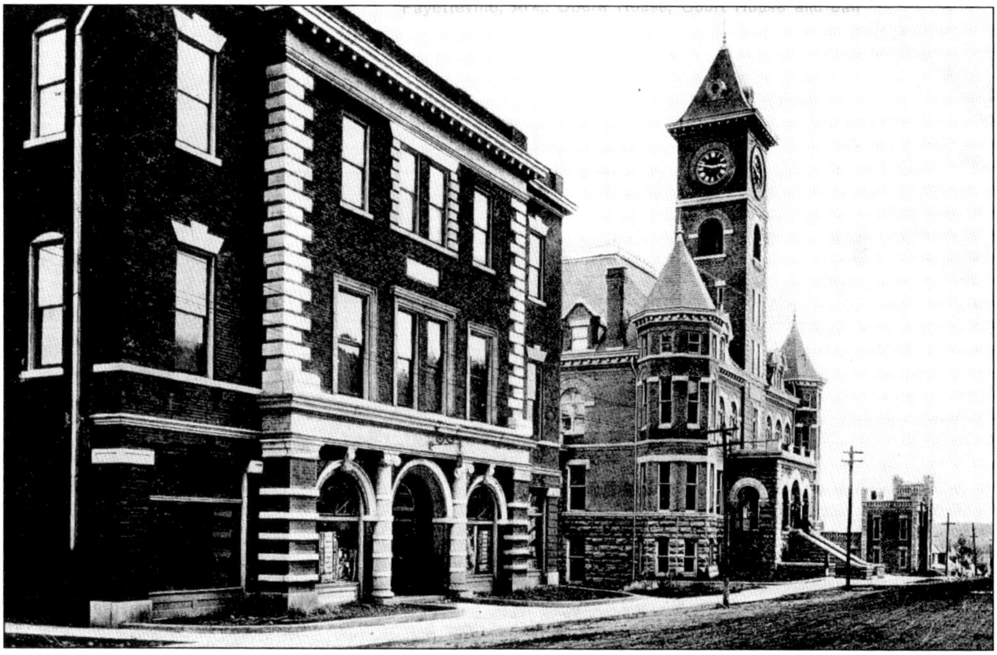

The cultural life of Fayetteville was given a boost in 1905 when the Knights of Pythias raised $25,000 to erect the Knights of Pythias Hall and Opera House, just up from the new courthouse, seen to the right. Local citizens would enjoy the plays of Shakespeare, the oratory of William Jennings Bryan, and music from big-city orchestras visiting Fayetteville. The building soon became known as the Ozark Theater, named for the Ozark Club and its membership of prominent citizens. (*c.* 1910.)

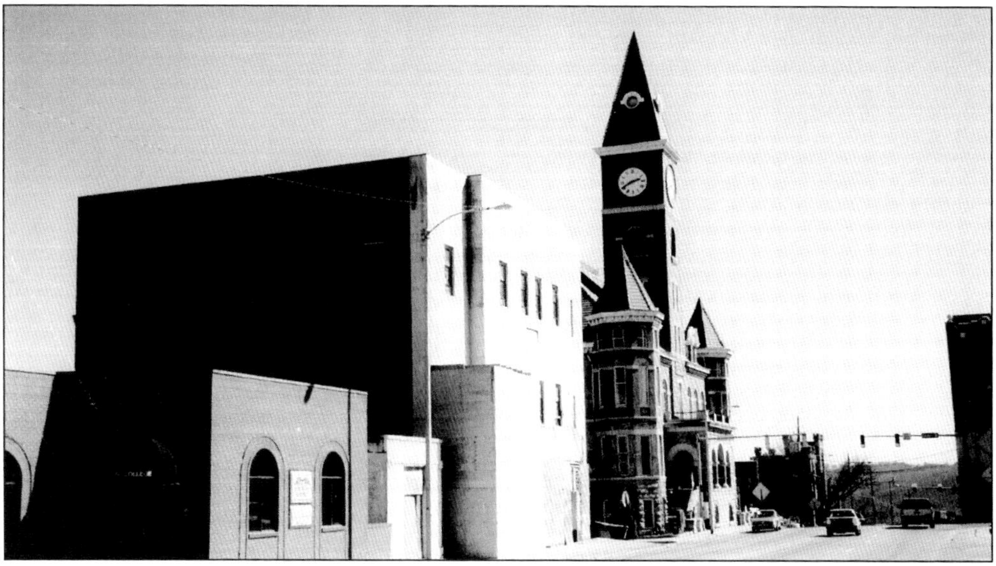

While the Washington County Courthouse has been restored and is still a proud landmark, the years have not been as kind to the Ozark Theater. In this 1997 photograph the building was a boarded, decaying shell threatened with demolition. Concerned citizens worked hard to save the historic structure, however, and plans were announced in mid-1998 to restore the Ozark as an office building. (Photo by Ray Hanley.)

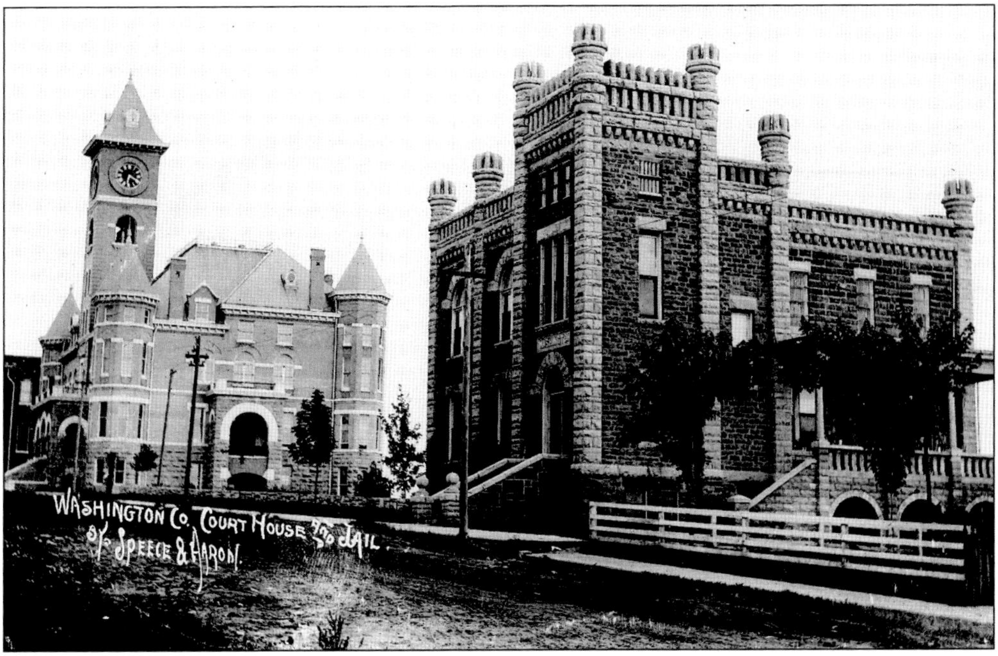

Washington County lawbreakers found themselves lodged in the shadow of the courthouse, in a fortress-styled jail that had been completed in 1897. Upon its opening the *Fayetteville Democrat* reported, "The lock-up will accommodate fourteen men and is constructed in the most substantial manner. The floor is of stone three feet deep and cemented. The iron gate windows have iron shutters—and when a man is safely inside he will realize that he is caught." Today the building houses the affairs of the Washington County Historical Society. (*c.* 1910.)

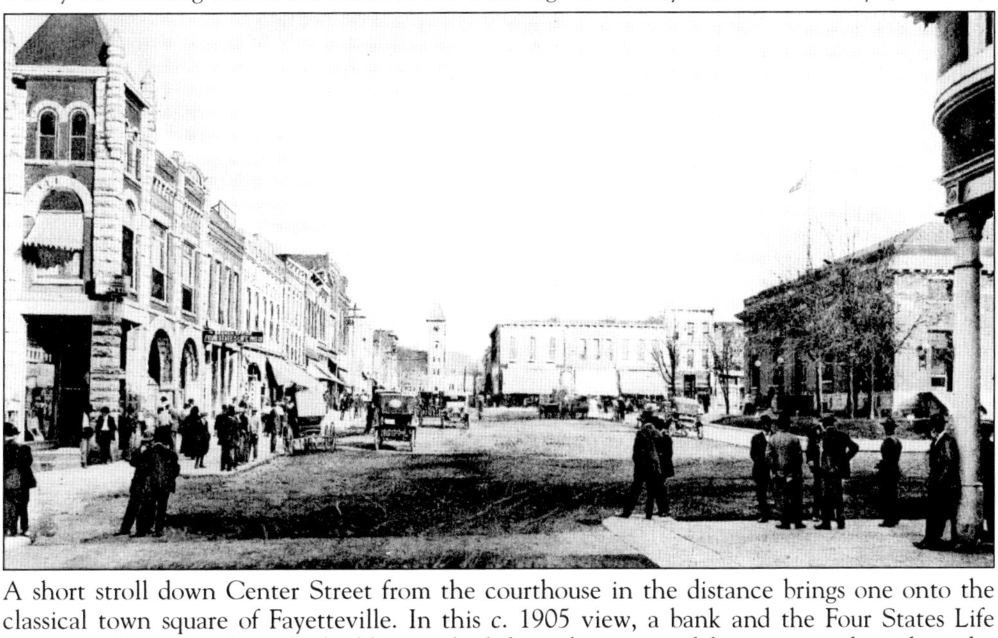

A short stroll down Center Street from the courthouse in the distance brings one onto the classical town square of Fayetteville. In this *c.* 1905 view, a bank and the Four States Life Insurance Company share the building to the left; in the center of the square to the right is the building that housed the town's post office. The raised walkway in the foreground would have served to protect the shoes of those crossing the street.

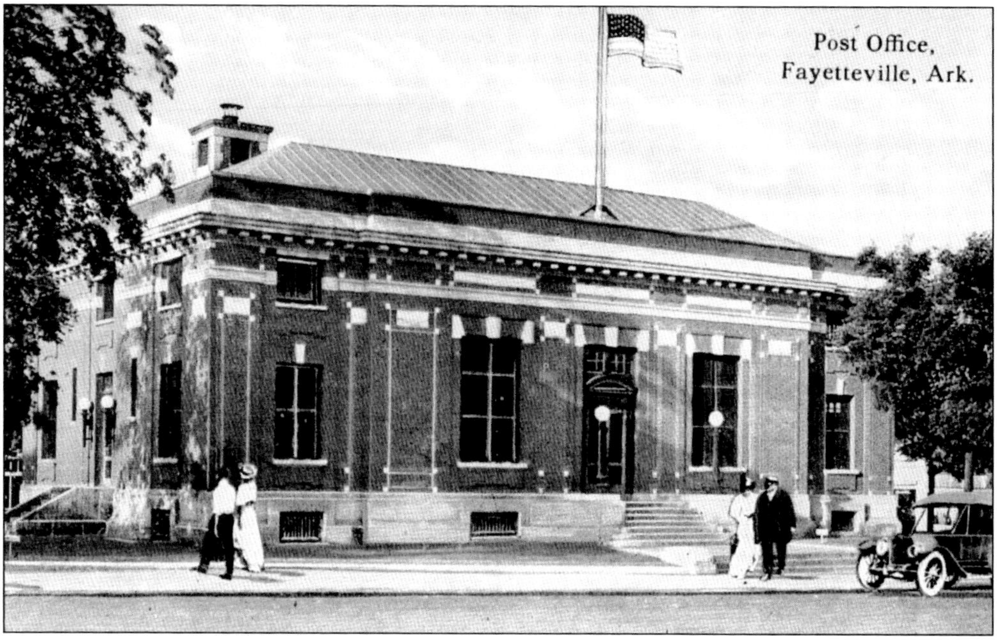

The Fayetteville Post Office, erected in 1911, occupied perhaps the most prominent spot in town, as an island unto itself in the center of the town square and surrounded by the city's business community. Today the building no longer handles the mail, but is a restored landmark containing a popular restaurant. (c. 1915.)

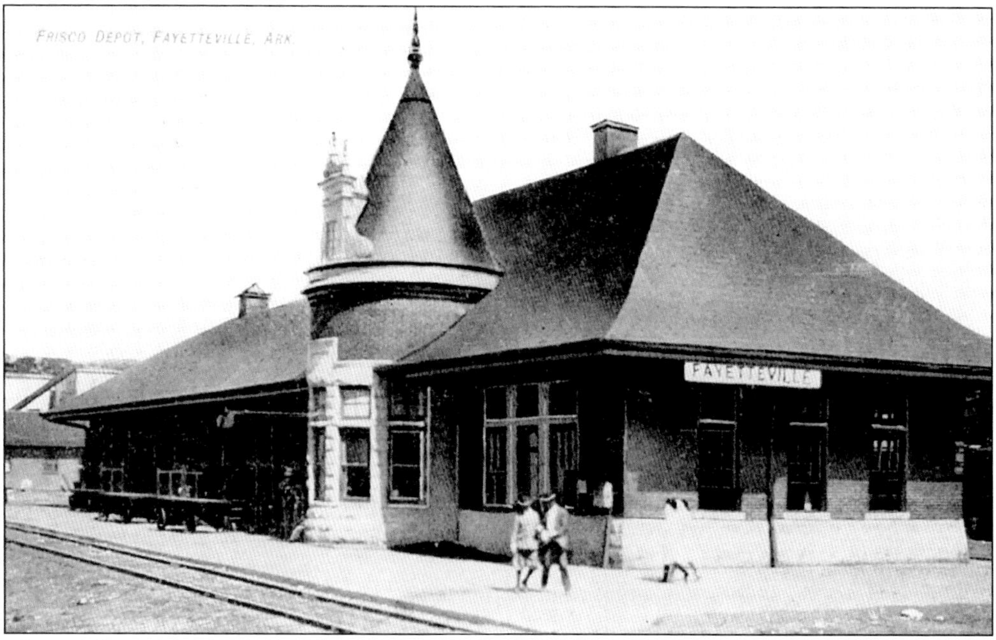

Most of the visitors and all of the mail to Fayetteville arrived by train at the depot of the Frisco Railroad. Erected to replace a depot that burned in 1897, this building would serve until 1925. A larger depot was then built around the one pictured on this card; it still stands today. The railroad was vital to the growth of the region, in an era before reliable roads. (c. 1908.)

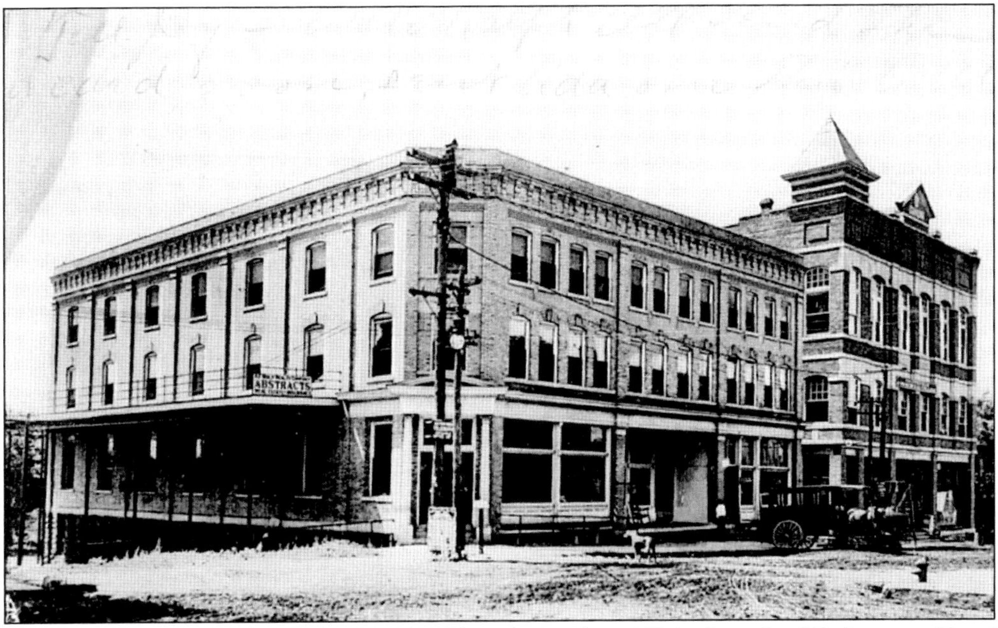

Visitors' choices of lodging was considerably enhanced in 1906 when the Washington Hotel was erected, along with the A.F. Wolf building to the right. A visitor in 1908 wrote, "Mabel is very sick, Dr. thinks she has scarlet fever, tell Mamma I'm alright. We will try and get home Monday." Today the hotel is gone, but the adjacent Wolf Building has been restored.

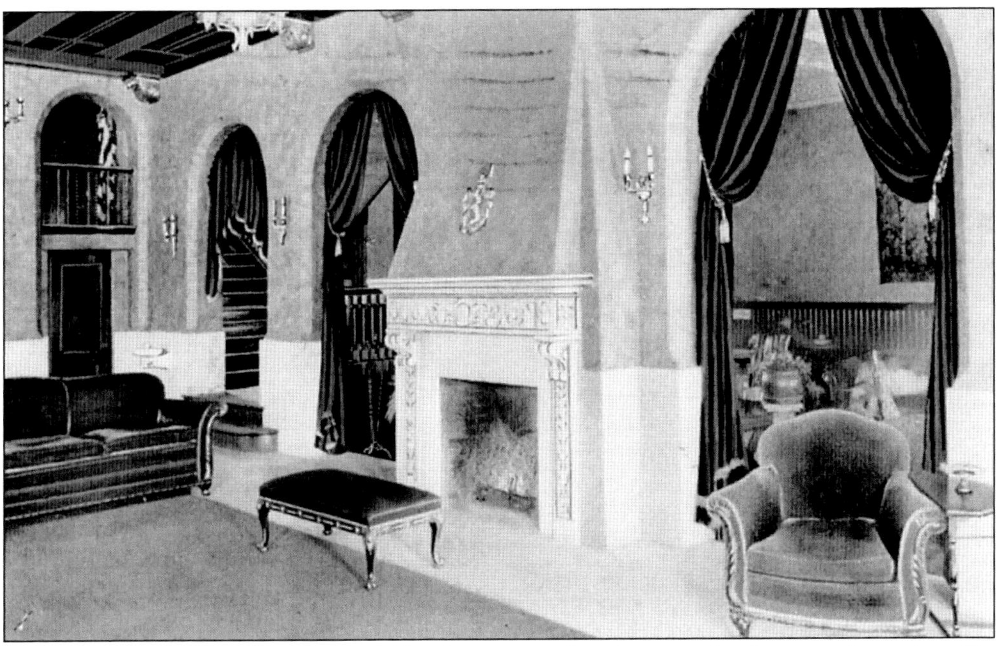

For almost 50 years the Washington Hotel was considered among the finest in the region. On the back of this 1933 card an ad reads, "The Washington has Simmons Beds and Beauty Rest Mattresses. It is 'first in service, first in hospitality and first in the hearts of its patrons.' " The hotel was razed in 1959 to make way for a Woolworth's store. The sender of this card, travelling from Texas to St. Louis, informed the folks back home that "we had only one flat so far."

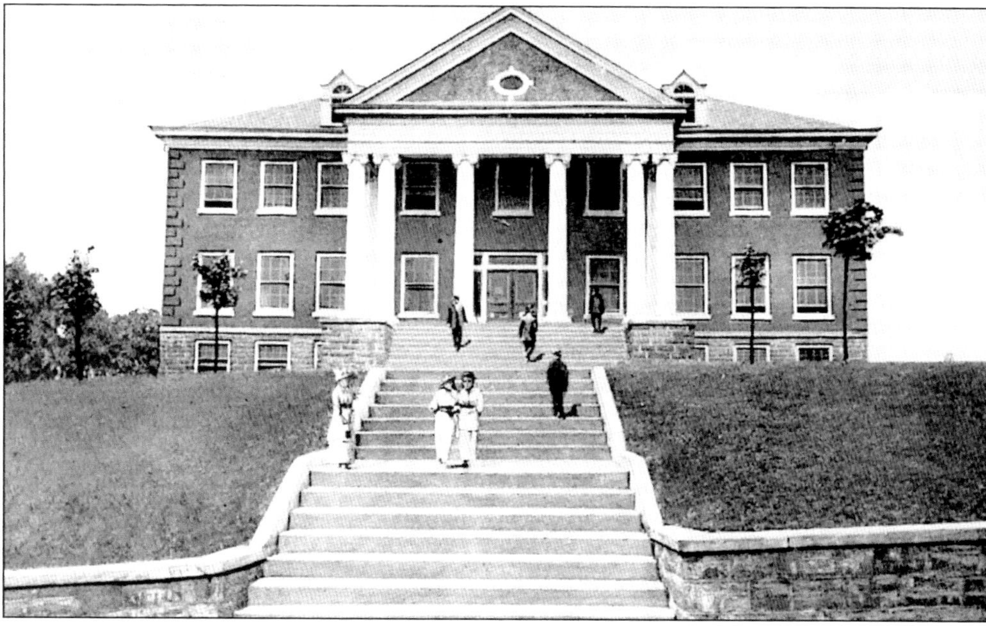

Area residents taken ill had little choice for treatment besides a physician's office, until the opening of the Fayetteville City Hospital on South School Street. Dedicated in 1907, the hospital couldn't open until 1912 because funds were lacking to equip and operate it. The writer of the card was not concerned with illness, however: "If he stays here long will put some fat on his ribs. Celebrating the corn we picked, berries all day yesterday, have bread baking and cobbler." The hospital building was razed in 1983. (*c.* 1910.)

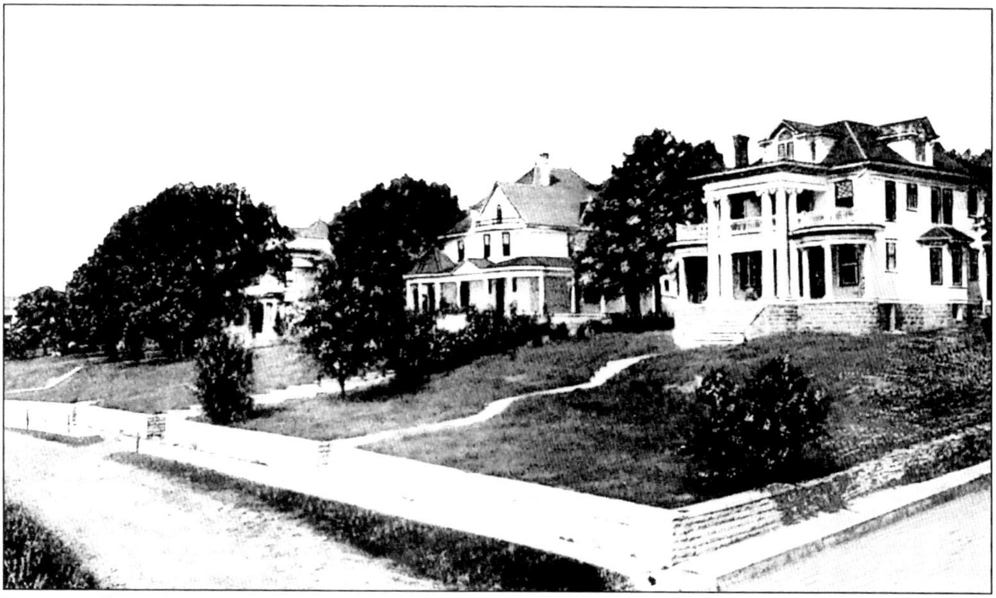

Fayetteville's Mount Nord, a small wooded rise north of the town square, was the site of choice for the finest homes in the city, and is today denoted as an official historic district consisting of five large homes. The land on which the great homes sit was part of a 40-acre grant by President Van Buren in 1838. The first of the homes was built in 1901 by James Bohart, president of the Washington County Bank. (*c.* 1910.)

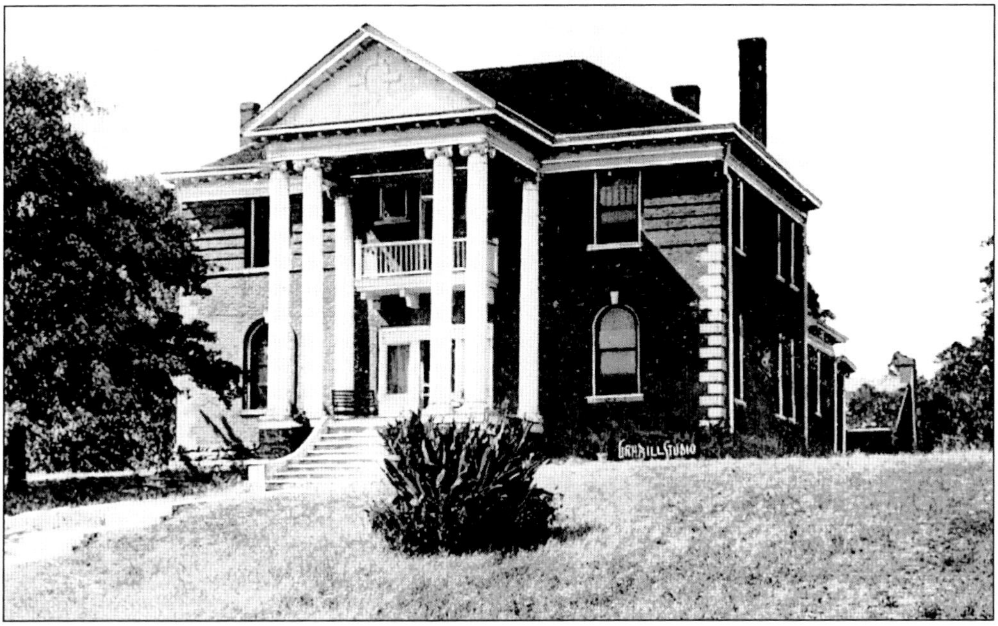

Among the fine homes located on Mount Nord was that of J.E. Mock, a real estate investor who also speculated in agriculture and commodities; the success of Mock's endeavors is evident in his home, shown on this 1912 card.

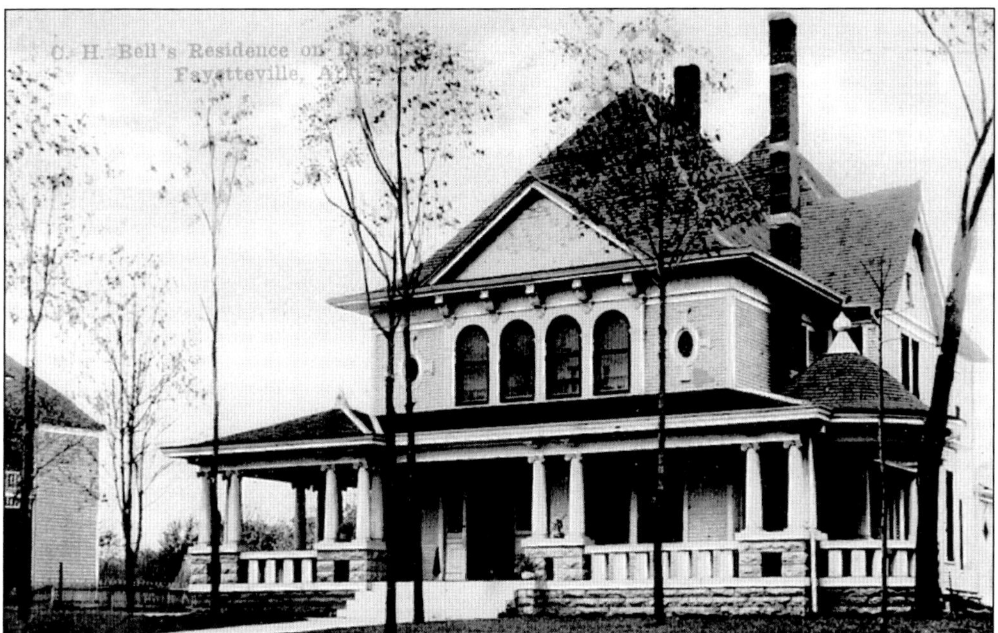

C.H. Bell's imposing home on Dickson Street boasted a wrap-around porch. Bell was prominent in the local community, serving on the city council, as one of the directors of Arkansas Ice and Storage Company, and as an elder of Central Presbyterian Church. (*c.* 1910.)

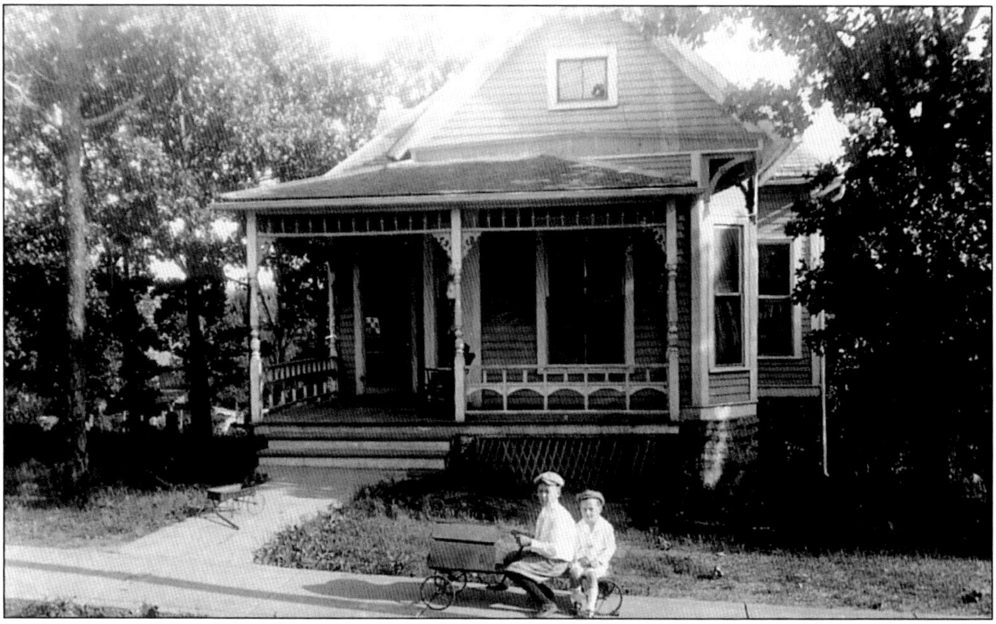

In the above c. 1910 photo, the camera captured two well-dressed boys, complete with caps, "driving" on the sidewalk in a homemade toy car. The house in the background, located at 113 West Lafayette Avenue, was built by A.M. Byrnes, a contractor who had helped erect the University of Arkansas' Old Main Building. Lumber left over from the campus project was used to build this house, along with two more just like it for his two daughters. In the 1997 photo below, the house was still standing and the small boys had long since grown old. Time had taken a toll on the white frame cottage—some of the ornamentation had been removed, the porch was sagging, and it had acquired a refrigerator collection. (Photo by Ray Hanley.)

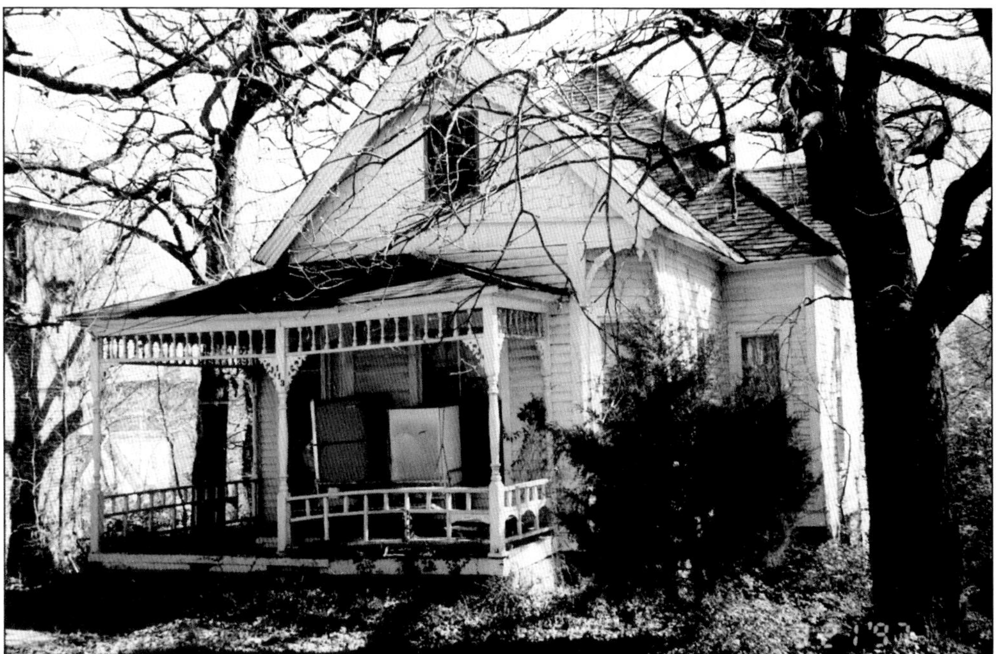

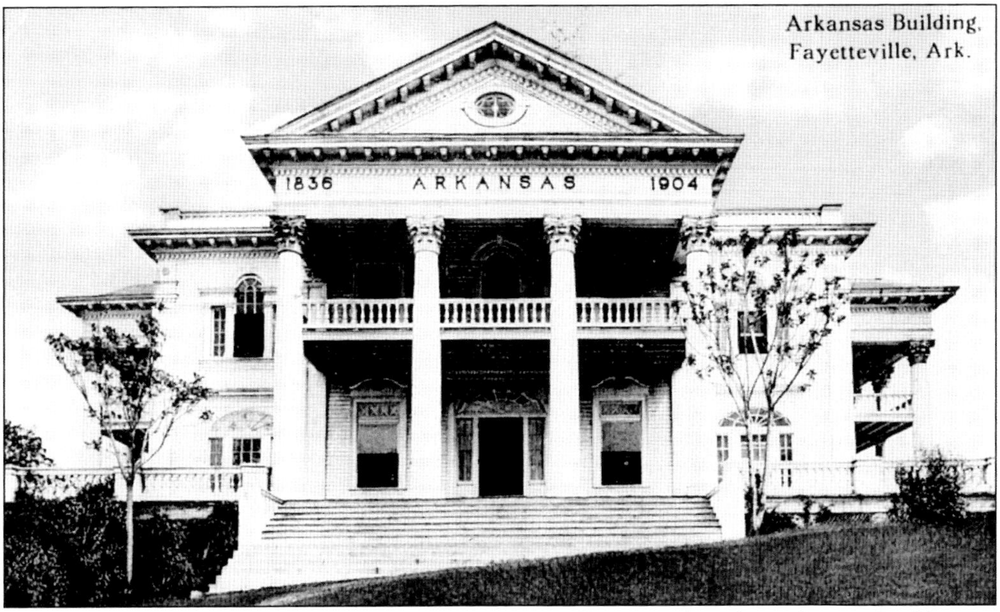

The elegant structure in these two views was originally erected as the Arkansas Building in St. Louis for the 1904 World's Fair. Designed by Little Rock architect Frank Gibbs and built at a cost of $119,000, the building hosted many receptions during the fair and was a magnet for the thousands of visitors from Arkansas. When the fair ended and the buildings were sold off to the highest bidder, Artemus F. Wolf, a Fayetteville real estate developer, won the house with a $1,700 bid. At a cost of $20,000 Wolf had the house dismantled, with the parts numbered and shipped in six boxcars to Fayetteville. Under the supervision of builder A.M. Byrnes (whose work is also seen on the previous page), the mansion was reassembled on Mount Nord; it would serve as the Wolf family home for a number of years. By the 1930s the home was relegated to use by college fraternities, and it soon fell into disrepair. A statewide effort to raise the $15,000 needed to restore the building failed, and in 1939 the grand structure was demolished. (Cards c. 1910.)

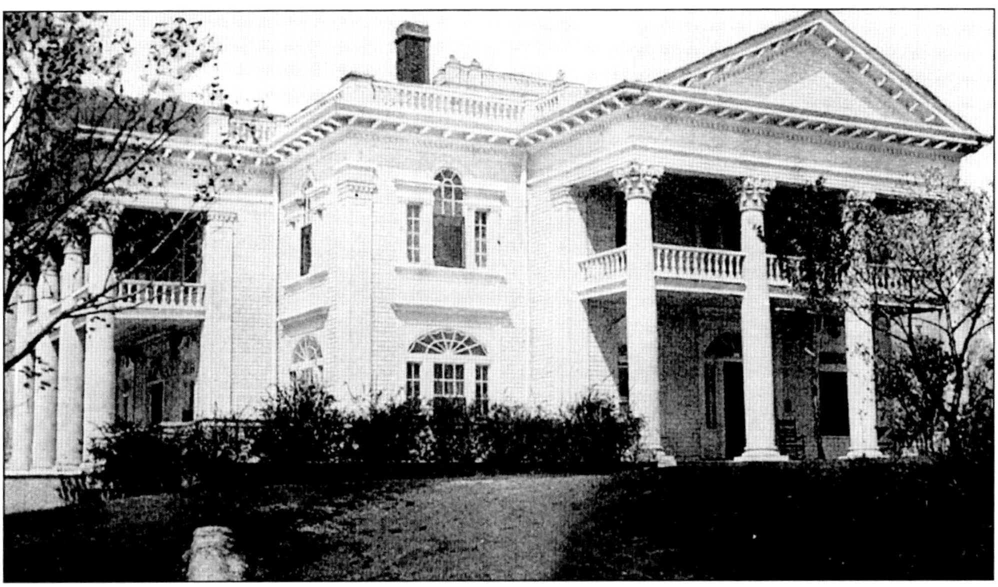

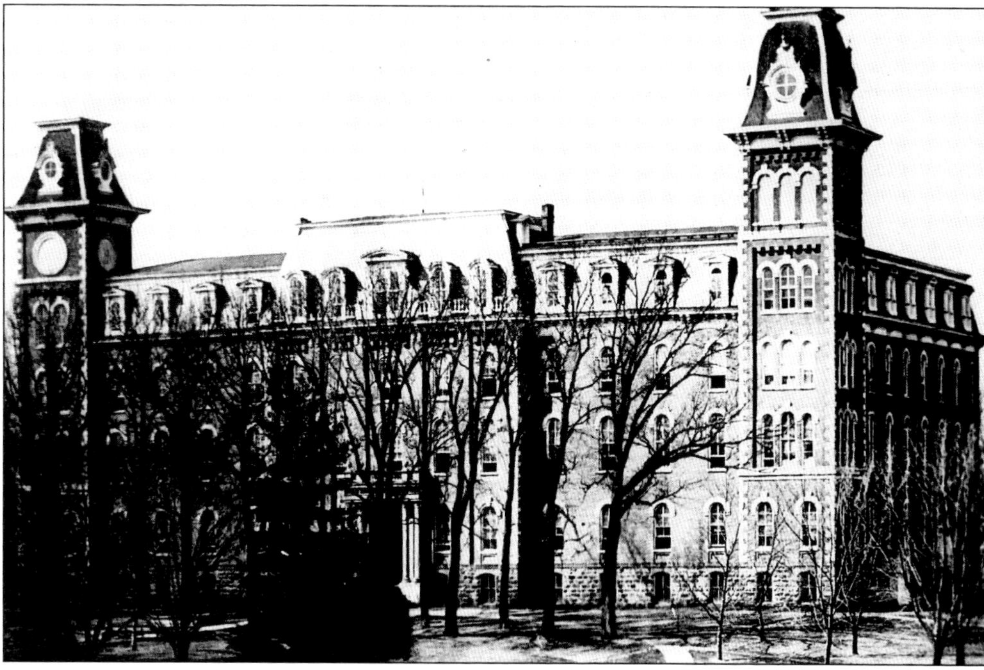

In 1875, when the first commencement was held at the University of Arkansas (U of A), it occurred in Old Main, today the oldest surviving building on campus. The 26,000-square foot building, which took two years to complete, stood 134 feet tall and measured 214 feet long by 122 feet wide. Two hundred fifty kegs of nails and 260,000 pounds of iron, along with tons of locally quarried gray limestone, went into the building's construction. Today the restored landmark is one of the most recognizable buildings in the state. (c. 1910.)

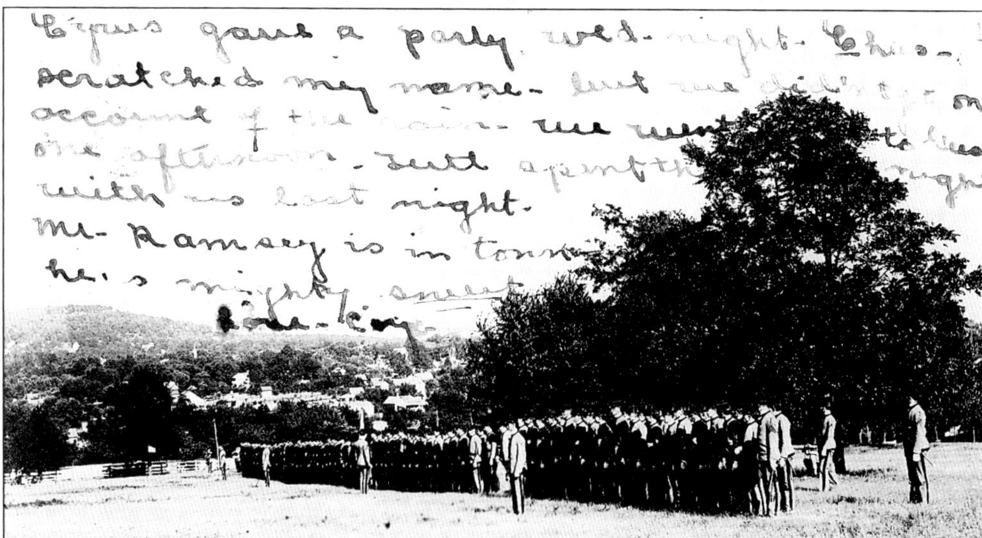

This military cadet unit was photographed in formation on the campus in 1909. Each university commencement during the early years of the century included a drill competition among the cadets. Individual contestants were lined up to receive various drill commands. Any cadet executing a wrong order dropped out, and the last man standing took home a trophy.

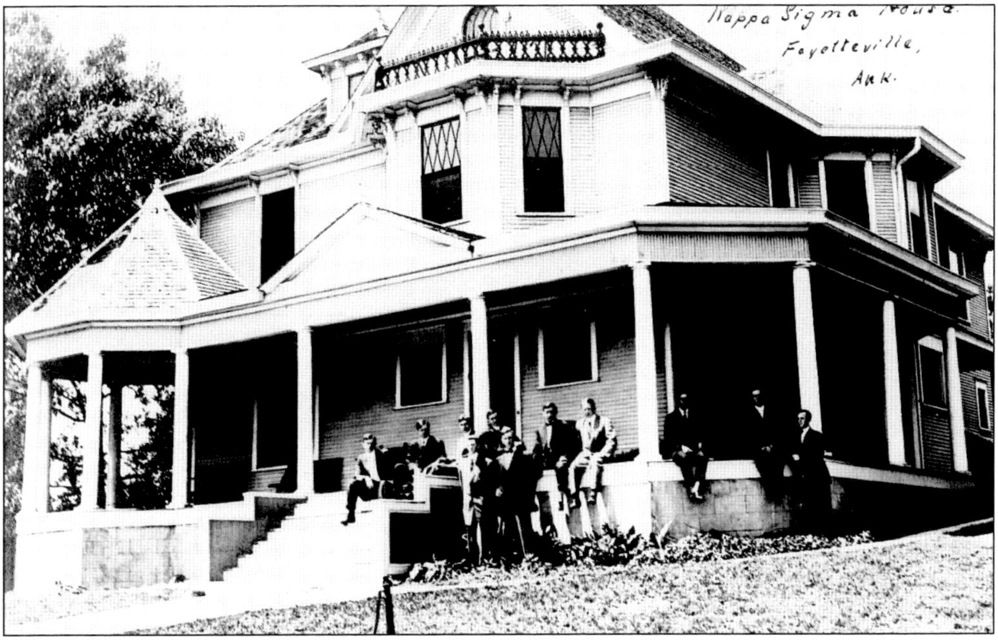

At the U of A, then as now, fraternity life was frequently a part of the college experience. The identities of these young men, posed on the porch of the Kappa Sigma House on Dickson Avenue, are unknown. "R.J.B.," the card's sender, commented to a young lady in Little Rock that they "had these pictures take last week."

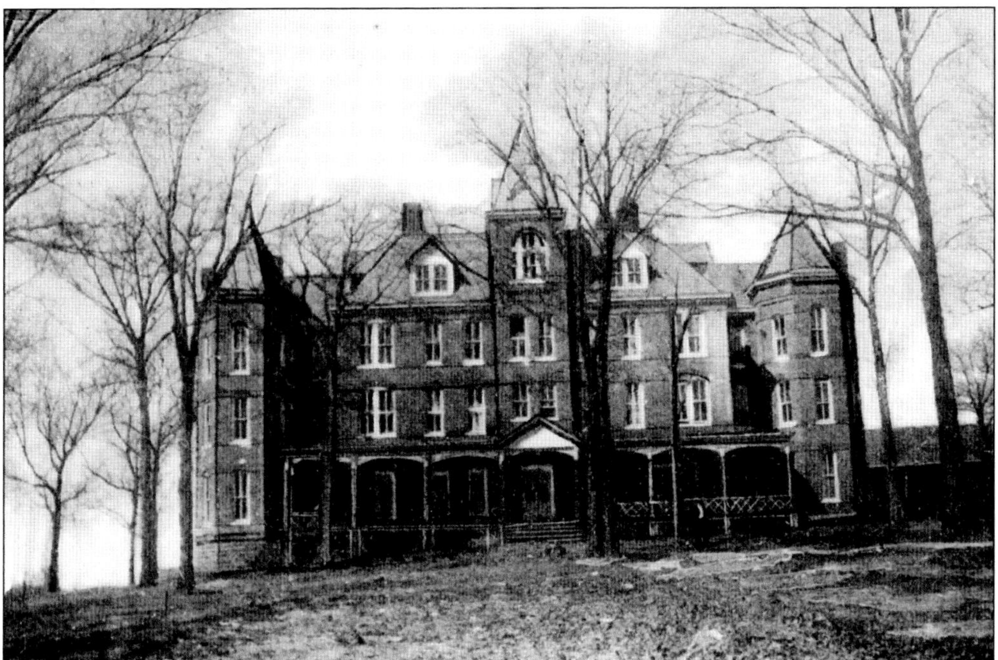

One of the boys' dormitories stood on a small rise, captured here in a stark winter scene. Like nearly all of the turn-of-the-century campus buildings, Buchanan Hall was razed many years ago.

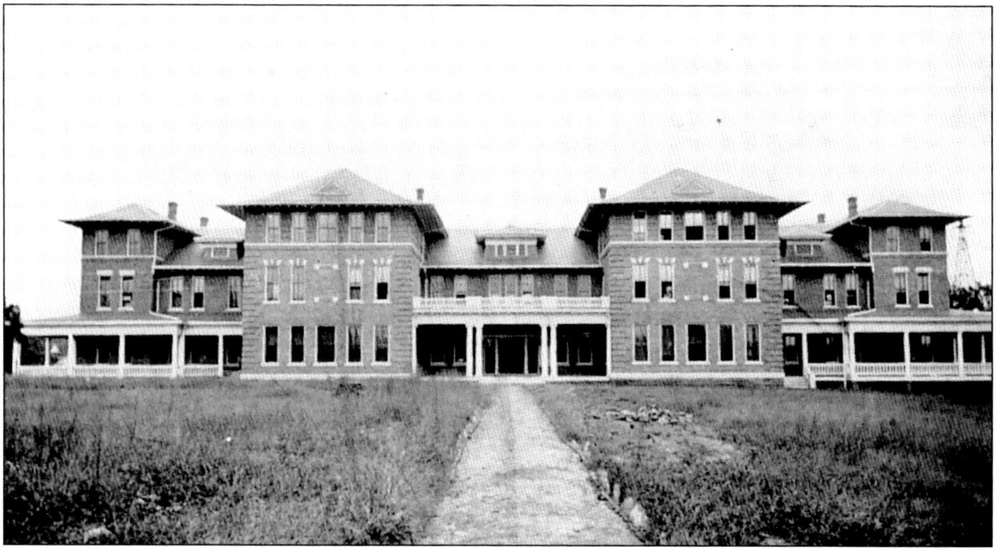

Carnall Hall is the second-oldest building on the U of A campus, after Old Main. Built in 1906, the historic women's dormitory was named for Ella Carnall, who had enrolled in the university at the age of 14 in 1877. The building, now in sad repair, has been closed since 1991. The dormitory is one of 145 buildings designed by famed architect Charles Thompson, and is on the National Register of Historic Places. Currently being debated is a decision to either restore or destroy the old building. (1908.)

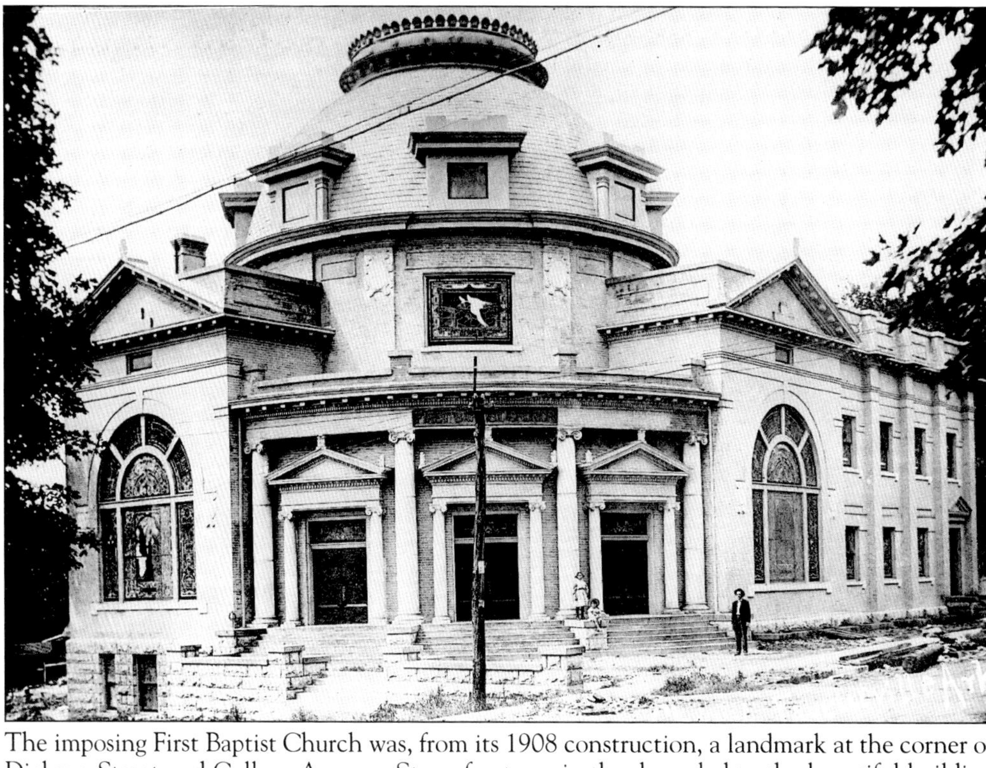

The imposing First Baptist Church was, from its 1908 construction, a landmark at the corner of Dickson Street and College Avenue. Stress fractures in the dome led to the beautiful building being demolished in the 1950s.

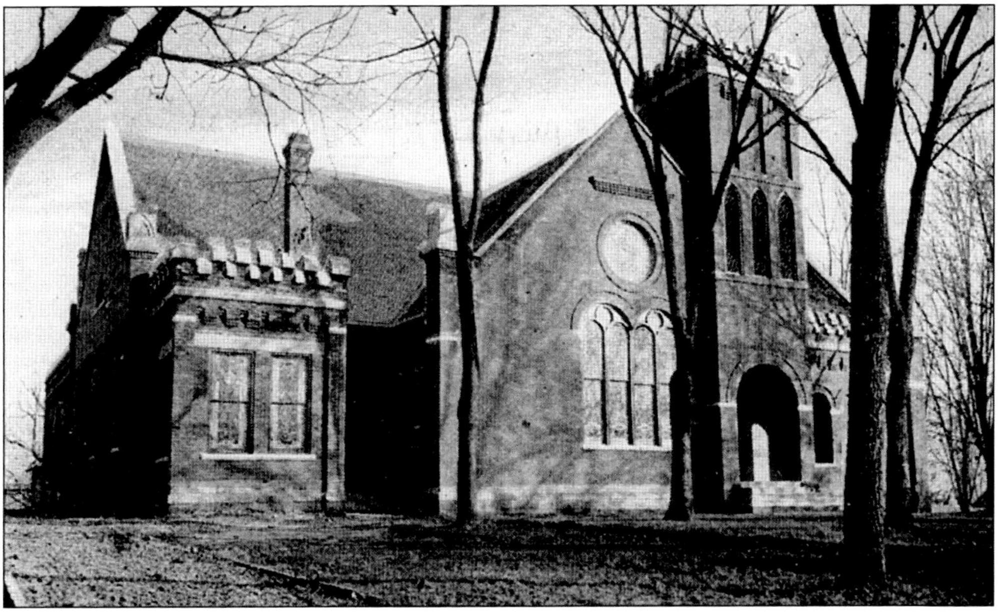

The First Christian Church was originally formed in Fayetteville in 1848. The church's building was used as a Union hospital during the Civil War and was then burned. Around the turn of the century, the church erected this handsome brick structure to serve its large congregation. "Would like to see your pretty face," are the words penciled on the reverse side and sent to Bessie Colclasure of Lawton, Oklahoma. (1910.)

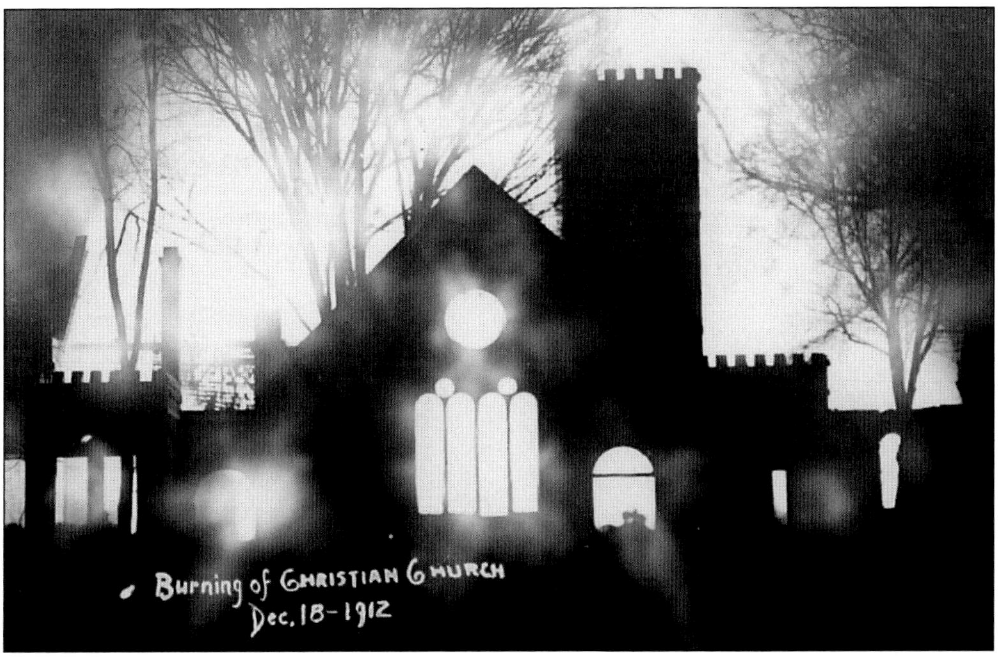

An on-the-spot photographer captured the "new" First Christian Church going up in flames on December 18, 1912. The inferno filled the church's interior in the cold night, seemingly framing every window, where shortly before stained glass had graced the openings. The dauntless congregation rebuilt its church, this time adding twin bell towers to the design.

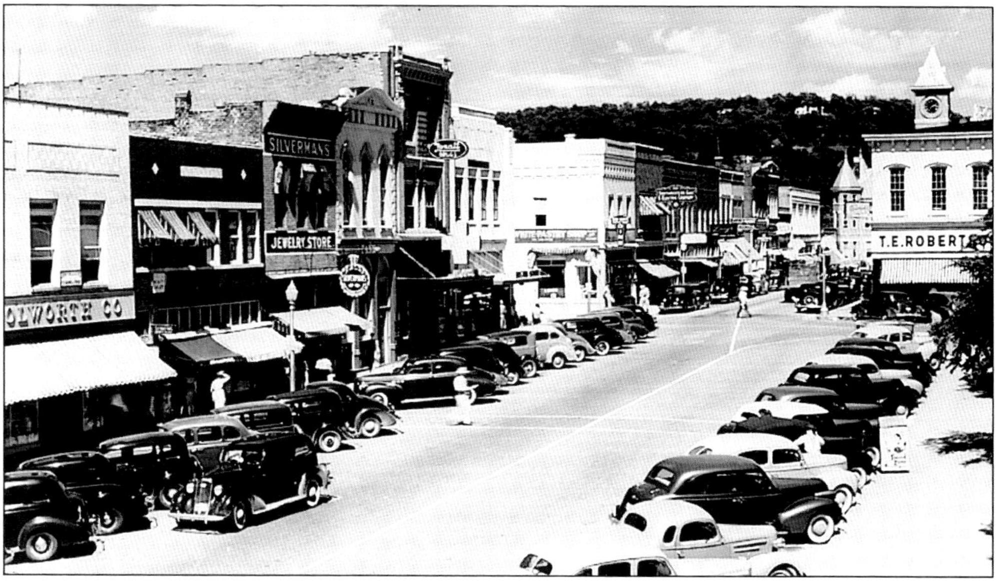

In a c. 1945 postcard, the Fayetteville town square was still the business center for much of the county, as bypasses and shopping malls were still some years in the future. The city's economy would expand rapidly after WW II, so that the population of the town surpassed 9,000. The boom represented good news for merchants such as Woolworth's and Silverman Jewelry on the right and T.E. Robertson's on the left.

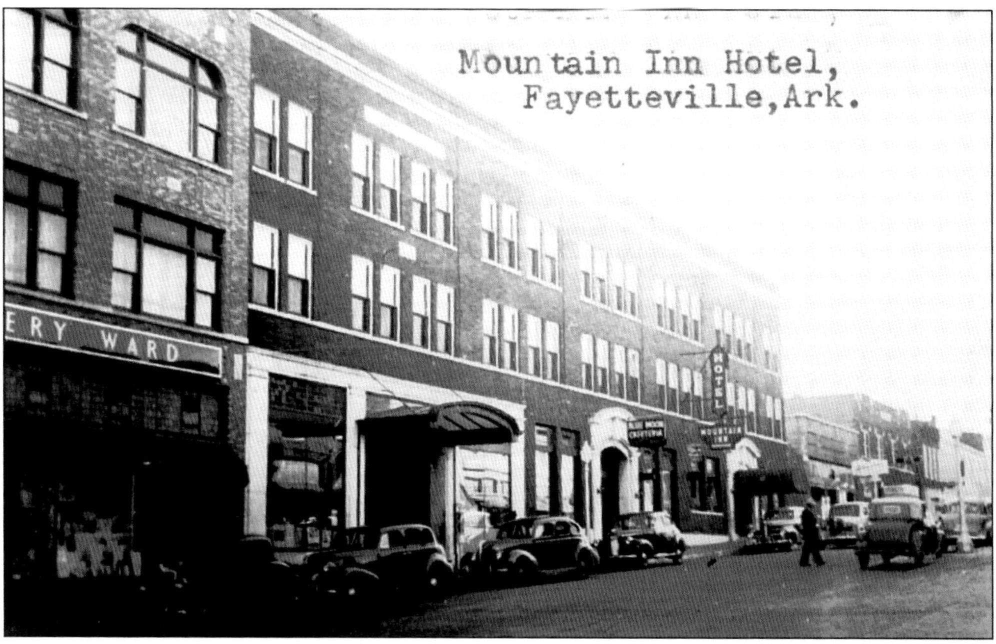

One of the most versatile structures in the downtown area surely must have been the Mountain Inn on Center Street. It began service in the 1880s as the Oriental Hotel, and gained another 60 rooms in the 1920s. Office space was also added on the building's east end. In this c. 1945 card the popular Blue Moon Cafeteria can be seen in the center of the building, with Montgomery Ward's store to the left. The hotel no longer operates but the building still stands.

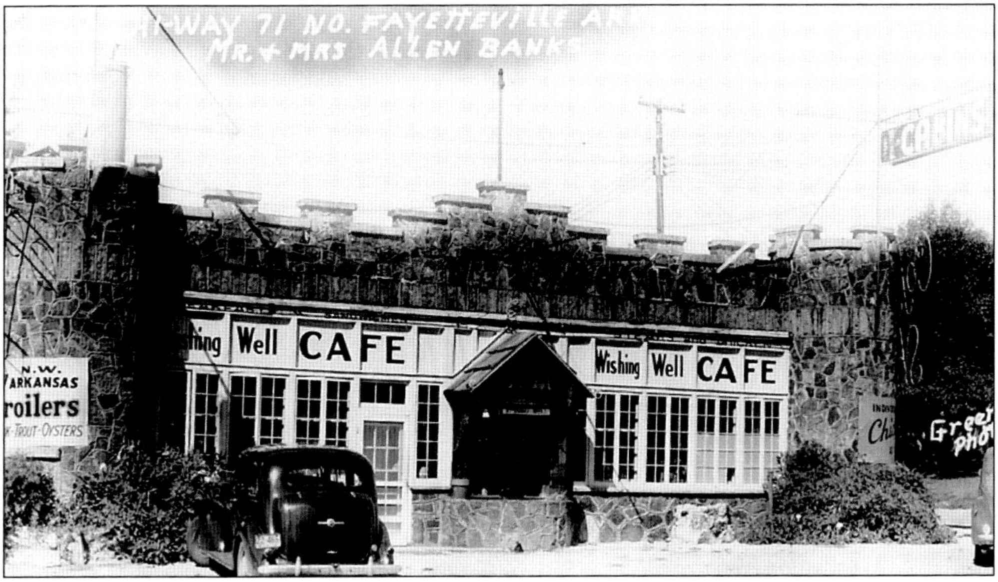

As business developed along Highway 71 north of the downtown area, a popular dining establishment was the Wishing Well Cafe. A sign to the right promotes cabins to let for "$1.50 and up." The sign to the left advises that the cafe serves northwest Arkansas broilers, steak, trout, and oysters, while large neon letters on each end of the building proclaim the presence of a "Coffee Shop" to road-weary travelers. The cafe, with its unusual interior/exterior wishing well, no longer stands. (c. 1945.)

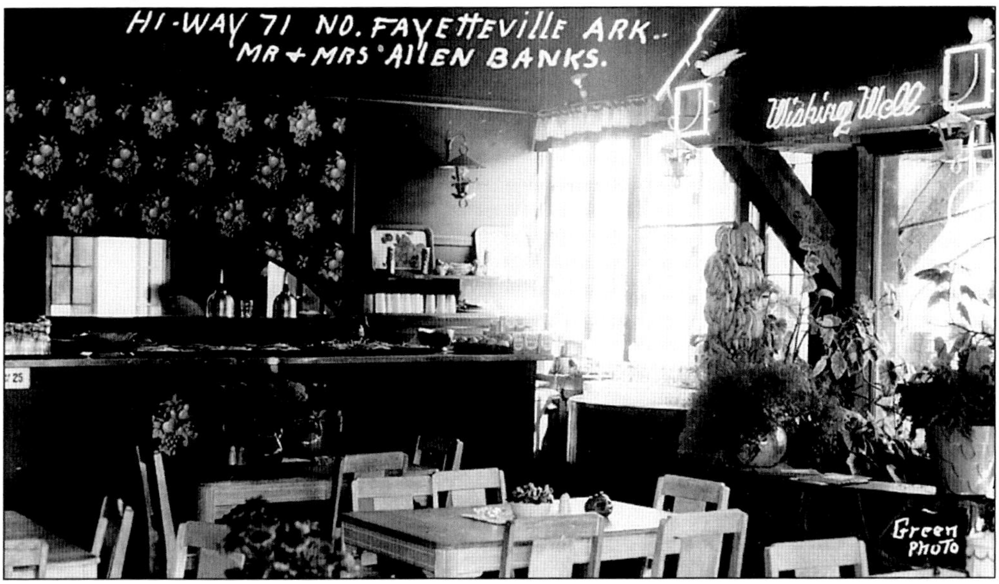

Mr. and Mrs. Allen Banks apparently took great pride in the interior decor of their Wishing Well Cafe; this c. 1945 postcard shows such decorative touches as plants, wallpaper, and country-style lamps. The sign on the counter to the left promotes shakes and sundaes for 25¢, while a huge bunch of bananas hangs near the namesake wishing well. Also visible are tiny cereal boxes on the counter, sparkling glasses near the window, and an assortment of meringue pies ready to serve—in the type of dining room that would largely fade away with the coming of franchised food restaurants in the 1970s.

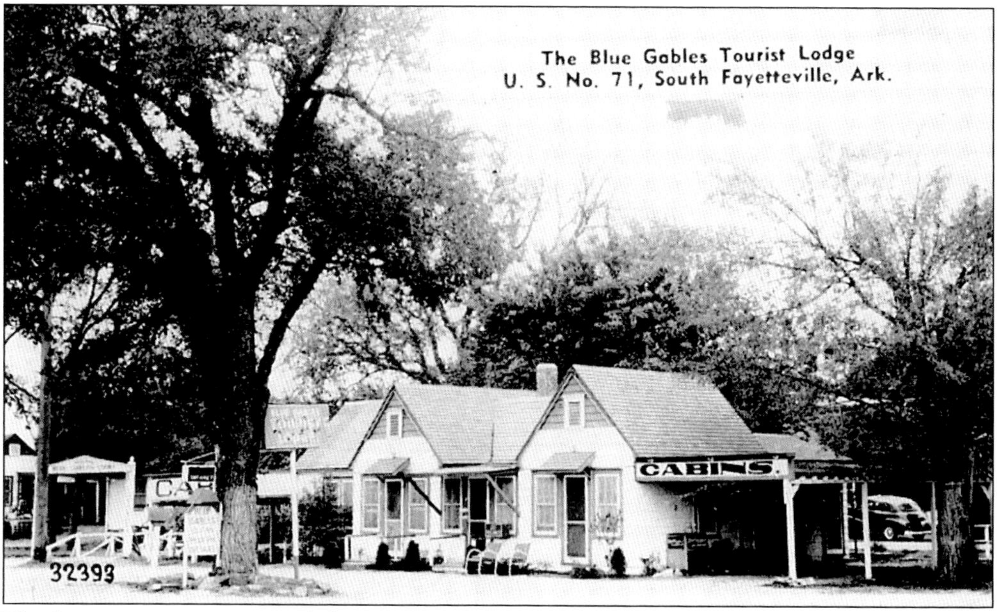

The large increase in automobile travel led to the opening of a number of tourist courts along the Highway 71 corridor through northwest Arkansas. Typical is this view of the Blue Gables Tourist Lodge, located at 805 South School Street. The ad on the back of the card proclaims the business to offer "Strictly Modern Cottages, Clean, Quiet." Today no trace of the Blue Gables remains. (c. 1945.)

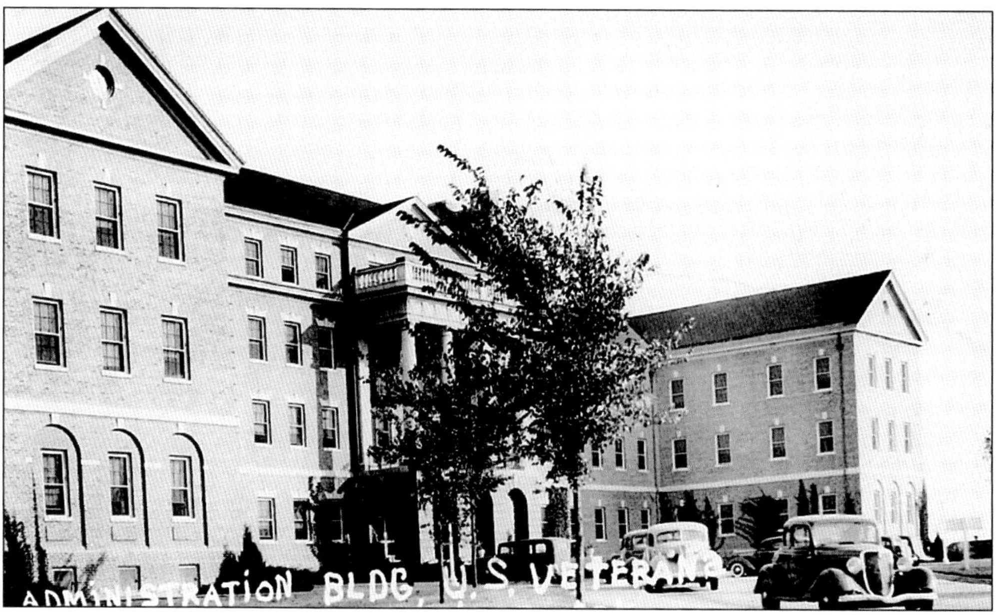

In the depression years of the 1930s a new Veterans' Hospital was erected just north of downtown. A patient named Randal Ross, mailing a card of this hospital in 1942, wrote: "Was operated on Wednesday morning. Am feeling fine but will spend at least two weeks in bed. Expect to get a good rest. The Chaplain here added the Upper Room to my library two days ago." (Card c. 1940.)

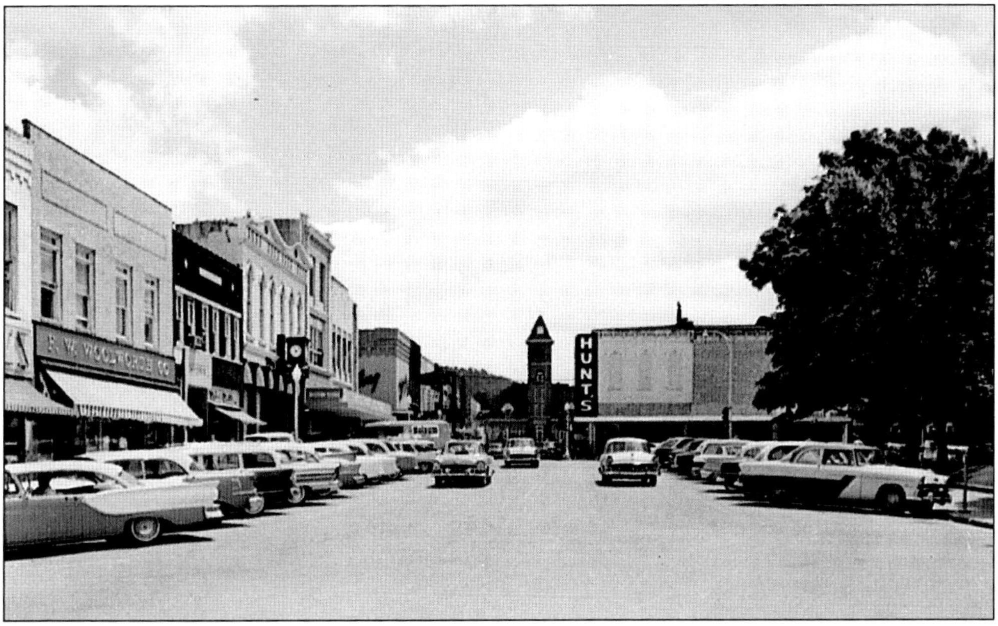

In a 1960 view looking east down Center Street, the photographer had almost the same view as was taken in the card on page 22 some 15 years earlier, and on page 11 in 1905. Woolworth's was still there on the left, the cars were now brightly colored, and Hunt's store had replaced T.E. Robertson's in the center of the photo.

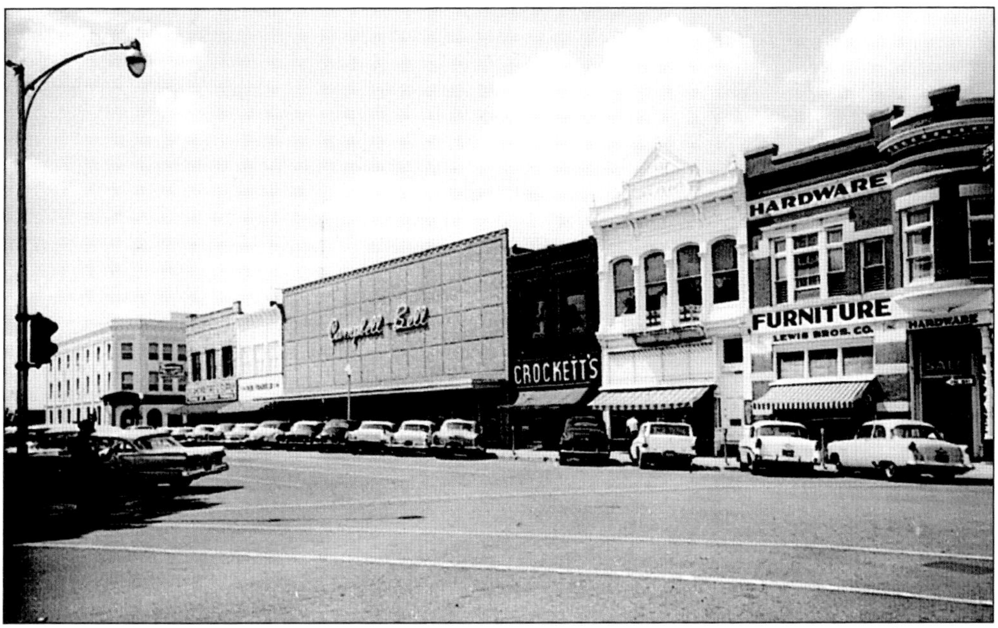

On the other side of the town square in 1960, cars still lined the street before the stores; the first shopping center was only a year or so from opening, thus starting the retail exodus from downtown. Businesses on the block seen here include Ben Franklin's, Campbell-Bell's Department Store, Crockett's, and Lewis Brother's Hardware and Furniture Store on the right corner.

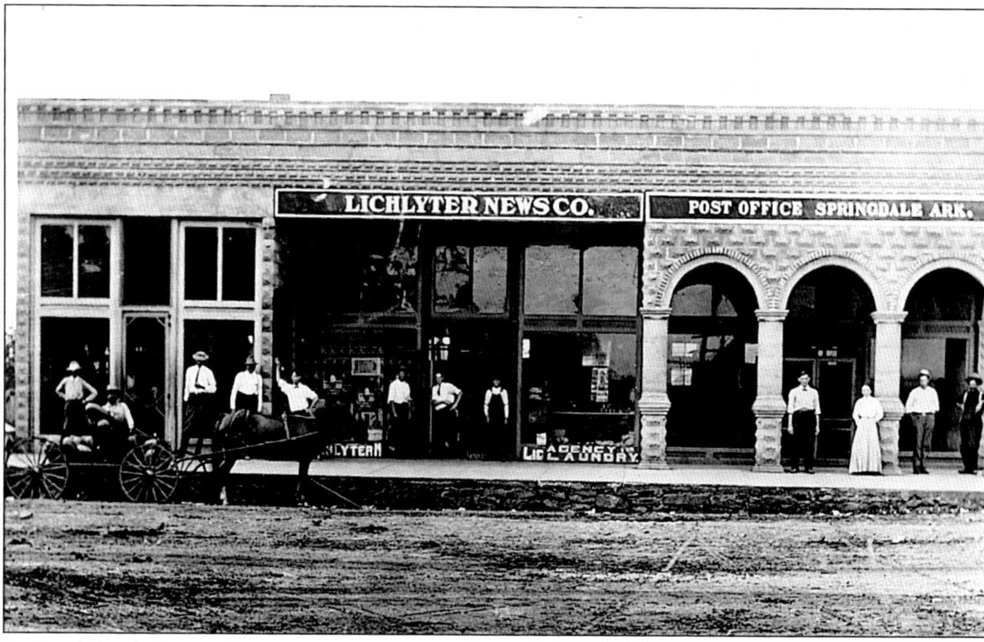

Springdale, Arkansas began its existence as the town of Shiloh, so-called from the founding in 1840 of "The Regular Baptist Church at Shilo." During the Civil War the church and many area homes were destroyed. When postal service was restored in 1871 the community was renamed Springdale. A man's 1912 message mailed from this post office to a young lady in Kansas read, "Do you remember a week ago tonight?"—a statement that leaves us wondering some 80 odd years later.

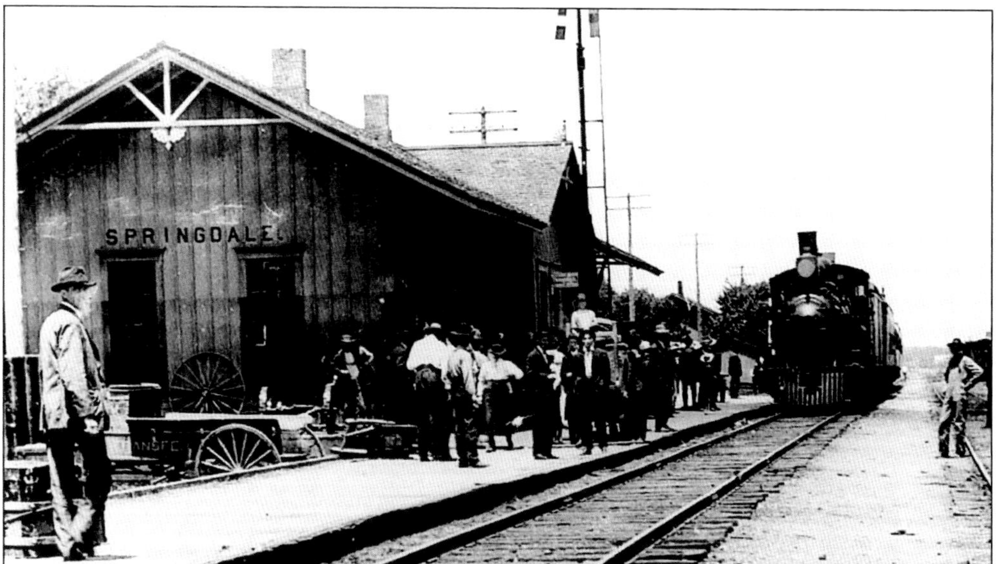

The Frisco Depot was hosting a crowd to meet the train pulling into the station. In the era before automobiles, the railroad connected Washington County to the rest of the nation, and its Springdale station allowed the area's abundant produce to be shipped. The station also served as a point of arrival for the many visitors that came to what would become the most rapidly growing area of Arkansas. This depot was torn down in 1922.

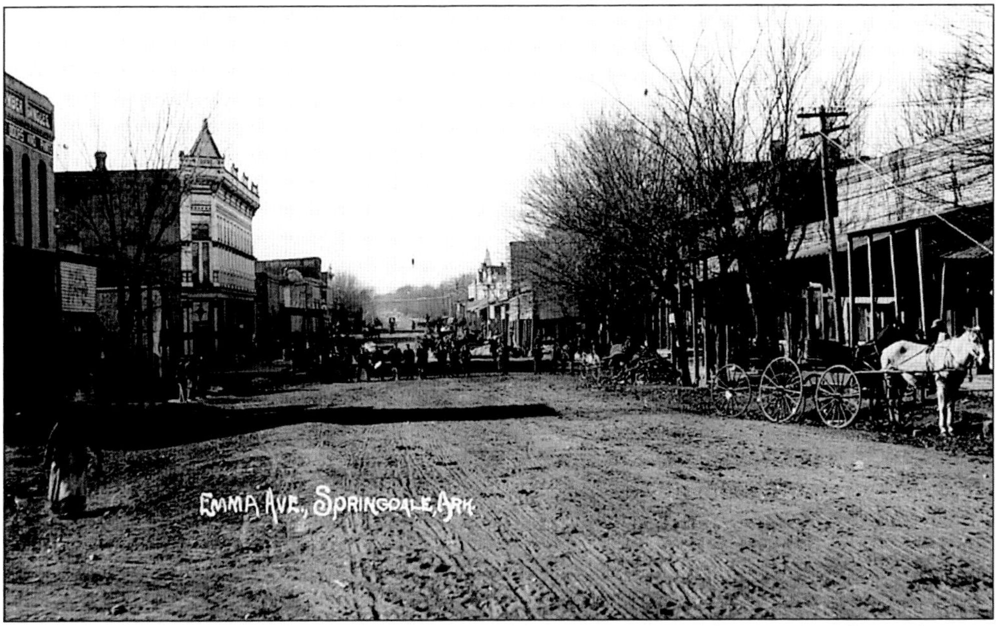

Emma Avenue was the major business avenue of Springdale. In the c. 1900 photo above, a marching band is approaching on the wagon-lined dirt street. The sender of the card wrote, "Ma is in such bad health, what seems to be the trouble is in her lungs. The rest of us are in tolerable good health, crops are looking pretty good." In the photo below, Emma Avenue was muddy and rutted with the tracks of the many wagons and buggies whose drivers were in town to transact business, perhaps in the bank to the right or in the stores to the left. The street would have been quite messy after a rain, but would have quickly become dusty in the hot Arkansas summers. (c. 1905.)

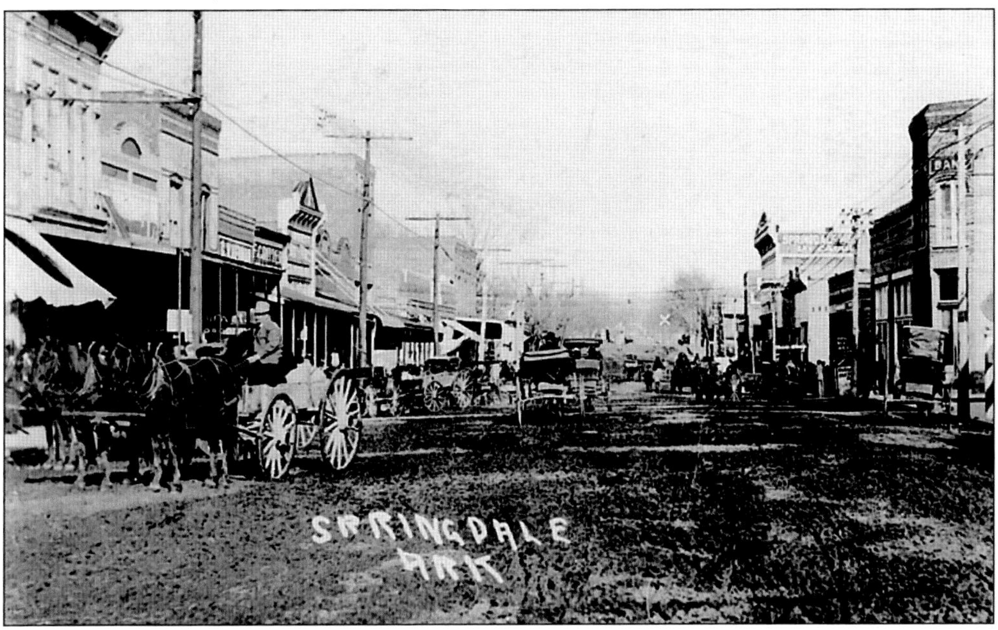

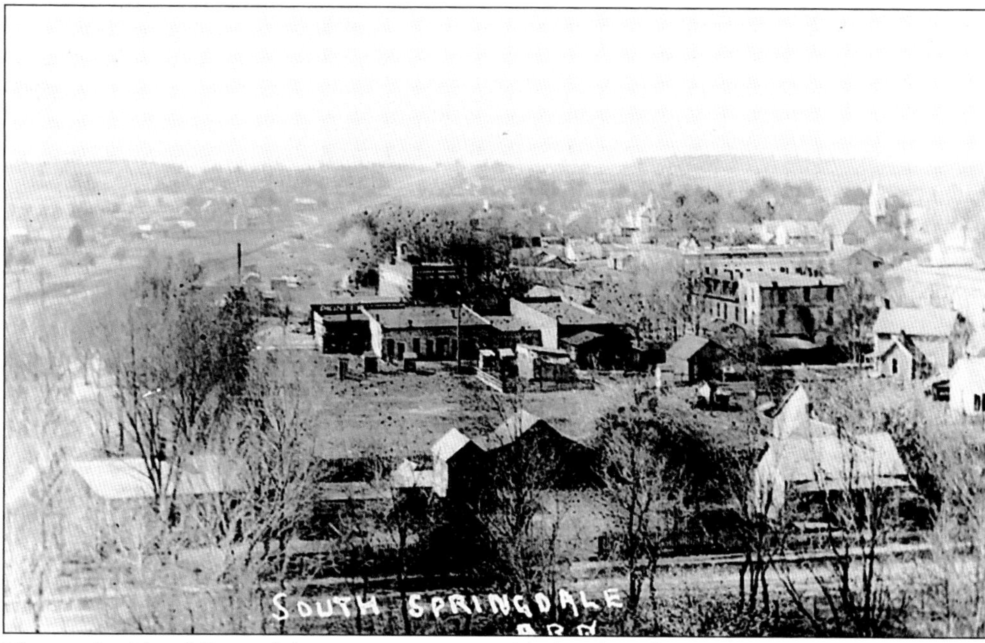

The south side of Springdale is seen in a view likely taken from a water tower. Homes and business establishments share close proximity and are connected by dirt streets. At least five outhouses are visible in the center of the photo. (*c.* 1905.)

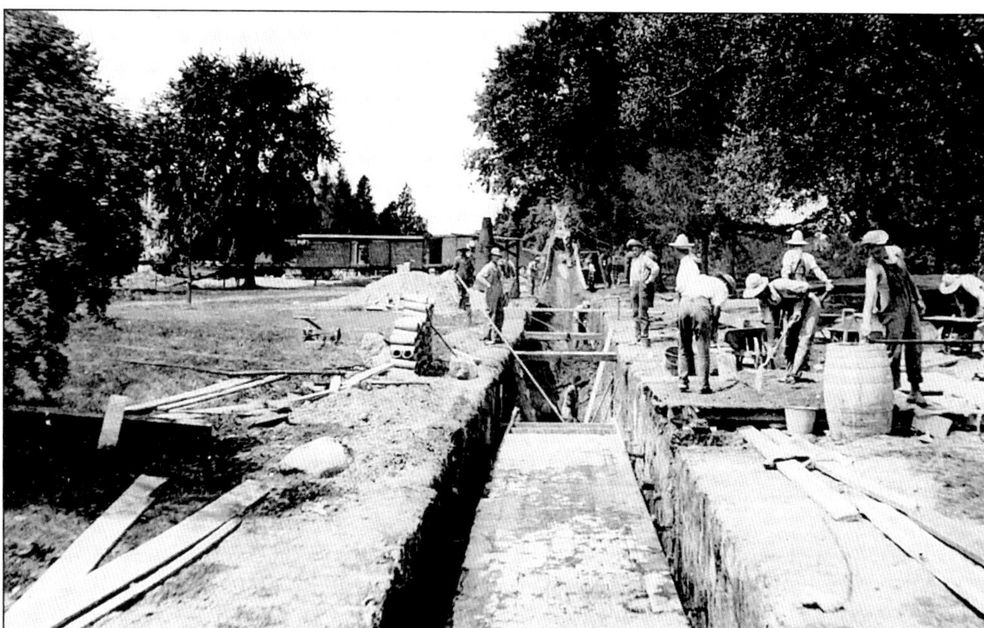

Springdale was intent on emerging as a first-class city, evidence of which is the installation of what appears to be a sewer line that would render the outhouses in the card above obsolete. In an era before today's modern machinery that is often taken for granted, the men in this photo exerted significant labor on this construction job. (*c.* 1910.)

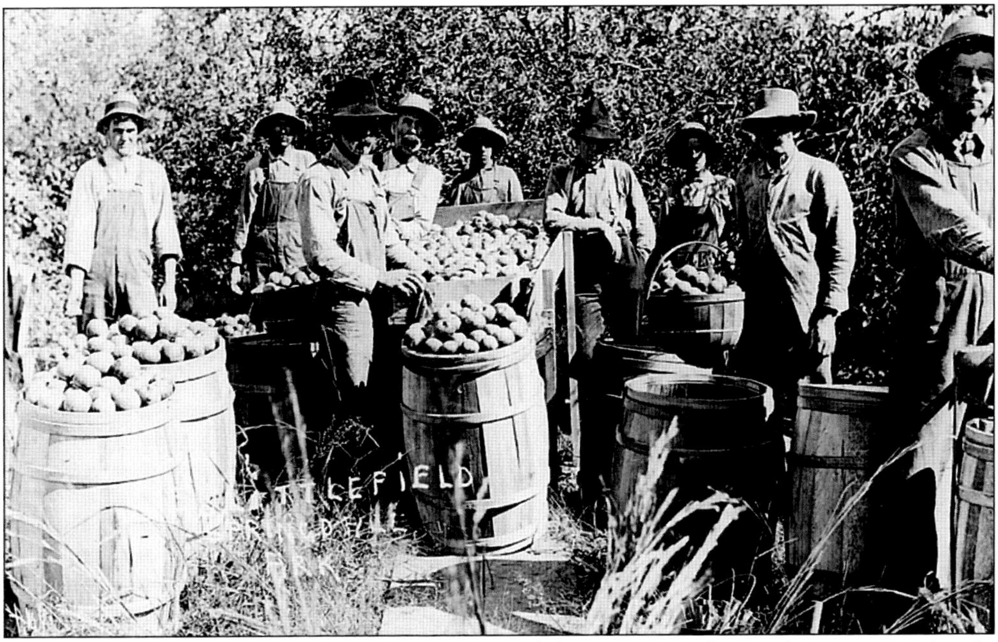

Early in the 20th century, northwest Arkansas led the nation in the production of apples. In 1900 alone, Washington County produced 615,000 bushels of apples, in a number of varieties. As seen in the postcard above, much of the fruit was packed in barrels made of Ozark hardwood staves, and then shipped to distant parts of the nation. The men seen here were laboring in the Littlefield Orchard in Springdale. The card's 1913 message read "Fine country, fruit of all kind, quality is good, prices is high. Will investigate some large orchards this afternoon." In the photo below is what was billed as the world's largest apple evaporator, owned by the Kimmont Walker Company. The evaporators were built to handle the "culls" and excess from the massive apple production of the area. By the 1920s apple production had almost died out of the region, due to bouts of disease and insects, and to the rise of the Pacific Northwest apple industry. (c. 1910.)

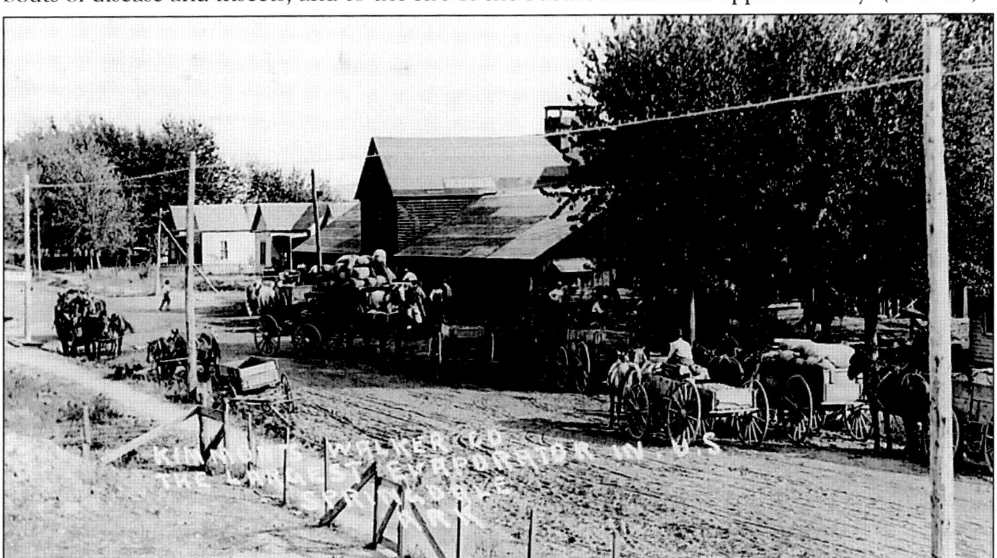

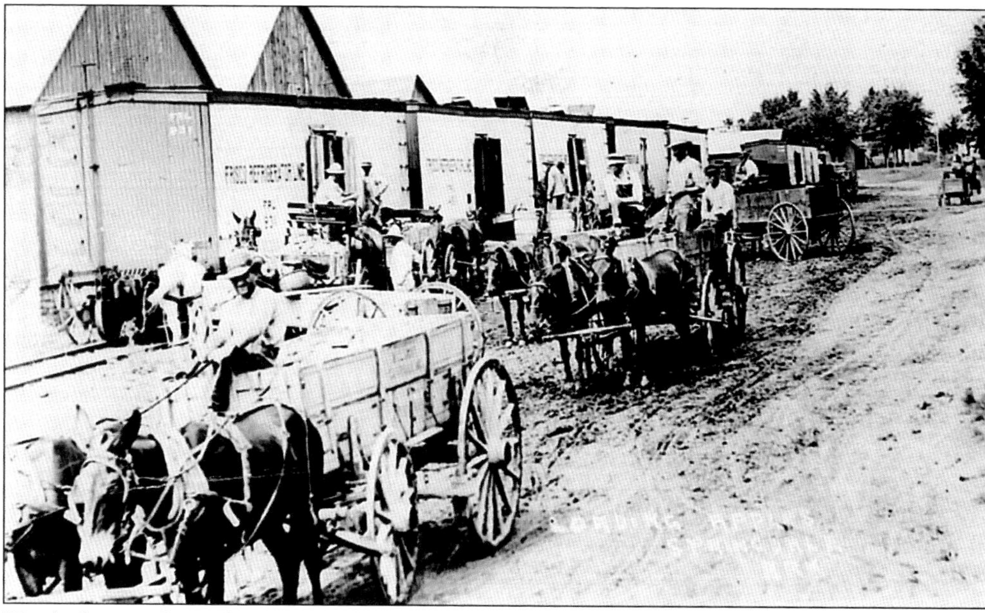

"Paul, this is where they put apples on the cars, I am hauling," reads a 1913 note written to Pennsylvania. The card illustrates the vital role of the railroad in shipping the apples hauled from orchards in fleets of mule-drawn wagons. On the side of the boxcar is painted "Frisco Refrigerator Line." Most likely the cars were kept cool with ice to preserve the fruit, in an era before chemical sprays were developed to extend the shelf life of produce.

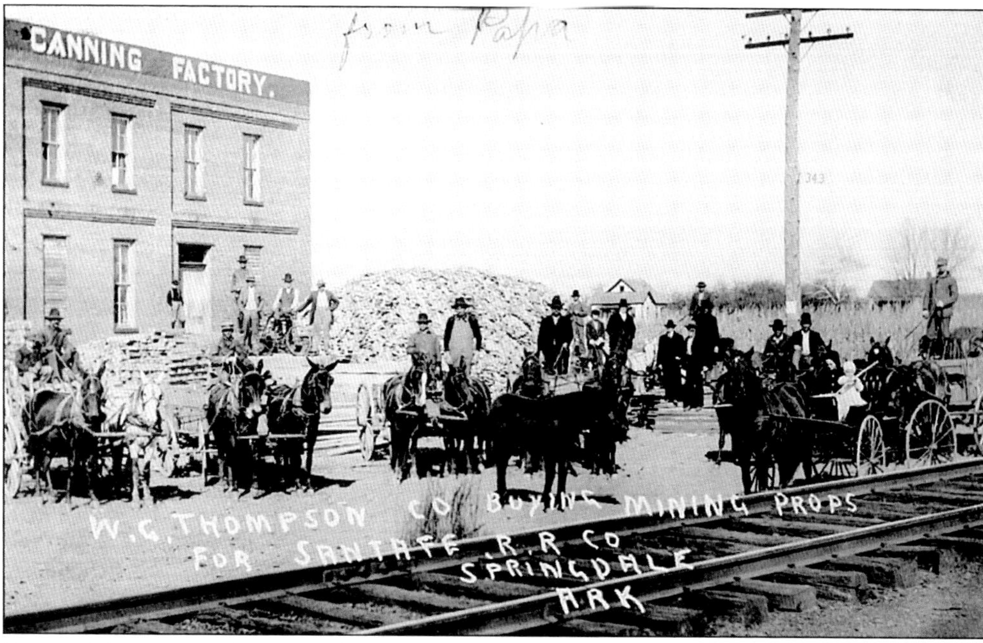

Some of the region's bounty of fruit ended up at the canning factory to the left; the canned fruit could then be easily shipped on the adjacent rail line. The large number of mule-drawn wagons had most likely been delivering apples to the factory. The message on the face of the card announces that, "The W.G. Thompson Co. buying mining properties for the Santa Fe Rail Road Company—Springdale, Arkansas."

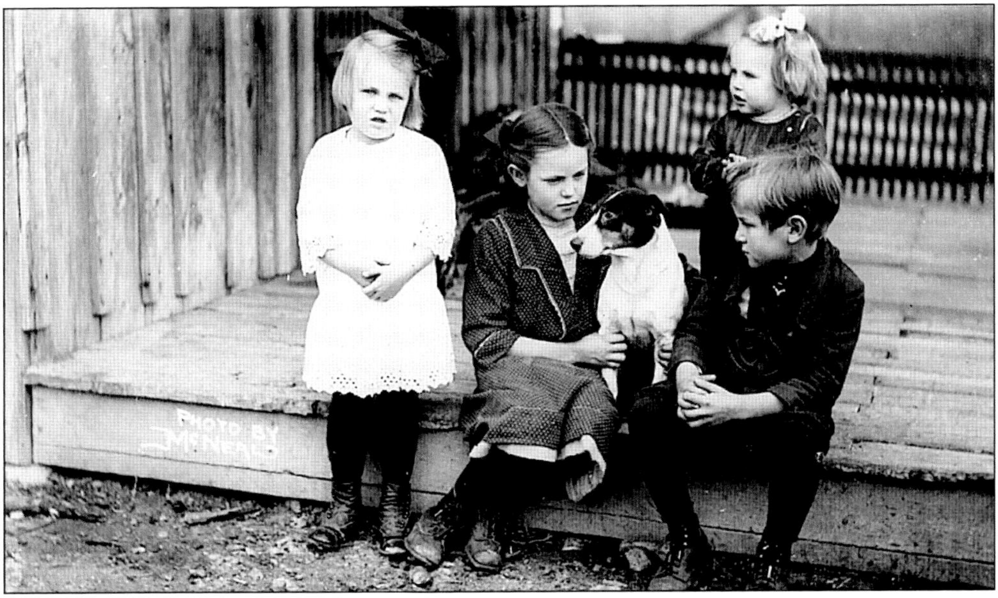

Then, as now, life in Springdale was a mixture of carefree, happy times tempered by times of trial and sadness. In the above *c.* 1910 photo, a group of children pose on the back porch with their family dog, in a setting that transcends generations. The girl in the center was gripping the dog's legs tightly, suggesting that holding still for a photo was not the animal's priority for that day. The card below, mailed in 1913, shows a crowd gathered on a rainy winter day at Springdale's cemetery, almost certainly to say farewell to a friend or relative. The message reads, "Mother has been quite sick for 2 weeks, is some better now."

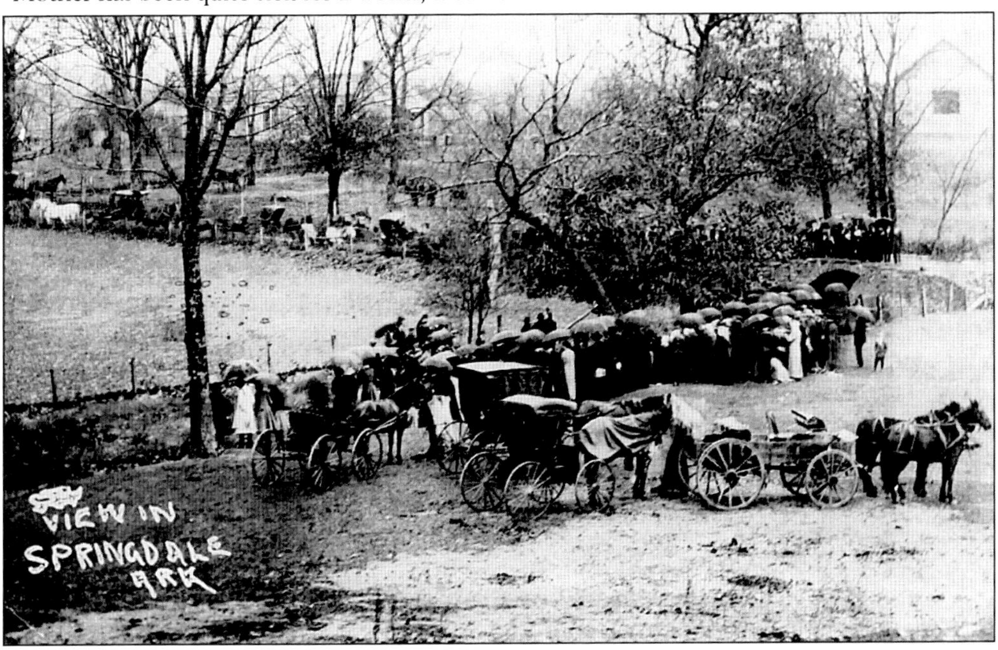

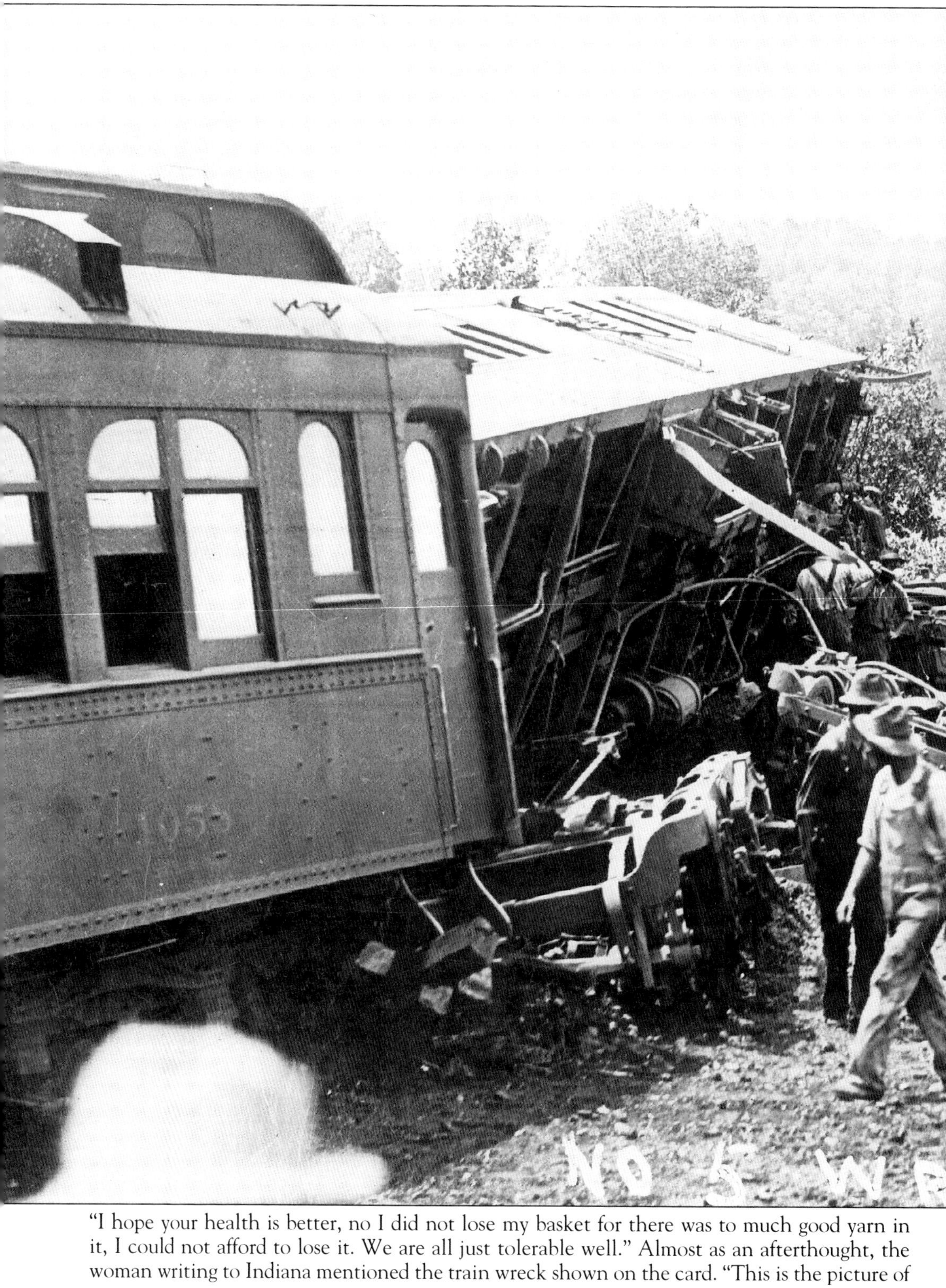

"I hope your health is better, no I did not lose my basket for there was to much good yarn in it, I could not afford to lose it. We are all just tolerable well." Almost as an afterthought, the woman writing to Indiana mentioned the train wreck shown on the card. "This is the picture of

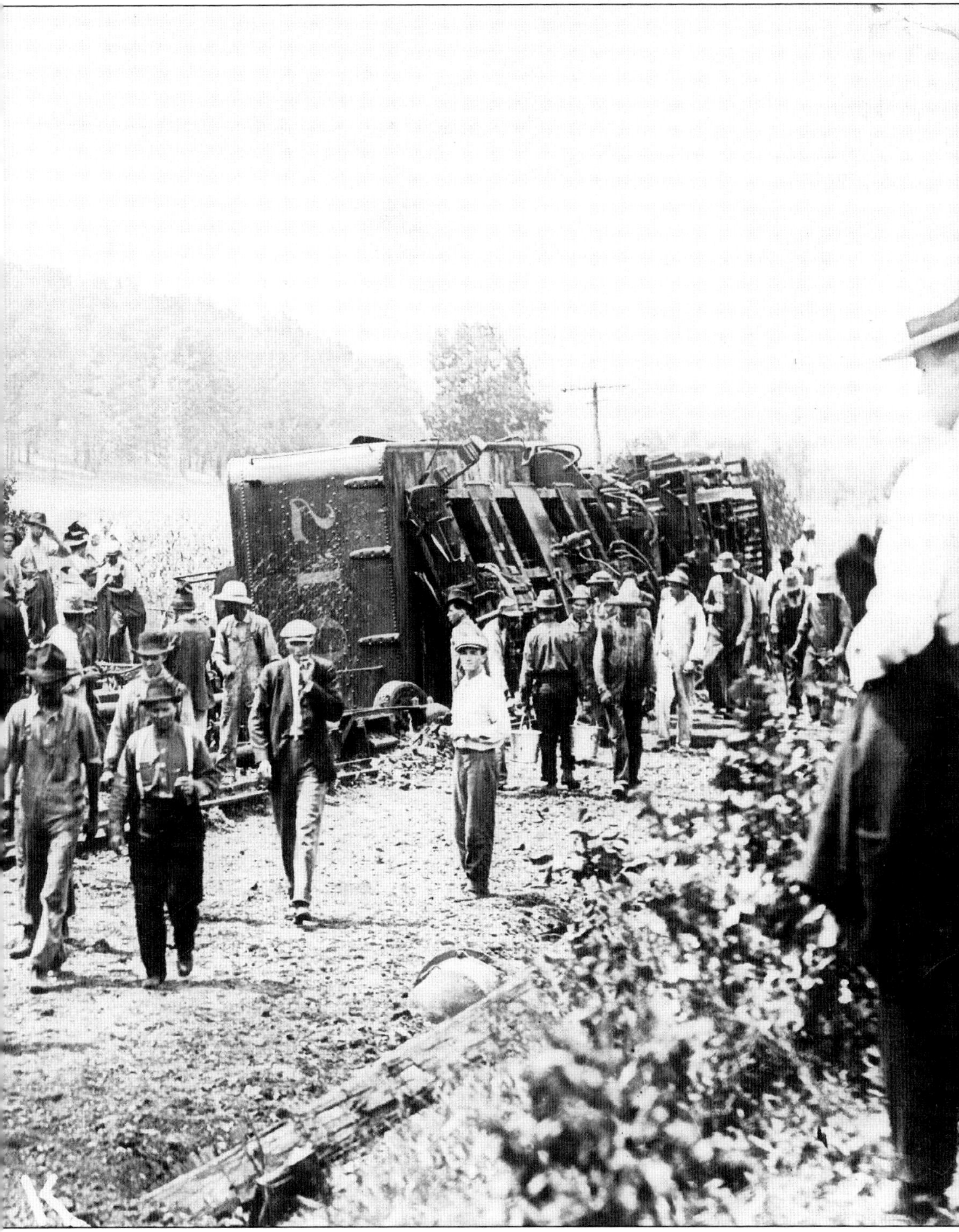

the Cannon Ball Wreck, it did not hurt anybody very bad." Such wrecks were not uncommon, due to the hazards faced by the numerous trains that crisscrossed northwestern Arkansas.

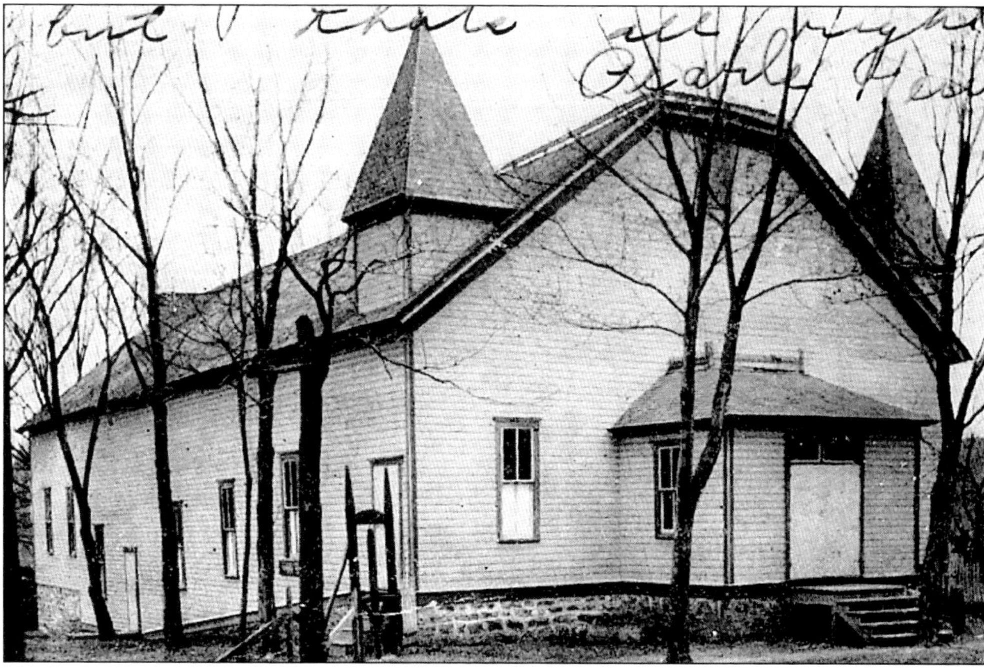

The Springdale Auditorium hosted what was, for several years, a major event in the community, the traveling Chautauqua. Thousands would fill the grounds to hear speeches by orators such as William Jennings Bryan, the prairie populist who ran unsuccessfully for president several times. A modern day re-enactment of the Chautauqua was held in Springdale in 1998, under the sponsorship of Springdale's Shiloh Museum. (1907.)

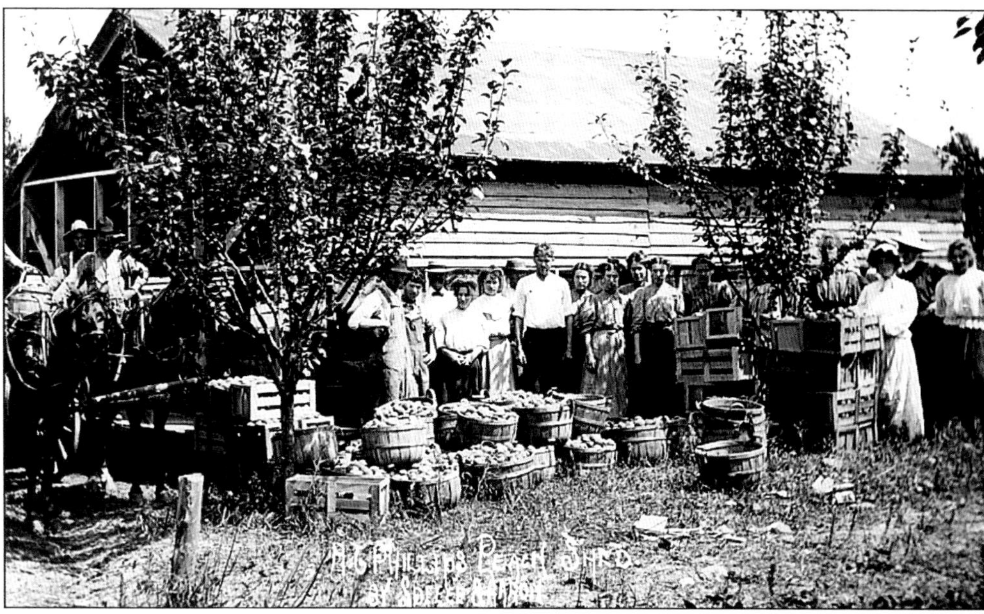

In 1909 there were reportedly 200,000 peach trees in Washington County, and many of these were in the A.J. Phillips orchards. In this 1912 card the harvested crop has been brought in to the packing shed. The penned message reads, "We have had some good old winter time, it was 10 below, we have about 18 inches of snow now."

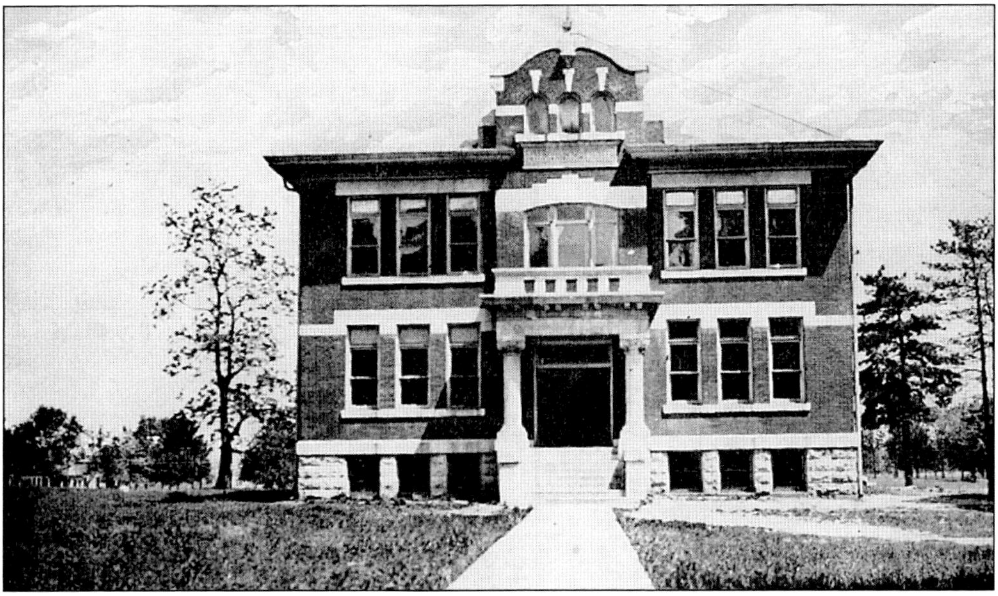

Springdale's sturdy brick high school still stands today, off of Business Route 71, some seven decades after this c. 1915 photo. If the school met the state average of the time, a teacher there would have earned around $400 for teaching a school year that lasted 124 days.

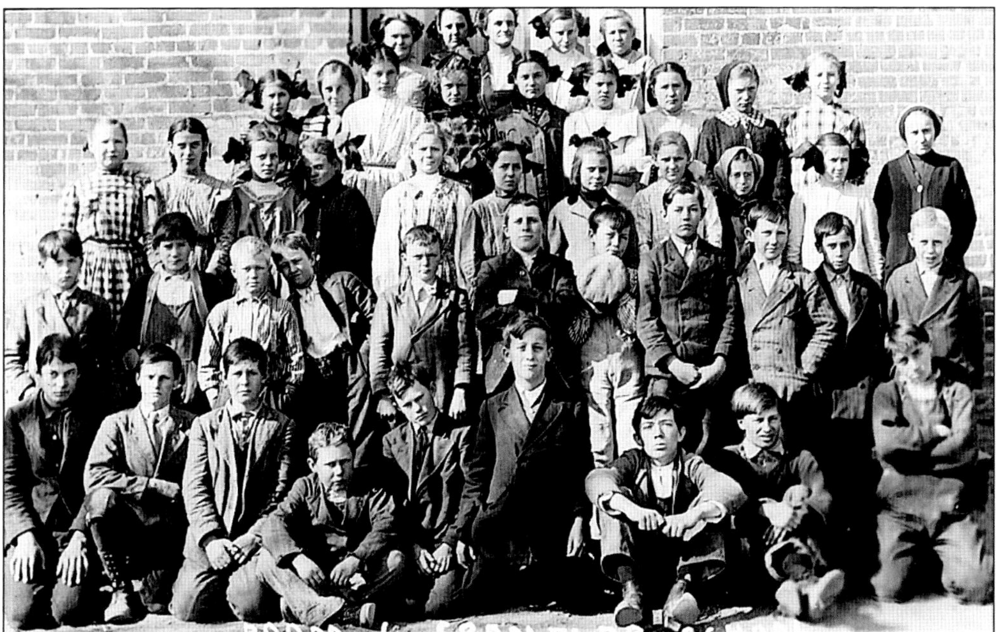

The class from Room #6 of Springdale's Grammar School posed on the steps of the school building in 1911. These children, with a multitude of expressions meeting the camera, were among 395,000 Arkansas public school children that year. For each of these, the state that year expended an average of $12 toward the cost of their education. Should any of these children still be alive today, they would be at least one hundred years of age.

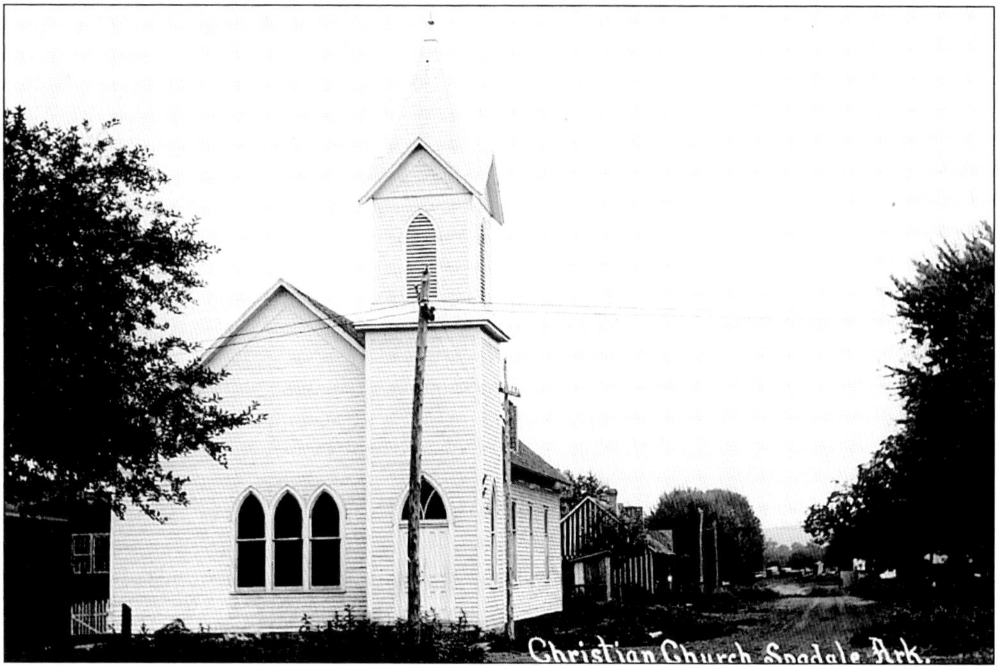

Typical of small-town white frame churches were these two in Springdale, nestled into quiet residential sections on rutted dirt roads that brought worshippers afoot and by wagon. Pictured above is the city's Christian Church, and below the Methodist Episcopal Church, before which is a plank walkway to aid in traversing the muddy pathway evident in the picture. Both churches are gone today. (c. 1910.)

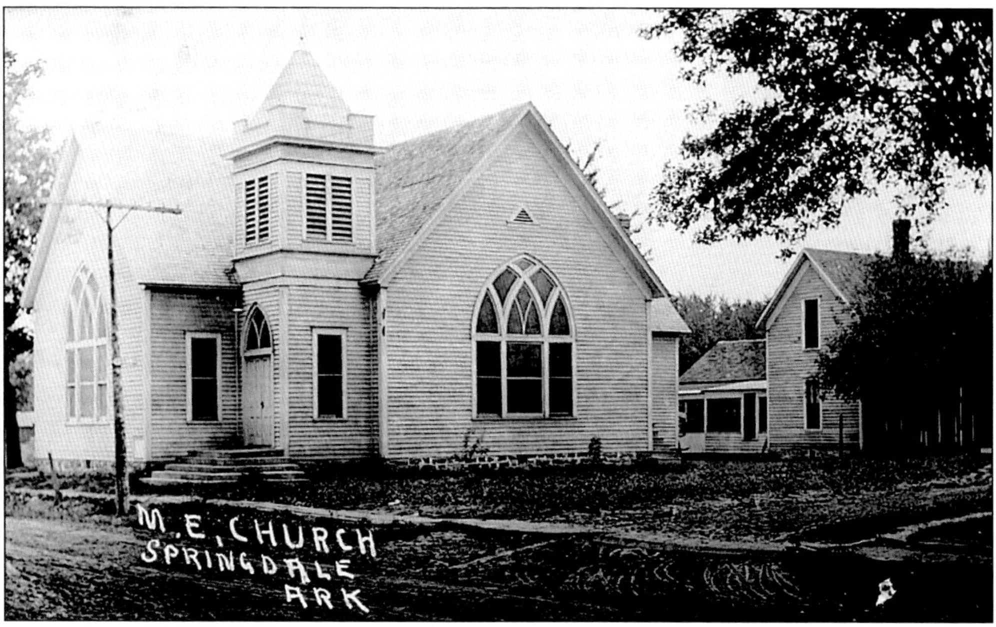

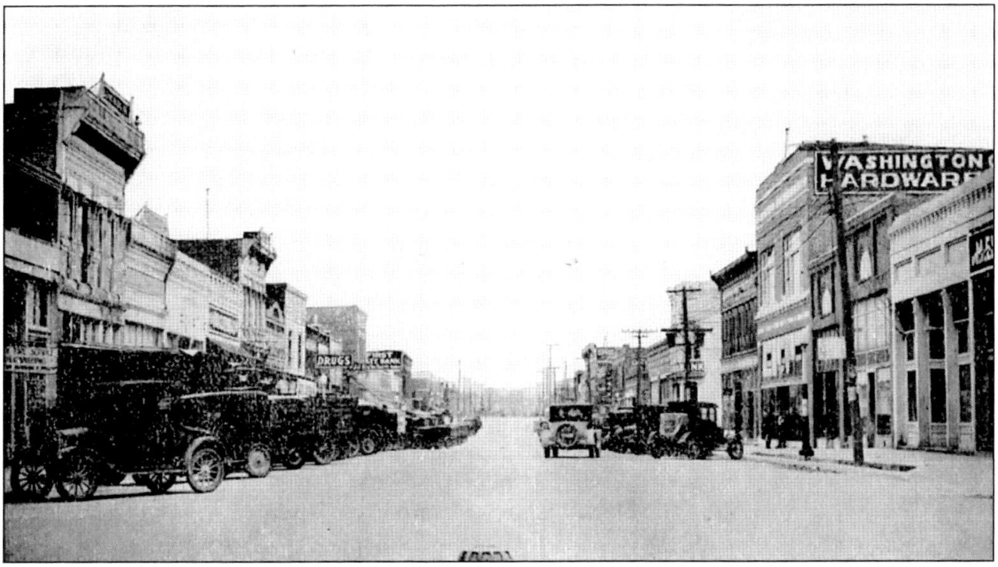

By 1930, Emma Avenue was paved and the automobile was beginning to make its mark. The turn-of-the-century buildings remained intact, as seen here, but the products sold in the stores were changing. The store to the very left sold car tires, while across the street, the Washington Hardware store would have had far fewer customers for the buggy harnesses and kerosene lamps it once stocked in quantity.

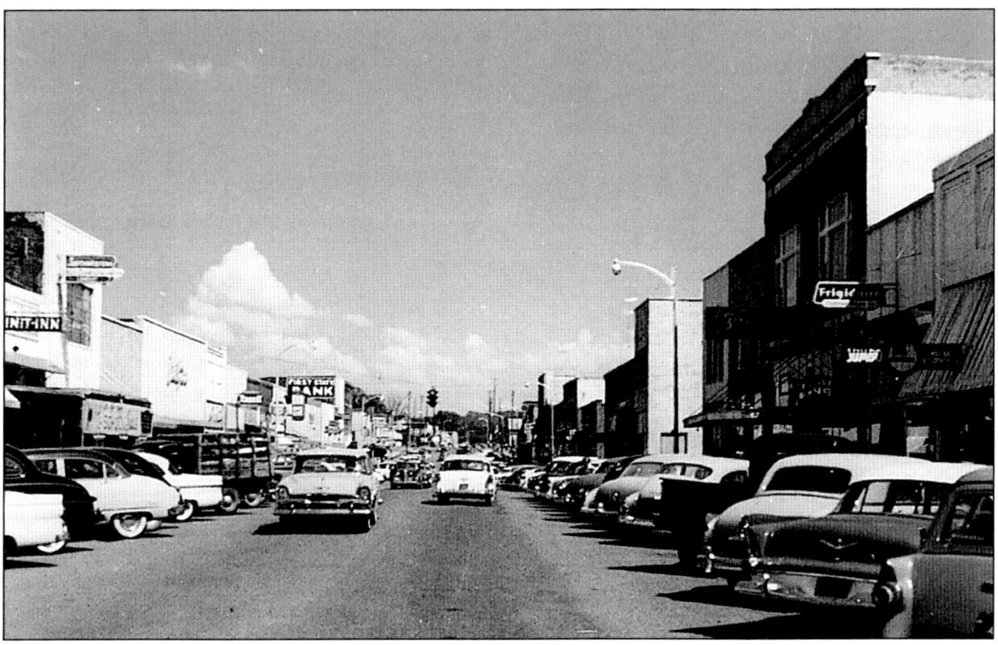

In a c. 1958 postcard view of Springdale's Emma Avenue, the changes are dramatic when compared to the image above and those found on page 27 of this book. In contrast to 50 years previous, this view finds automobiles and paved roadways where once only wagons churned a muddy street. The main retail district was still on Emma Avenue at the time of this photo, but today has primarily moved to outlying shopping centers.

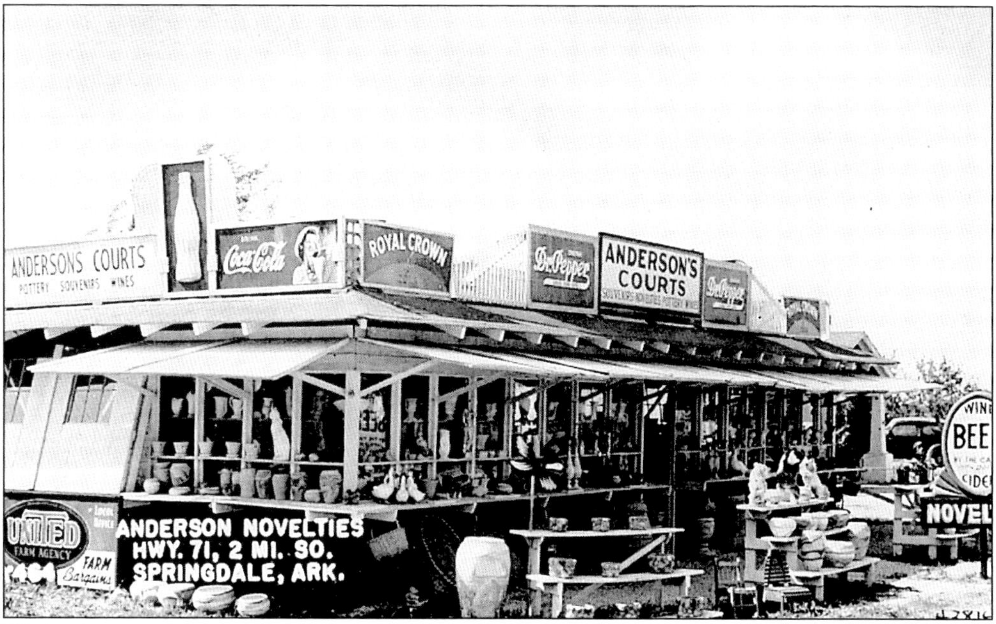

With the improvements to State Highway 71 and the rapidly expanding ownership of automobiles in post-WW II Arkansas, business expanded along the approaches to Springdale. In the photo above is seen a c. 1950 view of Anderson's Novelties, a roadside business selling pottery, soft drinks, and beer. The Anderson family also ran an adjacent motor court. In the photo below, also c. 1950, can be seen the Sunset Motel. It was typical of the tourist courts of the 1940s, where the cabins often had attached a small garage to shelter the guests' automobiles. Both businesses are gone today.

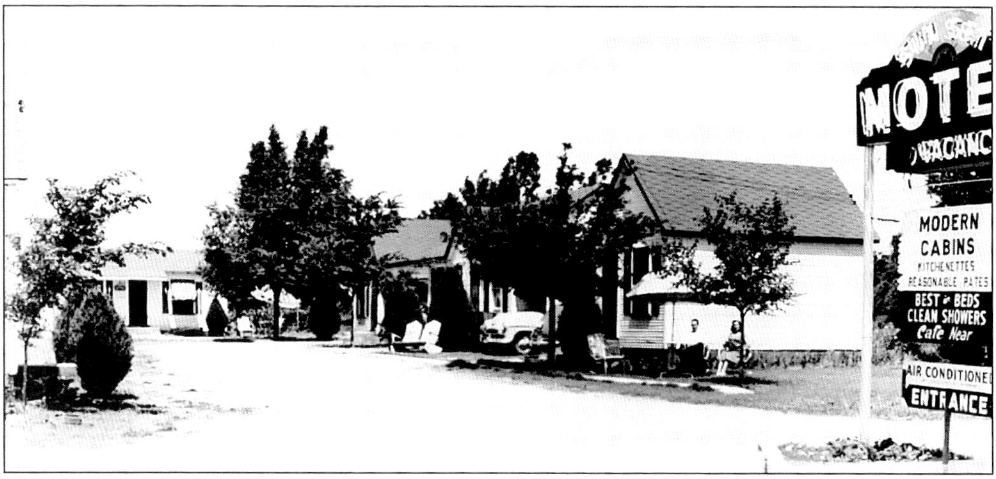

Two

Washington County

Small Towns and Crossroad Villages

While Washington County was home to the university town of Fayetteville and its growing neighbor Springdale, it also gave rise to a host of small, interesting towns that had a entirely different look. We are fortunate today that the postcard photographers found their way into these sometimes remote hamlets at the end of rutted wagon roads, to record scenes of rural Washington County for the future.

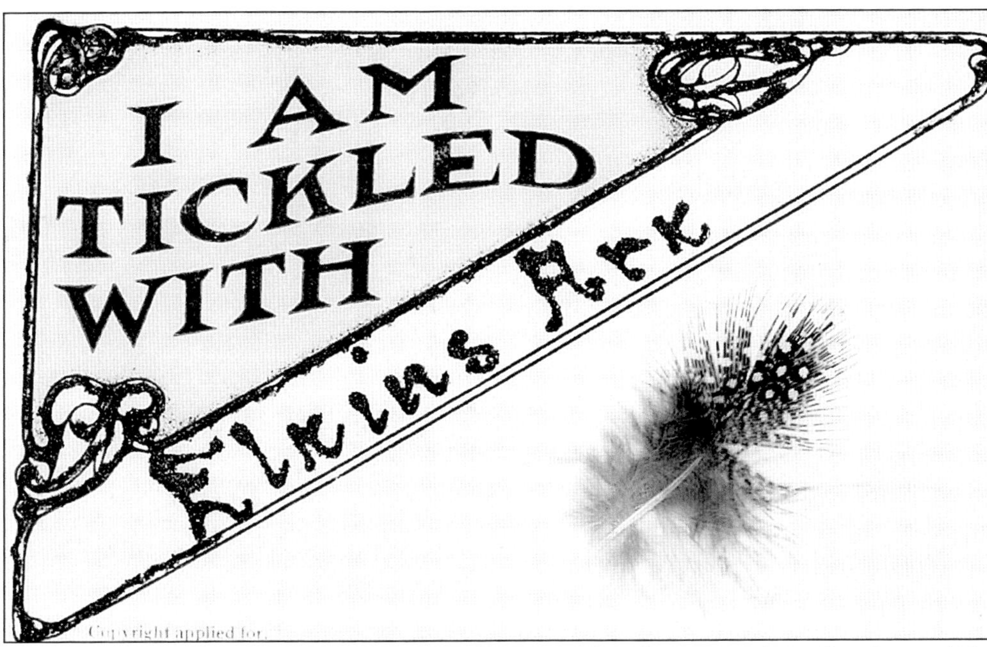

"I received your card today, it found us all well. In regard to the post cards I will make you 5 for 25 cents or 5 cents each for what you want. We had a box supper at Harris last Thursday night and a pie supper tonight. Well I can not make the cards until I get some, I order some Monday." John Davis, from the small town of Elkins, was running a postcard business from his home. An actual feather is glued on the face of the card.

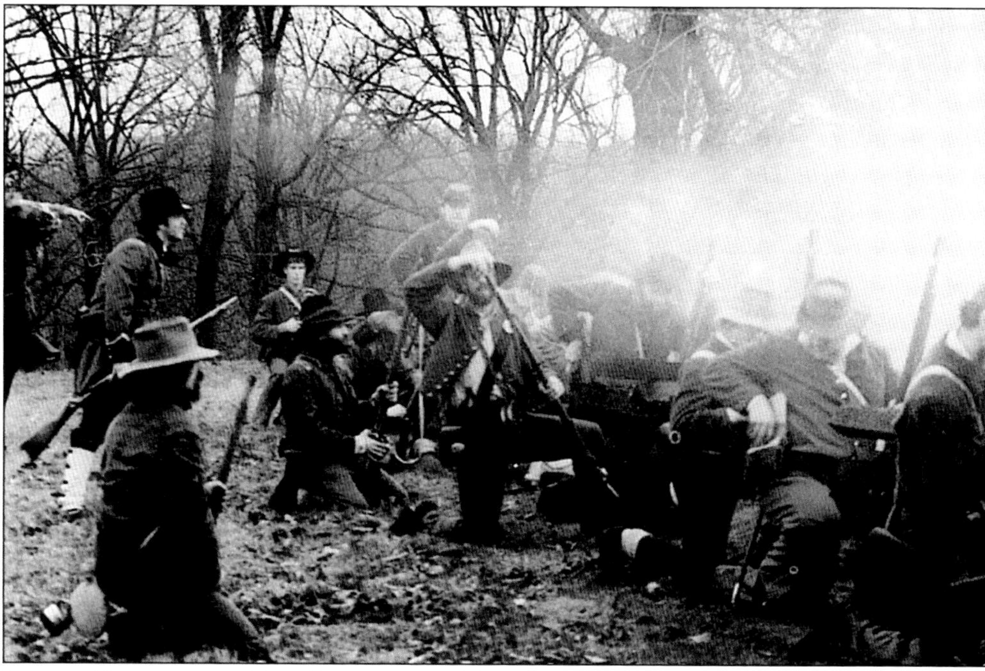

Prairie Grove, a small village west of Fayetteville, entered Civil War history on December 7, 1862. After a day-long, bloody battle in which 2,500 men were killed, wounded, or missing, Confederate General Thomas Hindman retreated, escaping under a flag of truce that had actually been called in order to search the darkened field for wounded men. Shown in this card is a modern-day re-enactment of the battle. (Card courtesy of the Arkansas Parks and Tourism Department.)

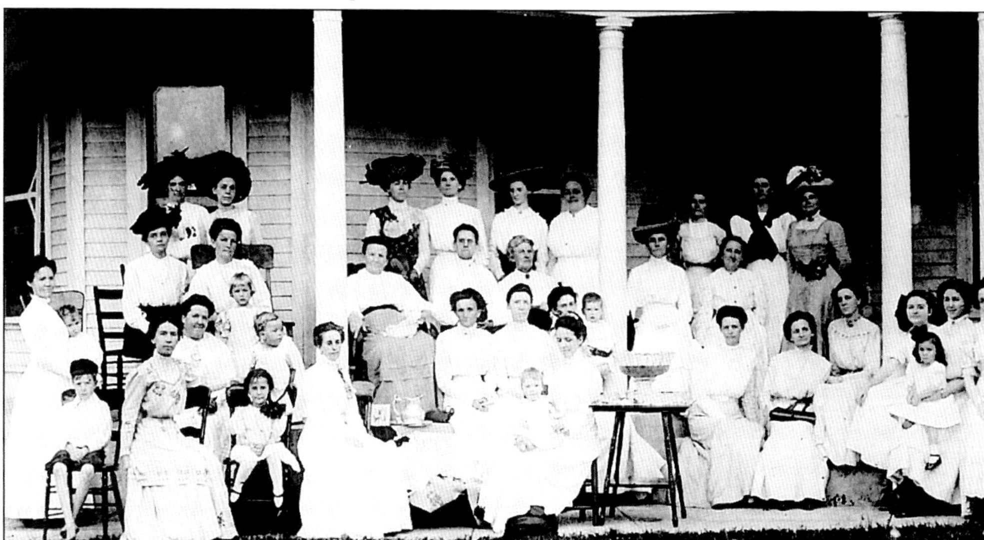

Members of the United Daughters of the Confederacy gathered on the porch of the home of S.H. Rogers in 1911 for a shower party. The Prairie Grove battlefield was designated a park in 1871 after the DOC purchased 9 acres on the site. Today the site is home to Prairie Grove State Park, which offers a museum commemorating the 1862 battle, along with frequent living history demonstrations.

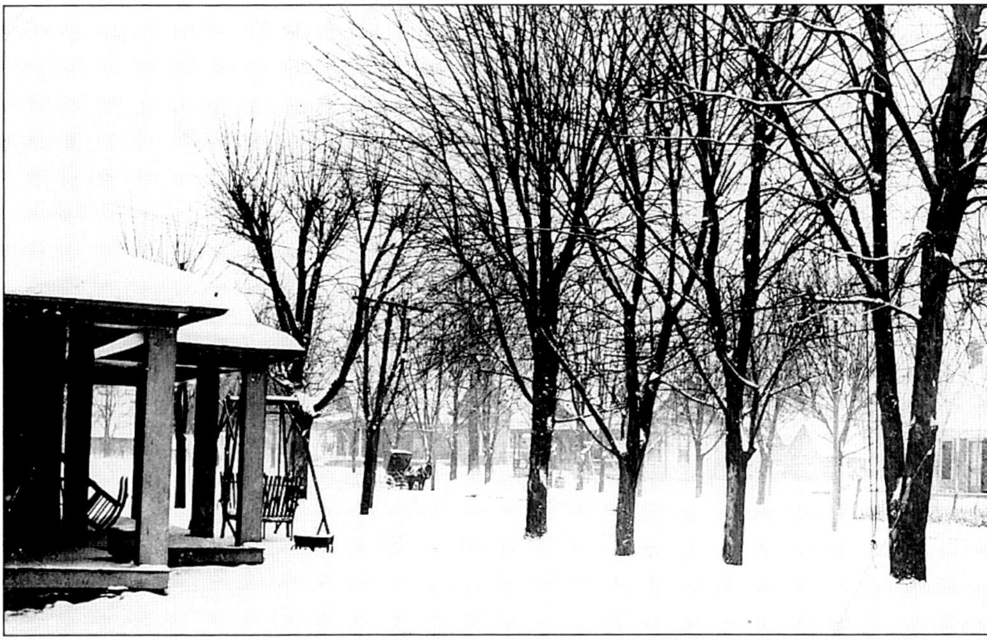

"Dear Mother—Not a Valentine in this burg, so will send a view," reads the 1921 message from Prairie Grove to Round Rock, Texas. Deep snow covered the small town, and the home's swing and rocking chair were still, awaiting the arrival of spring. Only a lone horse-drawn buggy was moving on the road the day this view was taken.

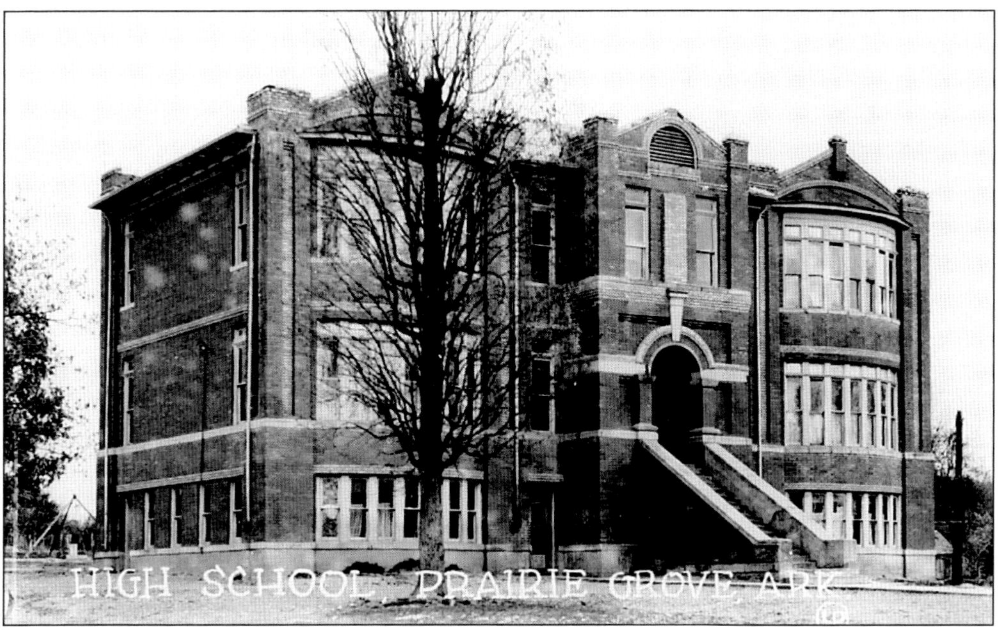

Prairie Grove had claim to a handsome high school for such a small town—in an era when the state had an astounding 5,110 school districts. If the school met the state's average in 1910, when the photo was made, each classroom would have had 40 students who climbed these steep steps every morning of the 107-day school year.

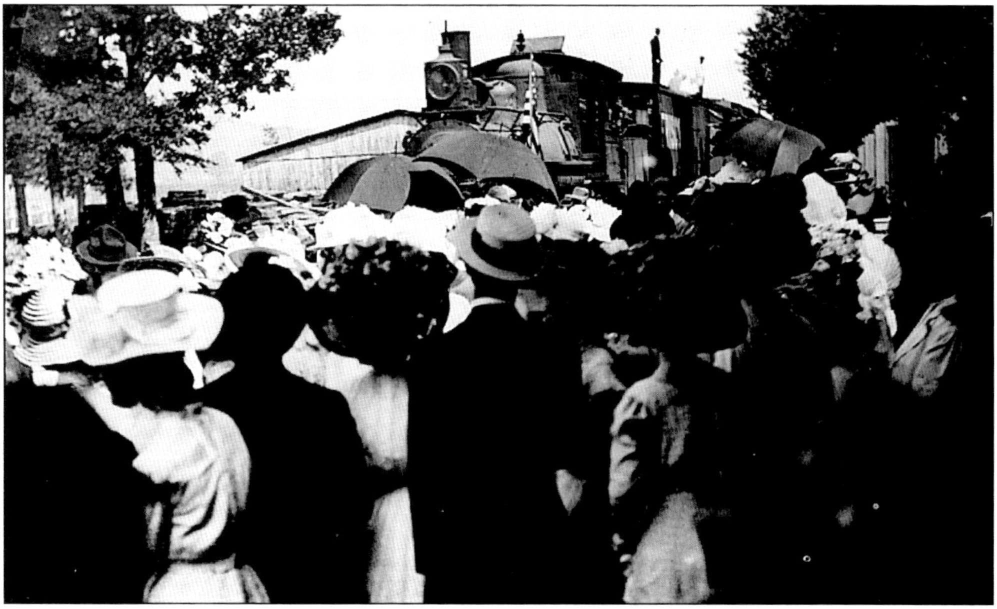

Elkins, a small community east of Fayetteville, found many of its citizens out to meet the train at the local station in 1909. The message to Missouri read, "I am sending a view of the train leaving the depot at Elkins, July 3, 09. Elkins is the next station to Harris, we are all well at present." In recognition of Independence Day, an American flag is affixed to the front of the locomotive as it prepares to steam on toward Fayetteville.

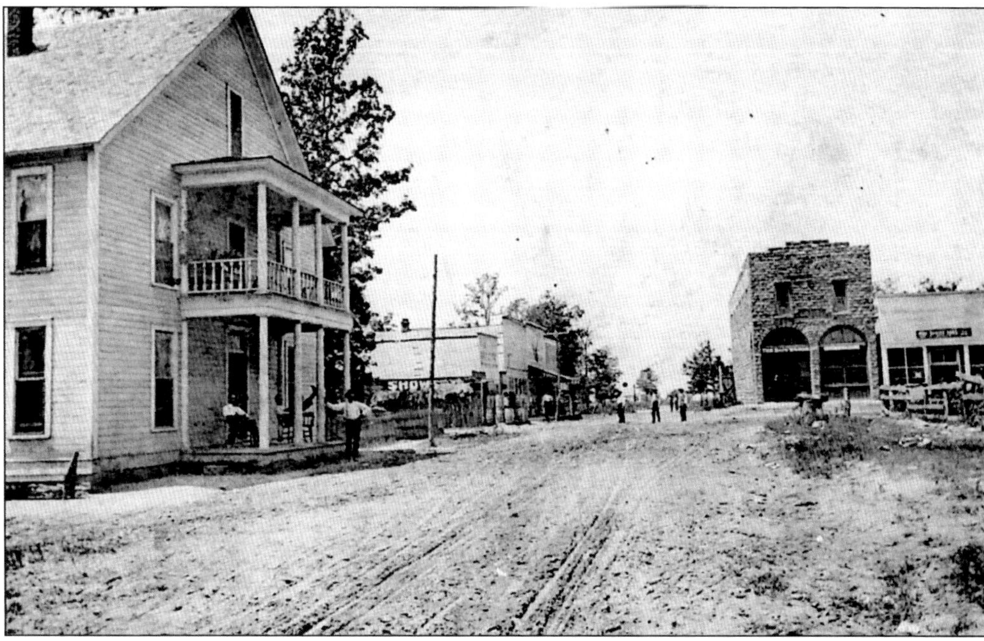

One legend has it that Lincoln, the small town located southwest of Fayetteville, got its name from a box of freight in 1885, while another claims that it was named for the martyred President. In this *c.* 1900 postcard, the Lincoln Hotel is seen at the left, with several guests lounging on its porch. The hotel offered meals for 25¢, and was popular with salesmen and railroad workers. Today the hotel is gone, but the stone building seen to the right still stands.

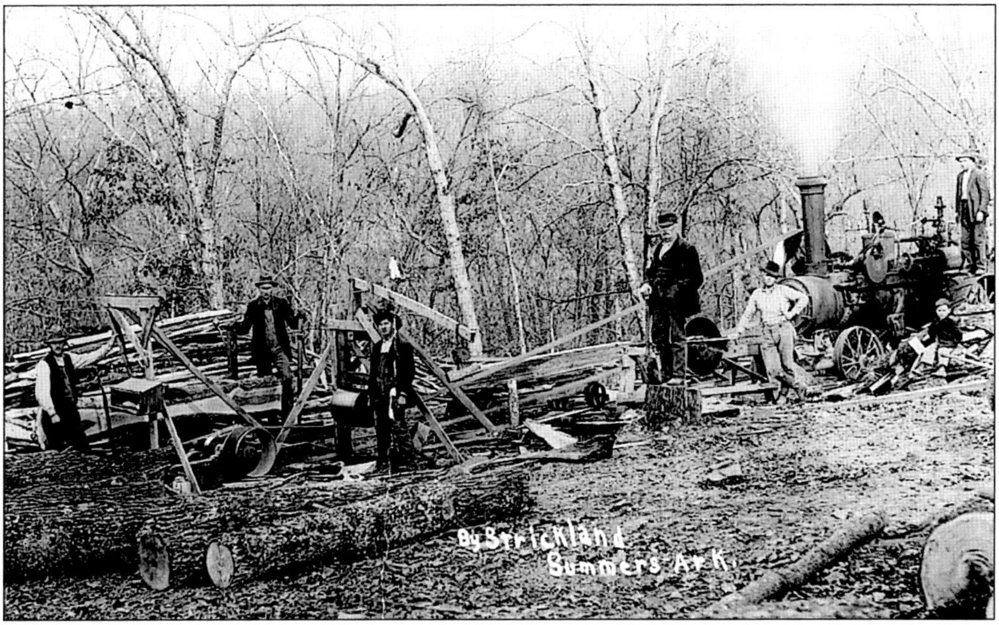

At the turn of the century, many men earned their wages cutting the great hardwood forests of Washington County. In the tiny village of Summers, southeast of Fayetteville, the men in the photo above were photographed sawing logs with a steam-powered, portable, wheeled sawmill. In the postcard below, a group of men take a photo break seated on a large pile of sawdust, evidence of how much lumber had been cut. The rapid cutting of the virgin hardwoods of Washington County was driven in part by new home construction, but also by demand for railroad ties; 1 mile of train track required 3,000 hardwood ties.

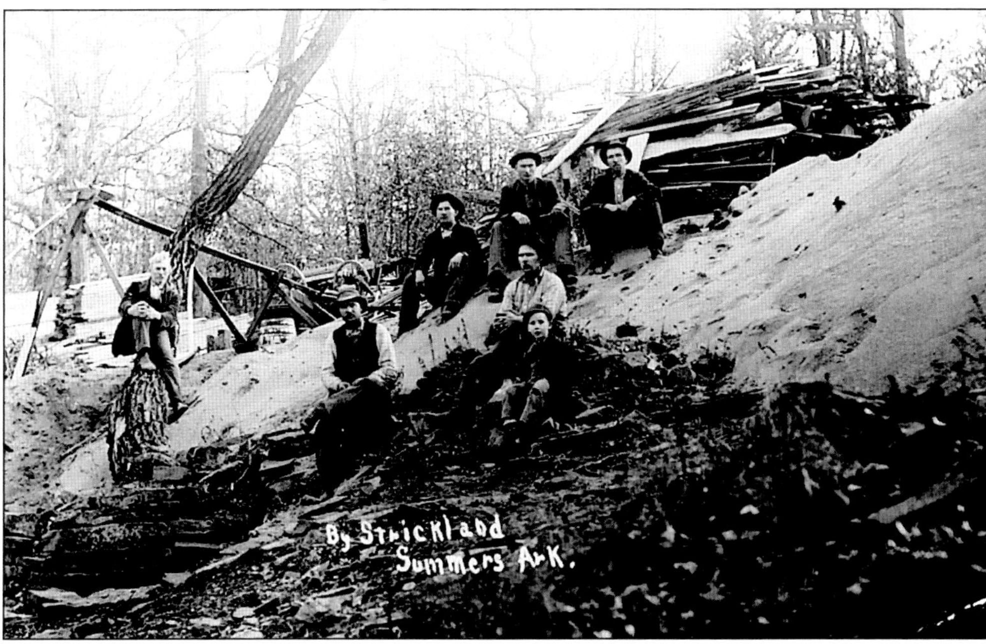

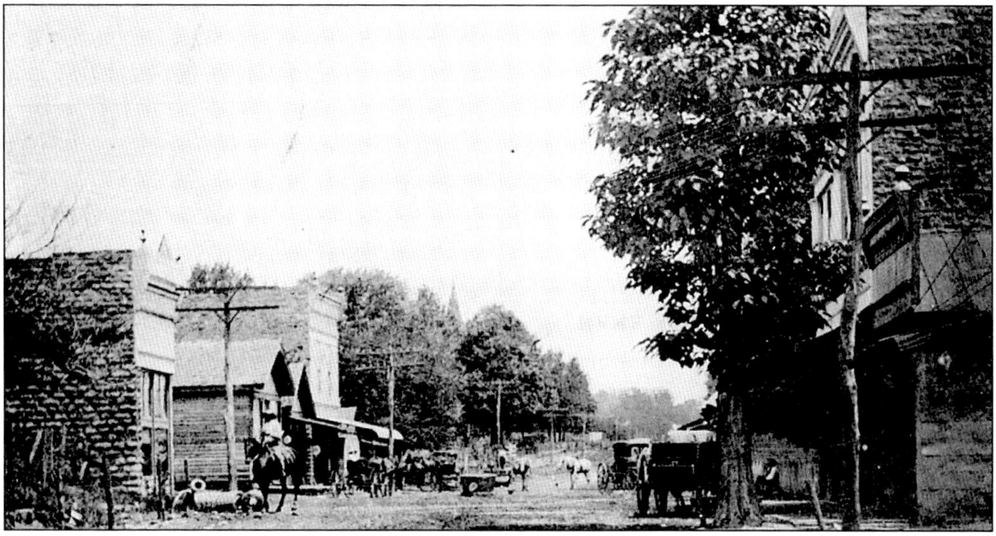

Cane Hill, in western Washington County, was a boom town originally named Boonsboro; it lay along the line of the Ozark & Cherokee Central Railroad until 1901, when shifting fortunes gave momentum to other communities. In the top, *c.* 1900 photo of the town's Main Street, a mounted horseman paused to stare at the photographer. In the lower view is seen the Bank of Cane Hill; at the lower right is seen the town pump, at which man and beast would have drawn water for refreshment from the dust and heat.

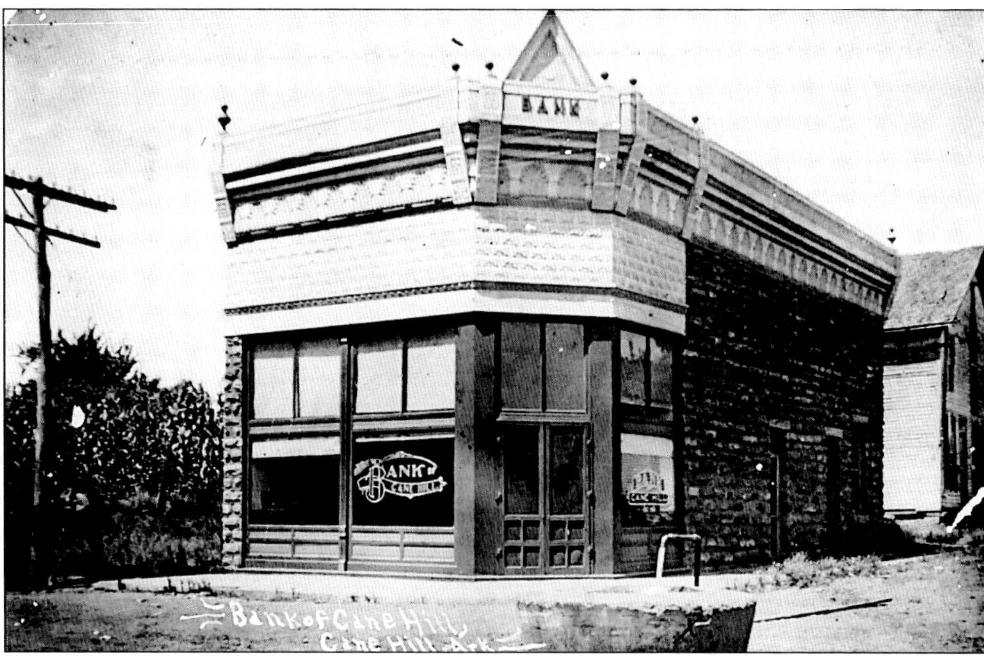

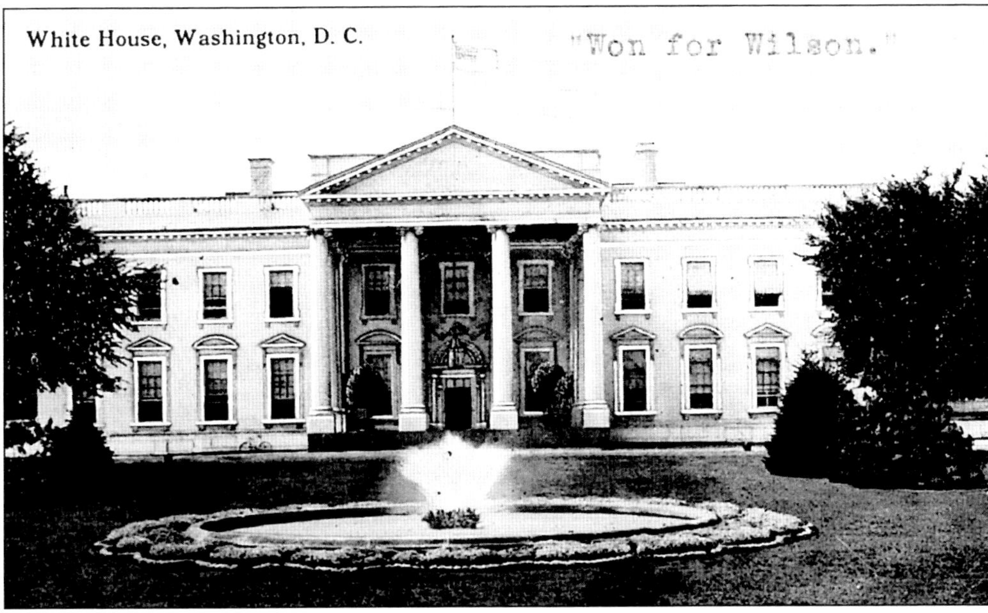

The community of Harris is now gone from most maps, and its post office closed in 1957, but interesting political commentaries appeared on these postcards received by the Bowen family in Harris: "Dear Harry, Nothing too good for the Wilsons. I hope your vote was among the balance of the good democrats? If you didn't vote for Wilson I think you should have. Yours, Fred." On the front of this postcard of the White House, Fred had typed, "Won for Wilson." (1913.)

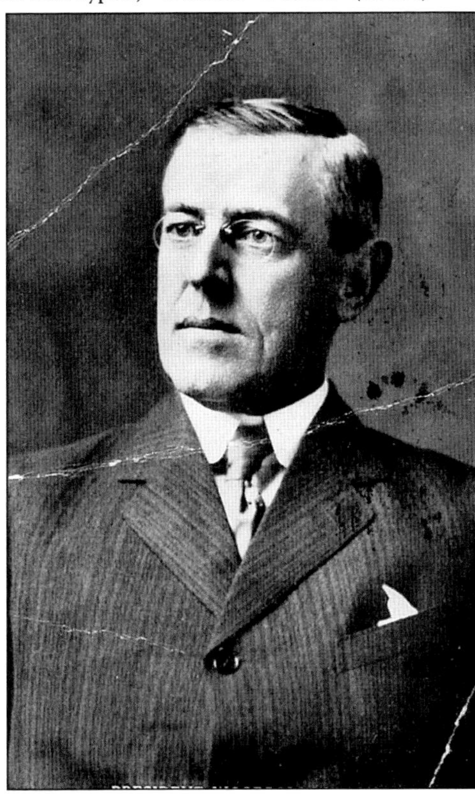

Three months later, Fred sent this note to his nephew, "Dear Fritz—What do you think of this Great Man? Wish you could be here to help us inaugurate him. Preparations are being made take care of the largest crowd Wash. has ever seen. Why not? See who he is.—Yours, Uncle Fred." In national elections Arkansas voted 100% for Democratic candidates, a carryover from Civil War reconstruction, until the Presidential election of 1968. Today northwest Arkansas is the most Republican-voting region in the entire state.

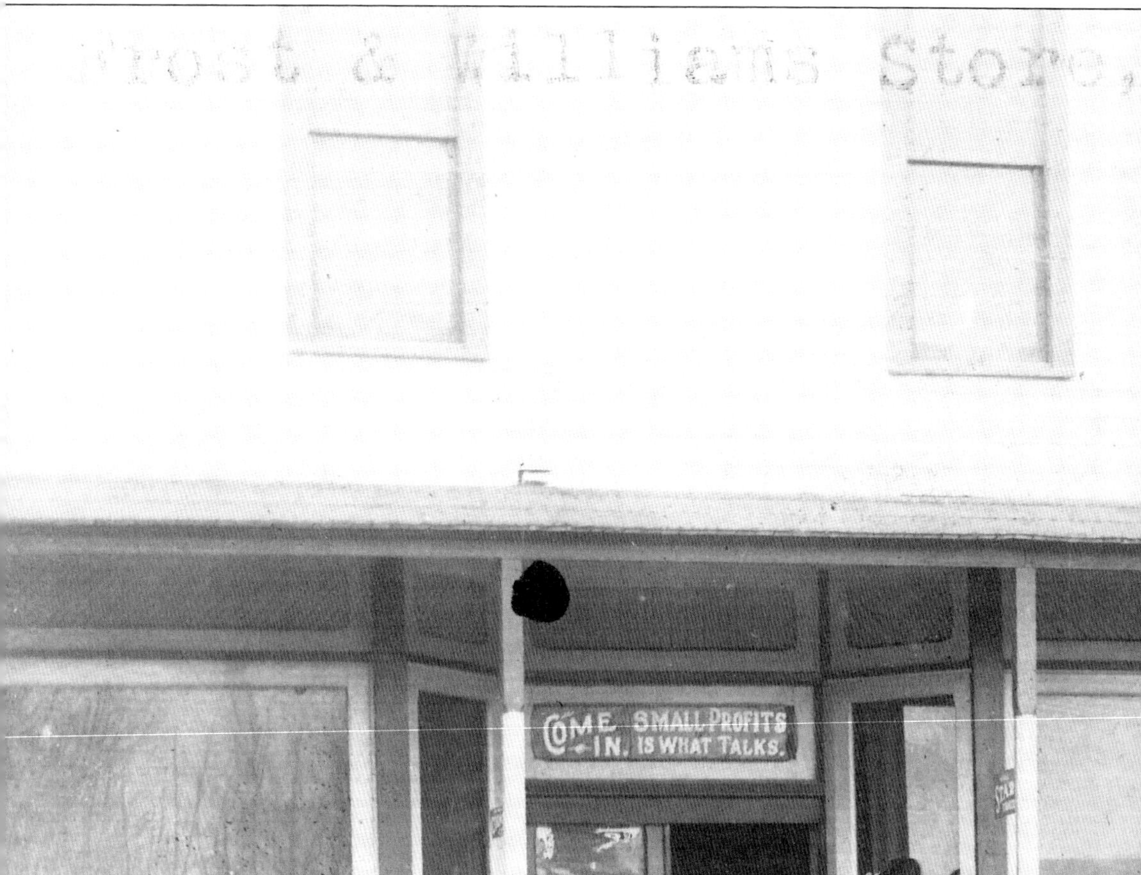

Greenland today adjoins the southern edge of the Fayetteville city limits, but in 1911 it was simply a small village a wagon ride away. The difficulty of traveling even a few miles helped preserve the customer base of Frost & William's Store. The sign over the door reads, "COME IN, SMALL PROFITS IS WHAT TALKS." Like most small-town mercantile establishments

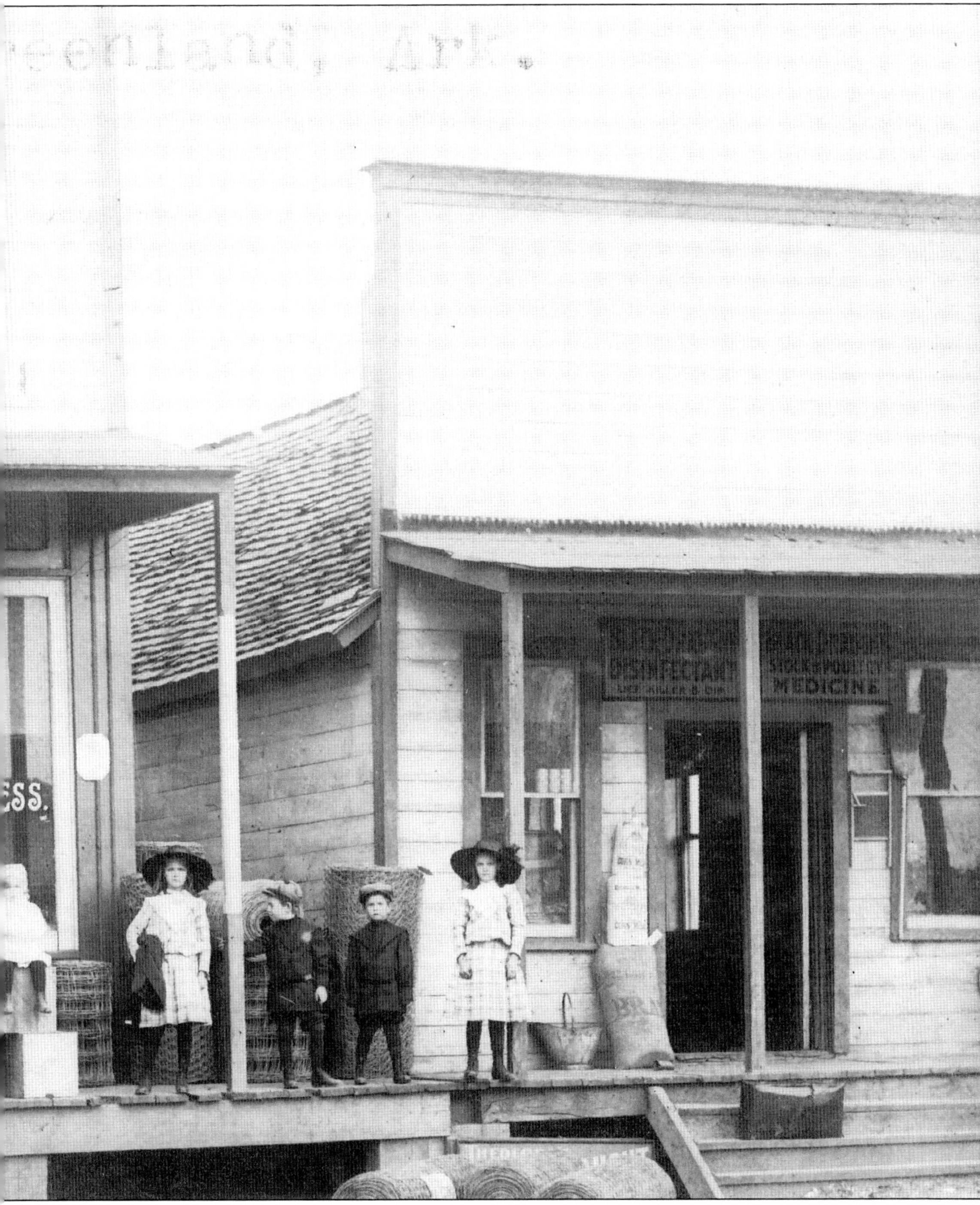

of the day, a wide variety of merchandise stocked the shelves, from buggy harnesses to clothing, plows, and even rolls of fence wire laying in the dusty street by the porch. The child in the black cap is seated on a box of Sunshine Biscuits. The message on this card advises, "You ought to be with us Easter. We are going to have our pictures made."

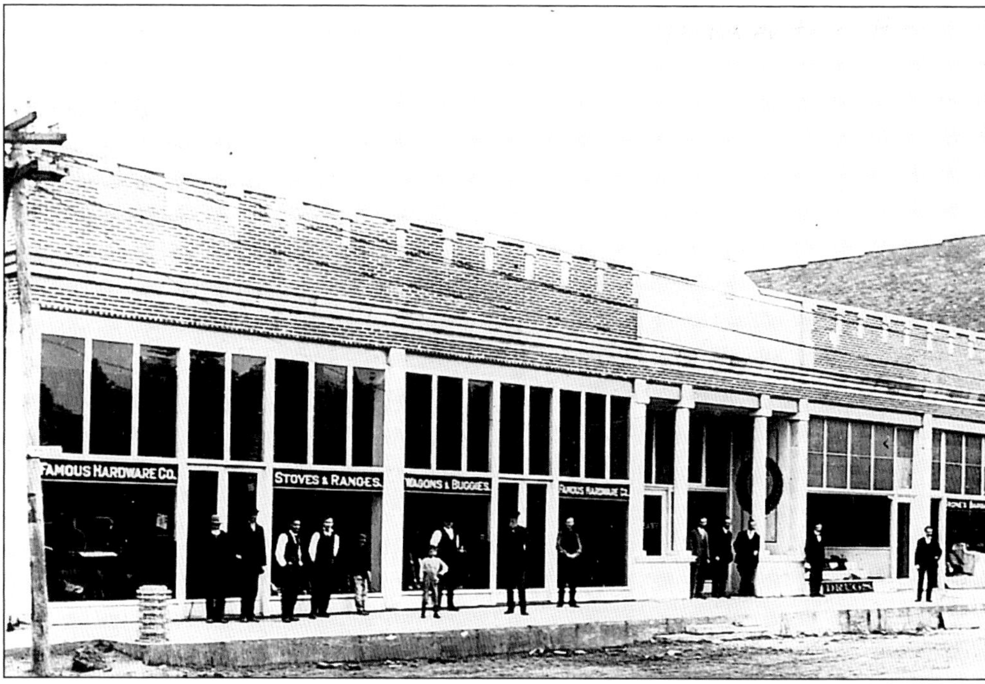

In 1913, Habberton was home to these men, some of whom probably worked in the Famous Hardware Company, which shared its long building with a drugstore. The Famous store advertised stoves and buggies among its wares. The town's post office closed in 1951, and the community has been absorbed by the eastward expansion of Fayetteville

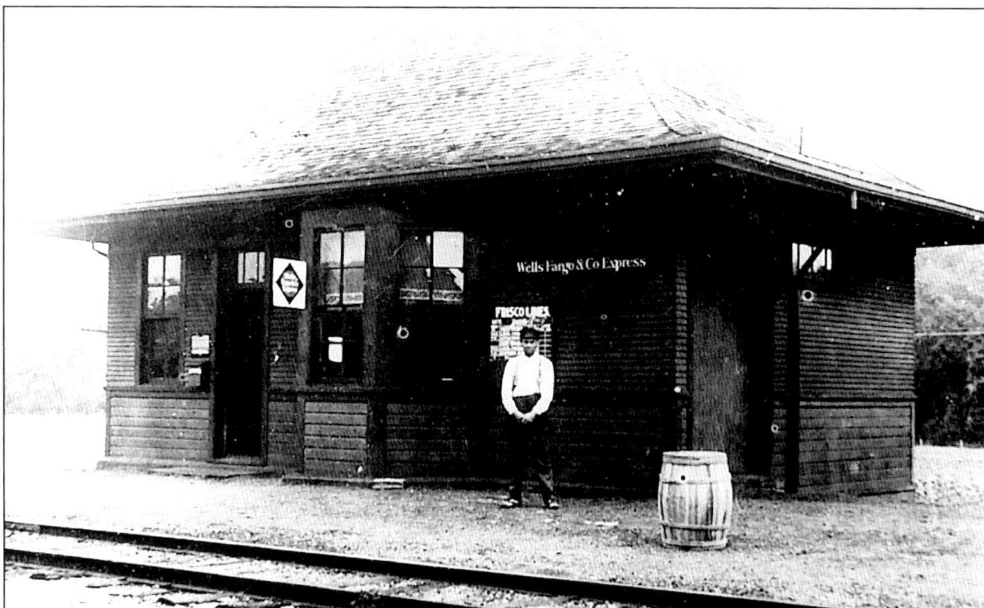

Woolsey, a small community south of Fayetteville, grew up around the Frisco Railroad depot. The depot attendant is standing before a Wells Fargo & Company Express sign. In 1930 the new Highway 71 would bypass Woolsey to the east; the town's growth stalled and faded in favor of other towns in the county. (*c.* 1920.)

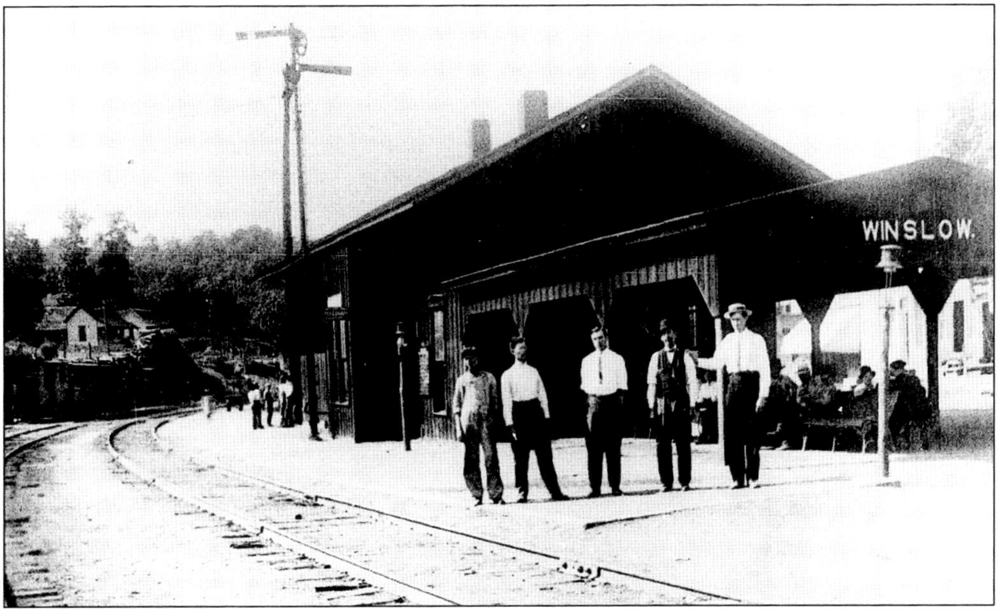

The town of Winslow is reported to be the highest incorporated city in Arkansas, and is listed also as the highest point reached by railroad between the Allegheny and Rocky Mountain ranges. The town was founded in 1876 as Summitt Home, but changed its name to Winslow in 1881 to honor E.F. Winslow, the president of the St. Louis & San Franciso Railroad, when the line arrived and brought promised prosperity to the town. (*c.* 1915.)

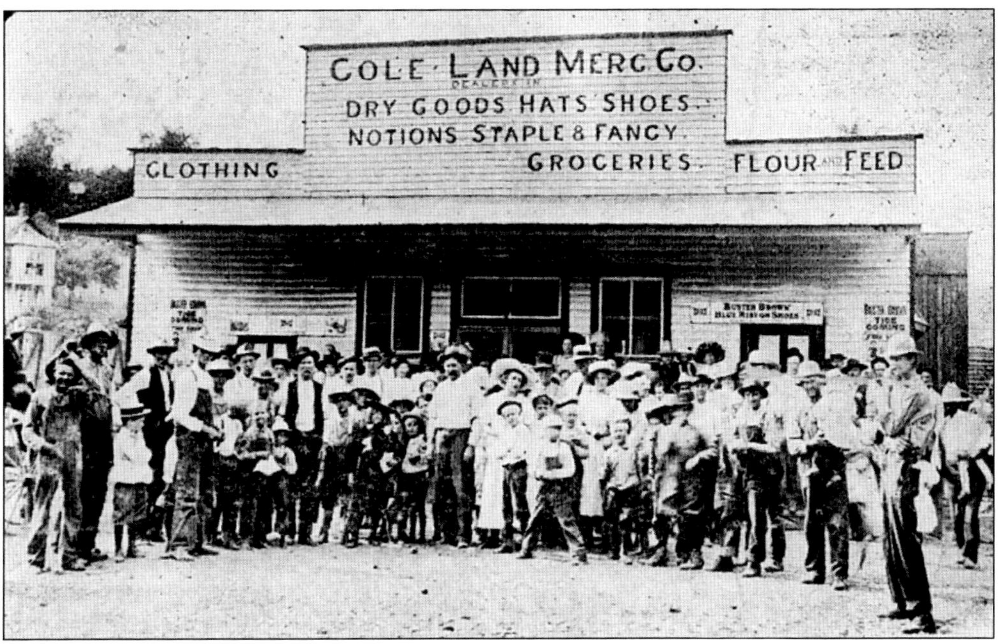

Winslow, located in southern Washington county, became a popular summer resort once the railroad arrived, putting its mountain-top breezes in reach of visitors. Residents and visitors alike would have shopped at the Coal Land Mercantile Company, which advertised dry goods, hats, shoes, notions, staple and fancy groceries, clothing, flour, and feed.

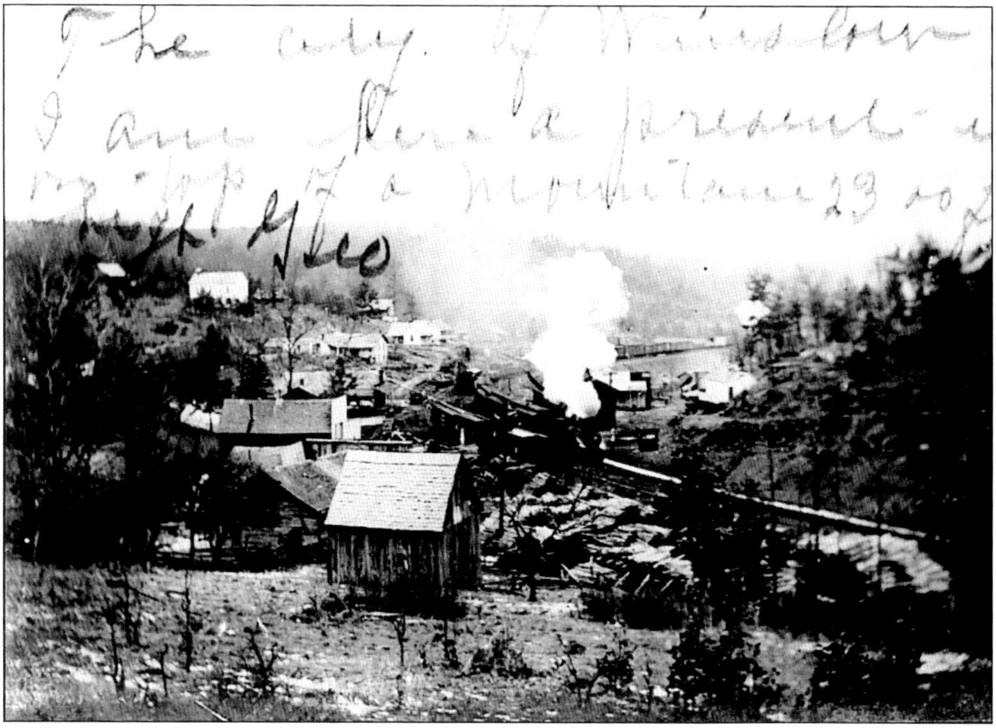

In a 1907 view the photographer looked down from the mountain side at a train steaming through Winslow; the message reads, "The city of Winslow, I am here at present—it is on top of a mountain 2,300 feet high." In the early part of the century, six Frisco passenger trains a day ran through Winslow. Until the mid-1920s the small railroad station was staffed 24 hours a day.

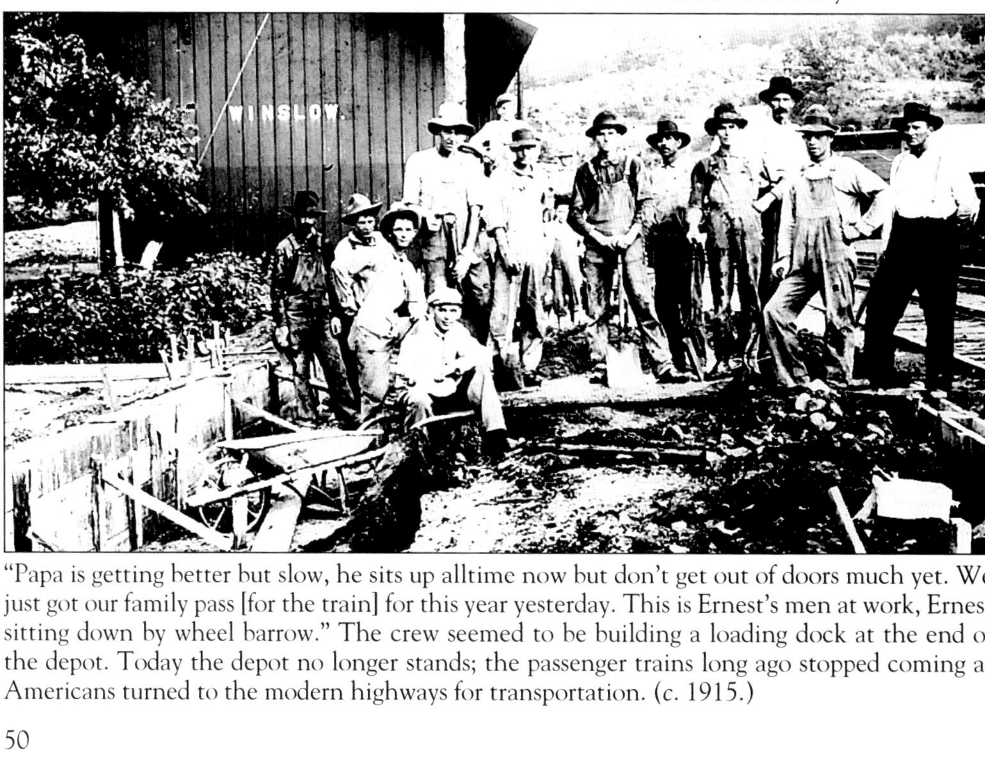

"Papa is getting better but slow, he sits up alltime now but don't get out of doors much yet. We just got our family pass [for the train] for this year yesterday. This is Ernest's men at work, Ernest sitting down by wheel barrow." The crew seemed to be building a loading dock at the end of the depot. Today the depot no longer stands; the passenger trains long ago stopped coming as Americans turned to the modern highways for transportation. (*c.* 1915.)

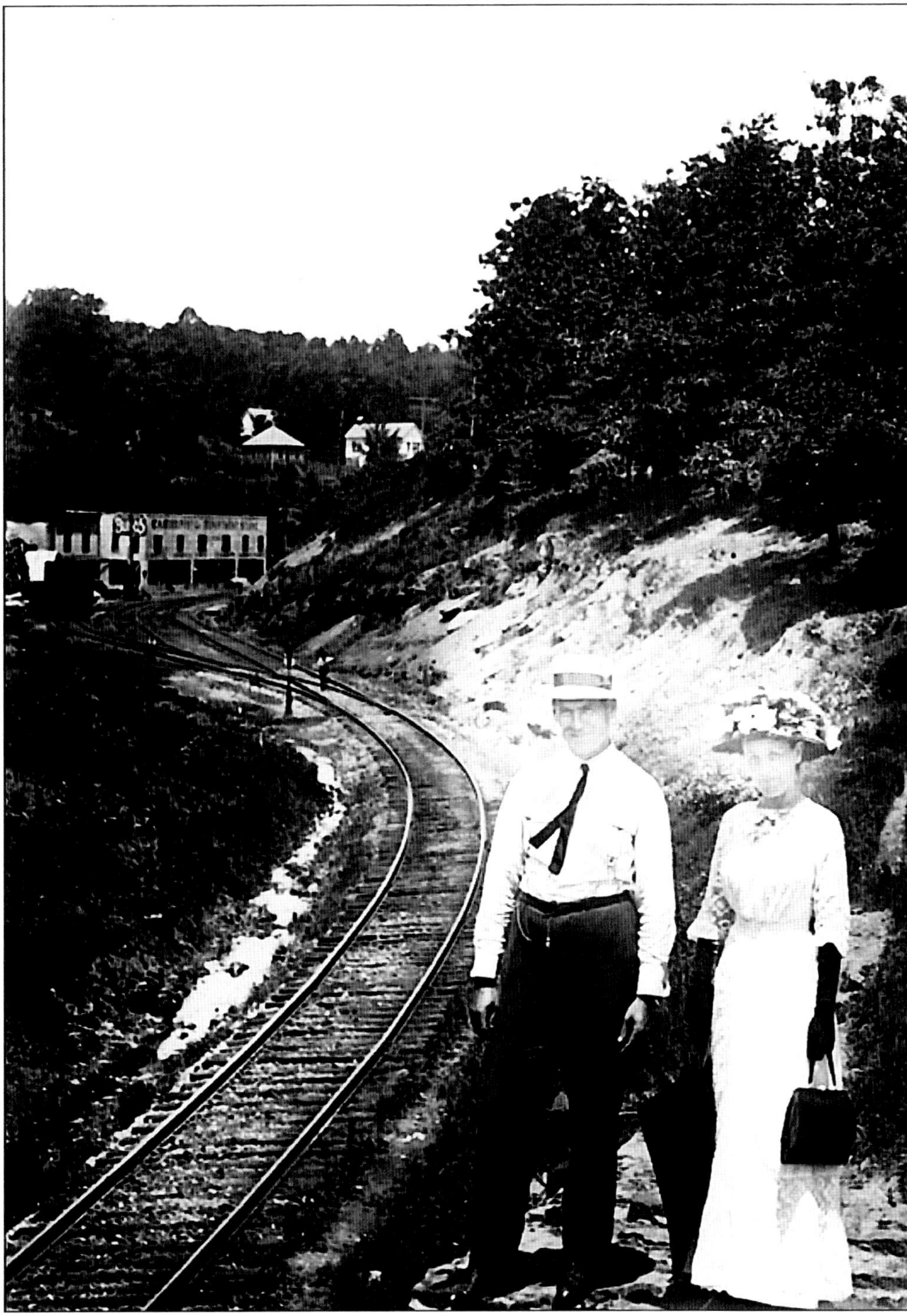

"Mr. & Mrs. Nathan Tracey taken at Winslow, Ark." No more is written or known about the couple that climbed a hill above the tracks in their best clothes; the woman sports a flowered hat, long black gloves, and an umbrella. Although their story is lost, it may be speculated that they were vacationing or perhaps on a honeymoon in the mountain-top resort.

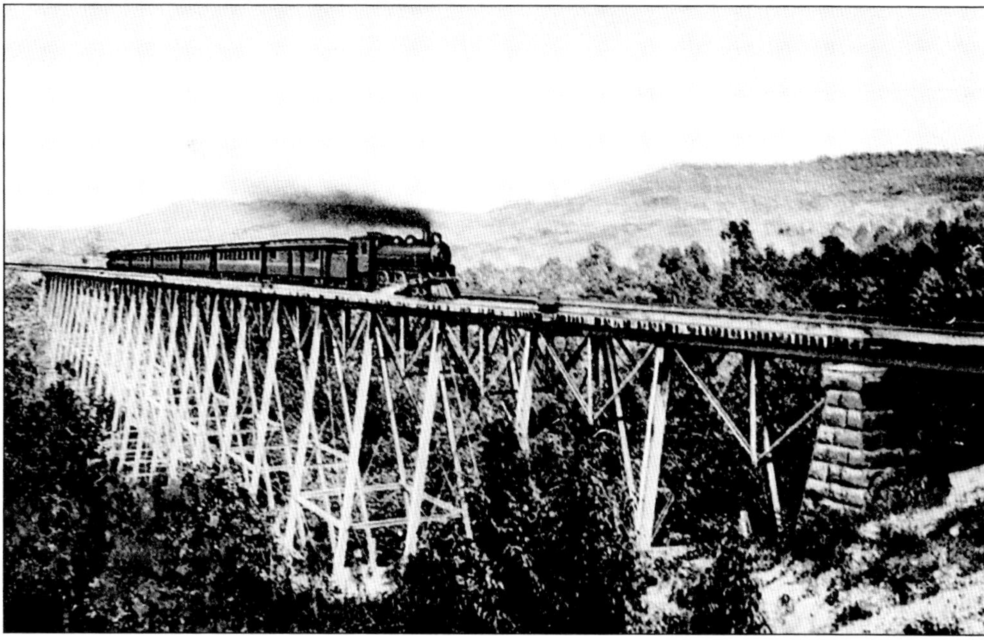

The Frisco Railroad made its mark on the approaches to Winslow in several major feats of engineering. In the above card, *c.* 1915, the steel viaduct trestle was one of three; it spanned 780 feet and was 140 feet high. In the 1912 card below is seen the Winslow Tunnel through the Boston Mountains; it took almost two years to complete its 1,780 foot length in the 1880s. The card's message reads, "Took 1 and 1/2 minutes to get thru this. Train was crowded & all windows & doors closed tight. We felt half suffocated, when we saw daylight again & windows flew open in a hurry. While we were delayed by freight wreck my fellow passenger wanted me to help her while away the time with a deck of cards. I told her my book was all sufficient for me, She is 45 yrs. I guess."

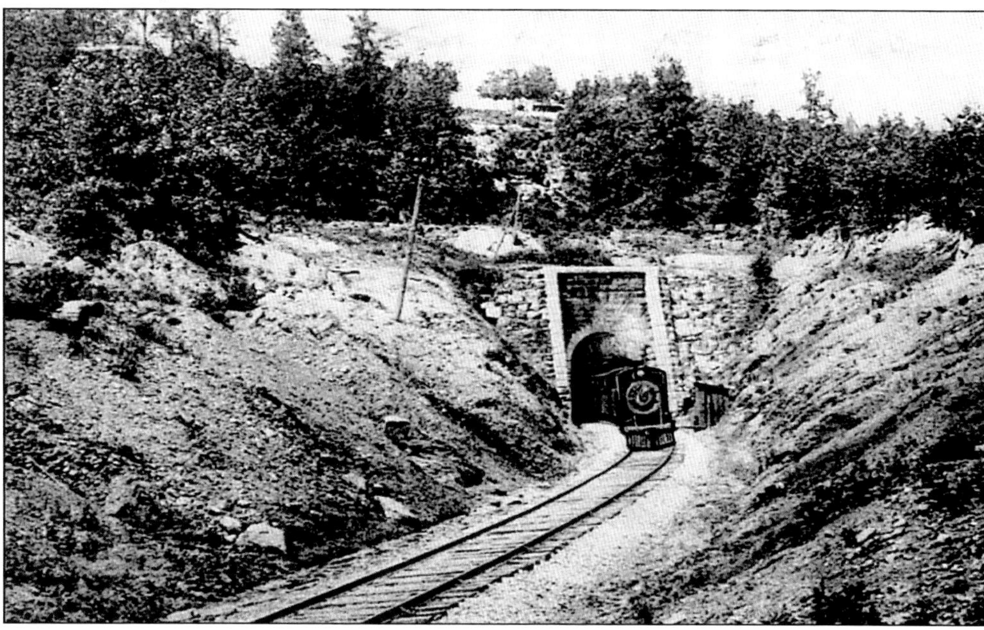

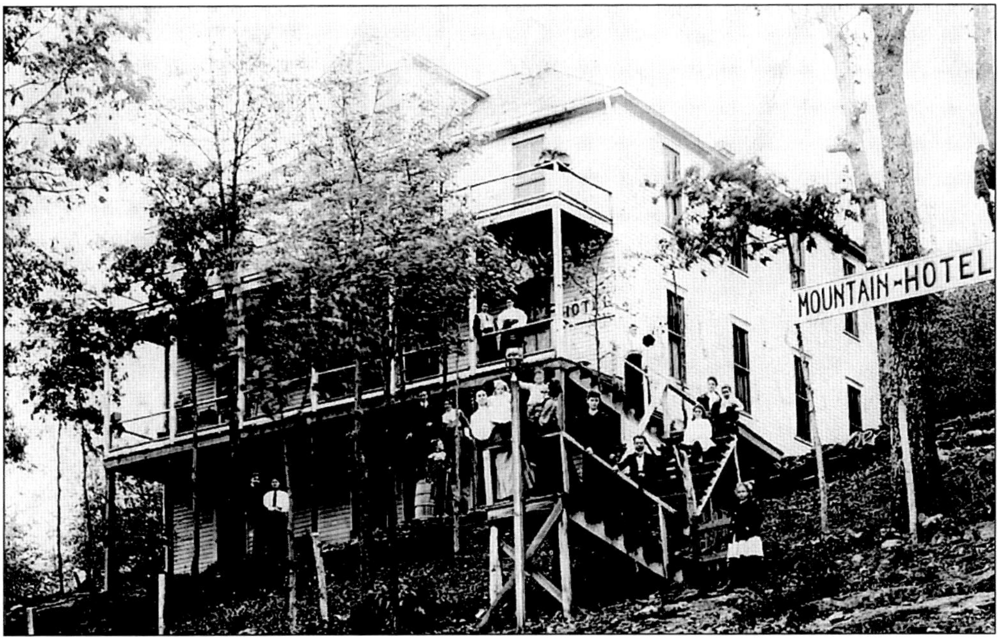

The Mountain Hotel was erected on the steep hillside above the Winslow depot, on a flat shelf that had been the original rail bed. The hotel opened in 1904 and served not only for accommodations, but also as the only dependable restaurant in town. The railroad agent at a station south of Winslow would take orders from train crews and passengers, and telegraph these to Winslow; the prepared food was then carried down the 200 steps to meet the arriving train. The hotel was lost in a 1923 fire.

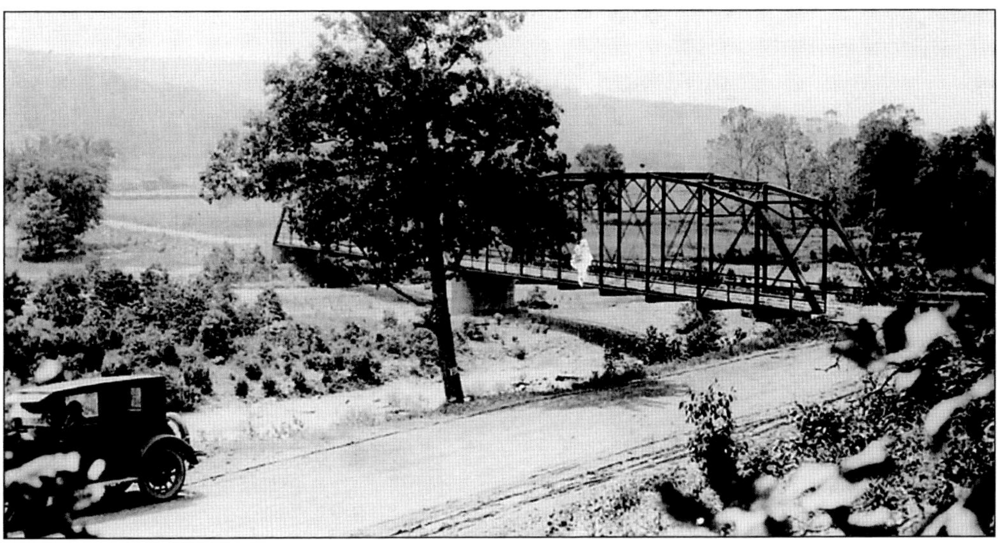

Although the last passenger train would not pass through Winslow until 1965, signals that the end of the great railroad era was approaching came as early as the 1920s. On this 1924 card the message read, "This is how we look since the completion of highway." The road would remain unpaved for another decade, but there was no going back. In this card, the automobile that had but a moment before crossed a bridge originally built for wagons and horses foreshadowed the future in ways few could imagine at the time.

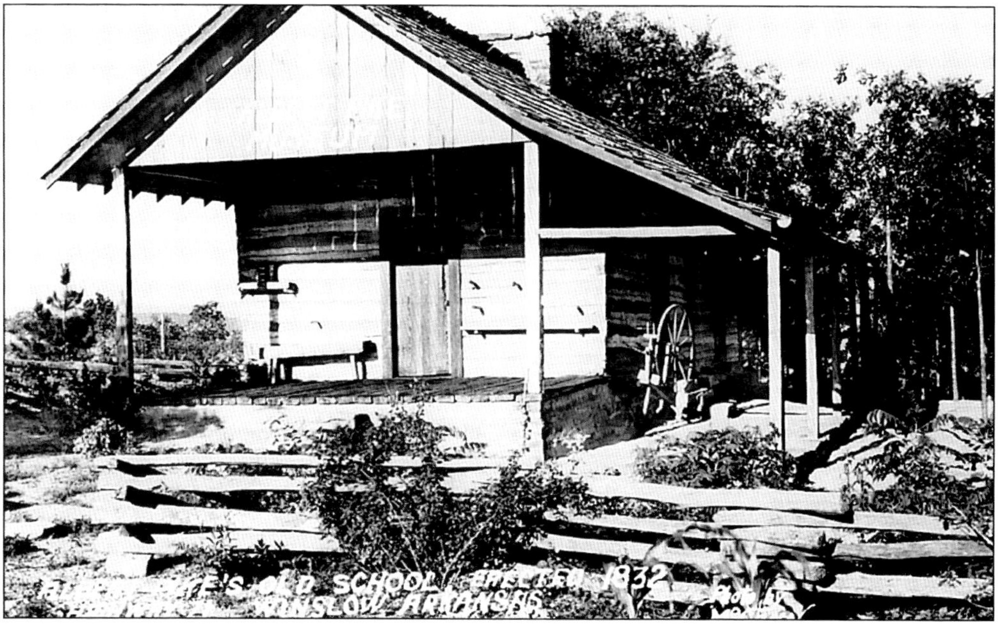

During the 1940s Winslow proudly showed tourists the relocated school at which, reportedly, Albert Pike taught in the 1830s. Pike was a poet and Confederate General who led Cherokee allies at the Civil War battle of Pea Ridge. He was a generally eccentric character and one of the more colorful men in Arkansas history. Pike once wrote a verse directed at a political opponent, claiming that the man "gets drunk once a week on whiskey and immediately sobers himself up completely on the very best wine." The original site of his school was some 40 miles south in Van Buren, but it was moved to this location south of Winslow in the 1930s for exhibition. In 1954 the building was moved to the U of A Campus in Fayetteville, and was relocated again in 1974 back to Van Buren, to its present-day home next to the Crawford County Courthouse. As seen below, the 1832 log building was appointed with many of the tools and implements that would have been used in Pike's time. (*c.* 1940.)

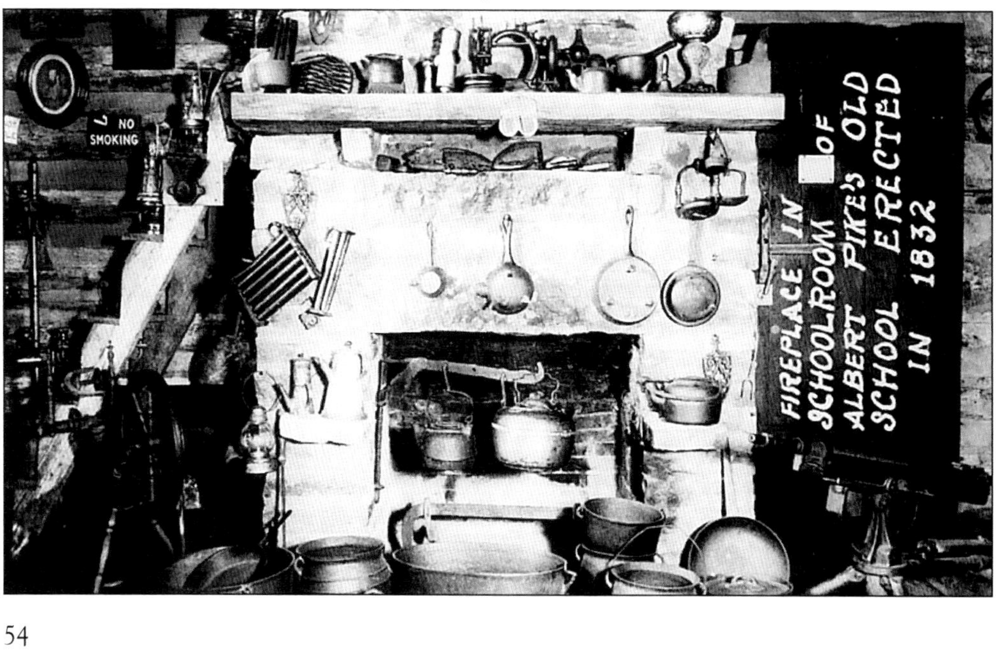

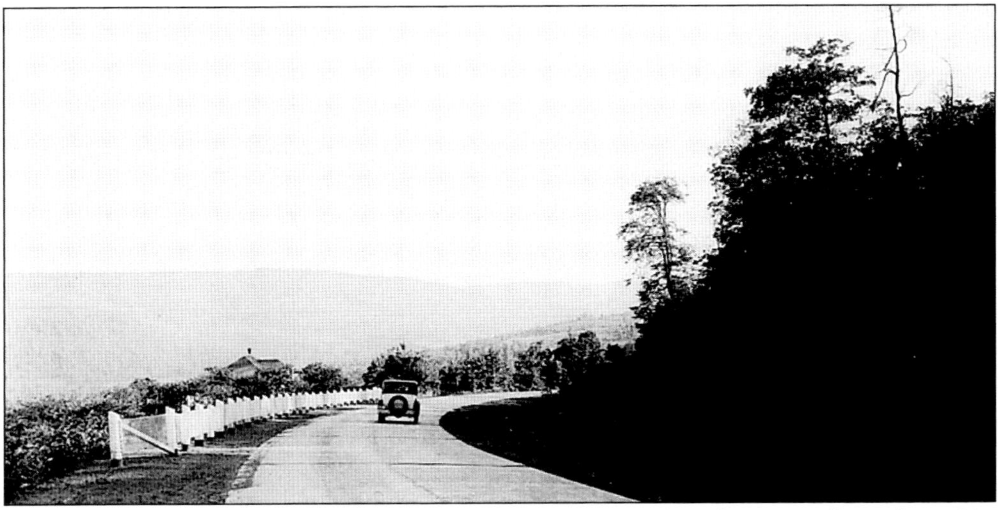

With the completion of paved Highway 71 between Fort Smith and Fayetteville in the 1930s, the volume of automobile traffic passing by Winslow picked up dramatically. In this c. 1935 scene, the driver of the roadster would have marveled at the view as he sped around the curve on the narrow concrete roadway, with the Boston mountain range of the Ozarks visible at every turn. As the 20th century drew to a close, Highway 71 was being bypassed by a new interstate to the west, in the valley below this curve.

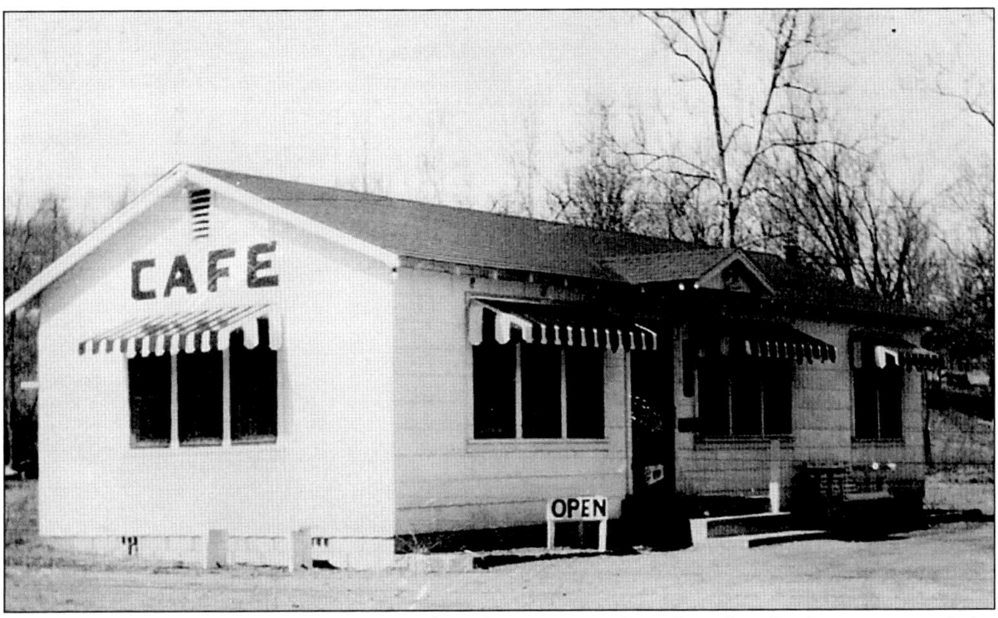

The end of the passenger train era was at hand, as improved roads and multiplying automobiles took away rail passengers. Other passengers would have depended on the bus that stopped at Anderson's Cafe and Bus Stop. "Try Anderson's home cooked food and fried pies one time and you'll come back," were the words on the back of the card. Today the bus no longer stops in Winslow.

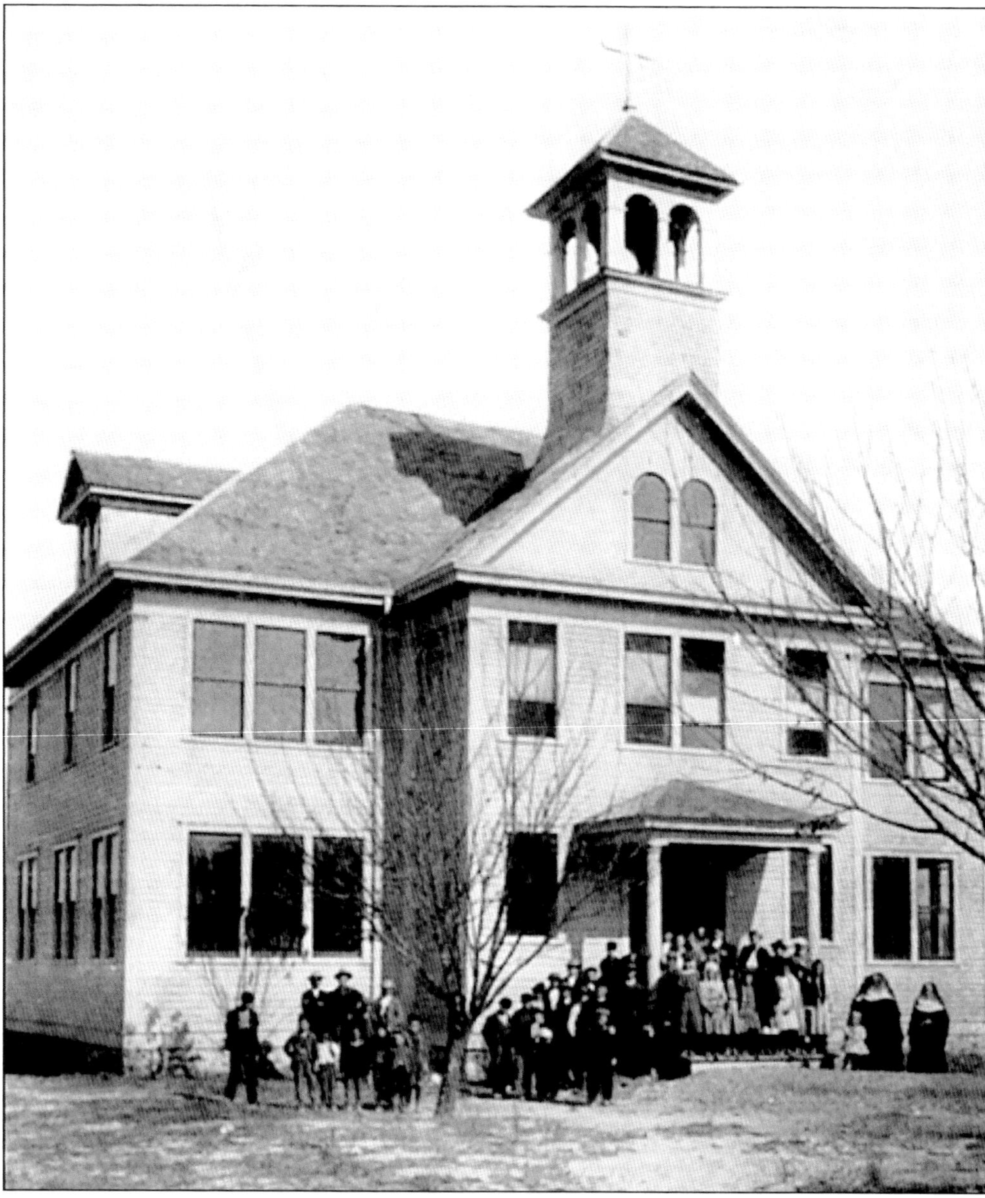

Tontitown was established in 1897 by Father Pietro Bandini, an Italian Roman Catholic priest. Father Bandini had been sent from Rome to investigate reports of starvation and malaria in a settlement of Italian immigrants who had attempted to colonize land in Chicot County, in deep southeastern Arkansas. Father Bandini's findings were sufficient to cause him to relocate the 35 families to land he had bought in Washington County, where Tontitown was formed as a new home. The priest became the town's first mayor, and selected its name in honor of Henri de Tonti, a lieutenant of the explorer La Salle and the founder of Arkansas Post. The new community thrived, and the immigrants there would be the first in northwest Arkansas to grow grapes as a cash crop. They were also the first to introduce to Arkansas the lawn game, bocce, which had been popular in Italy. This *c.* 1905 card shows the town's Catholic school, St. Mary's Academy, with nuns in full habit to the right—one sign of the success of the community and its faith transported from across the sea.

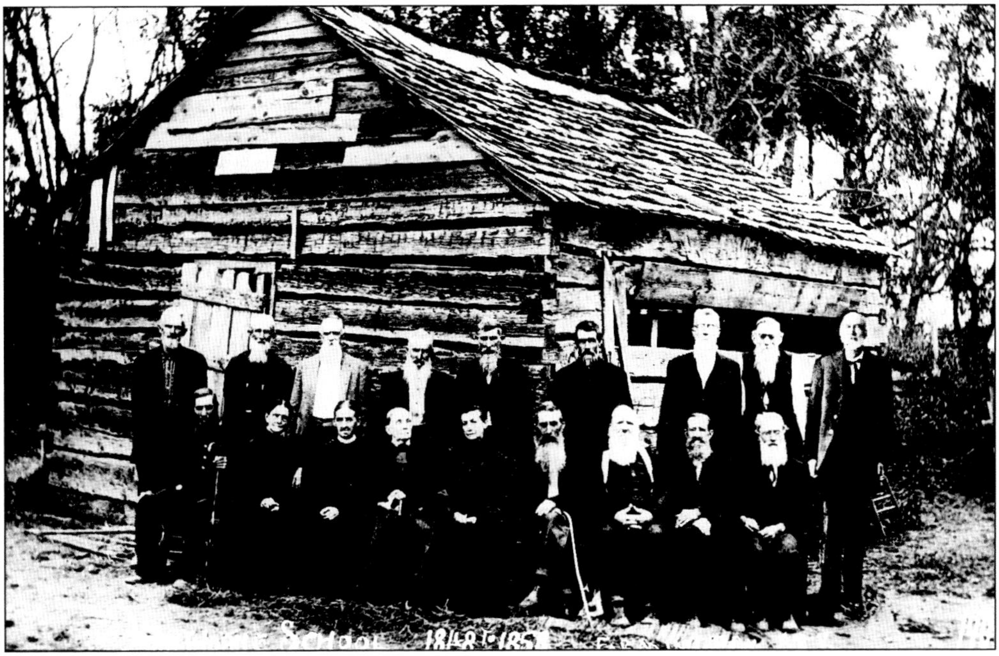

Farmington was reportedly given its name because it was a "farming town," but today it adjoins the western edge of Fayetteville, having been caught in the rapid growth of the region. The Hawthorne School, in use between 1848 and 1858, had been the forerunner of the Farmington School District. Presumably, based on the caption of 1909, these elderly men had attended the school during the pre-Civil War era.

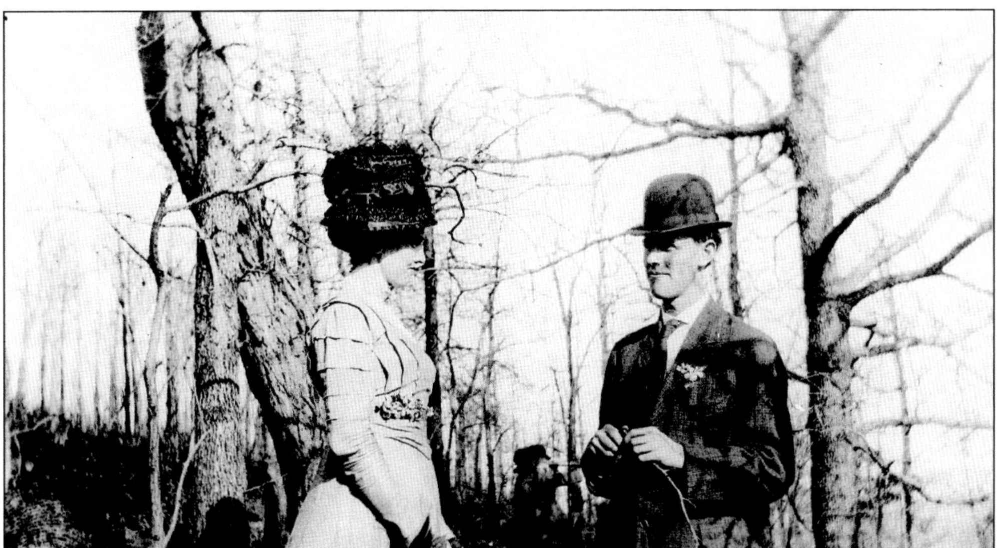

On a wooded hillside outside of Fayetteville in Washington County stood "C.E. Blacklock and Miss Tharp, Afterwards Mr. and Mrs. C.E. Blacklock." The couple had been photographed for a postcard, apparently just before taking marriage vows. (c. 1910.)

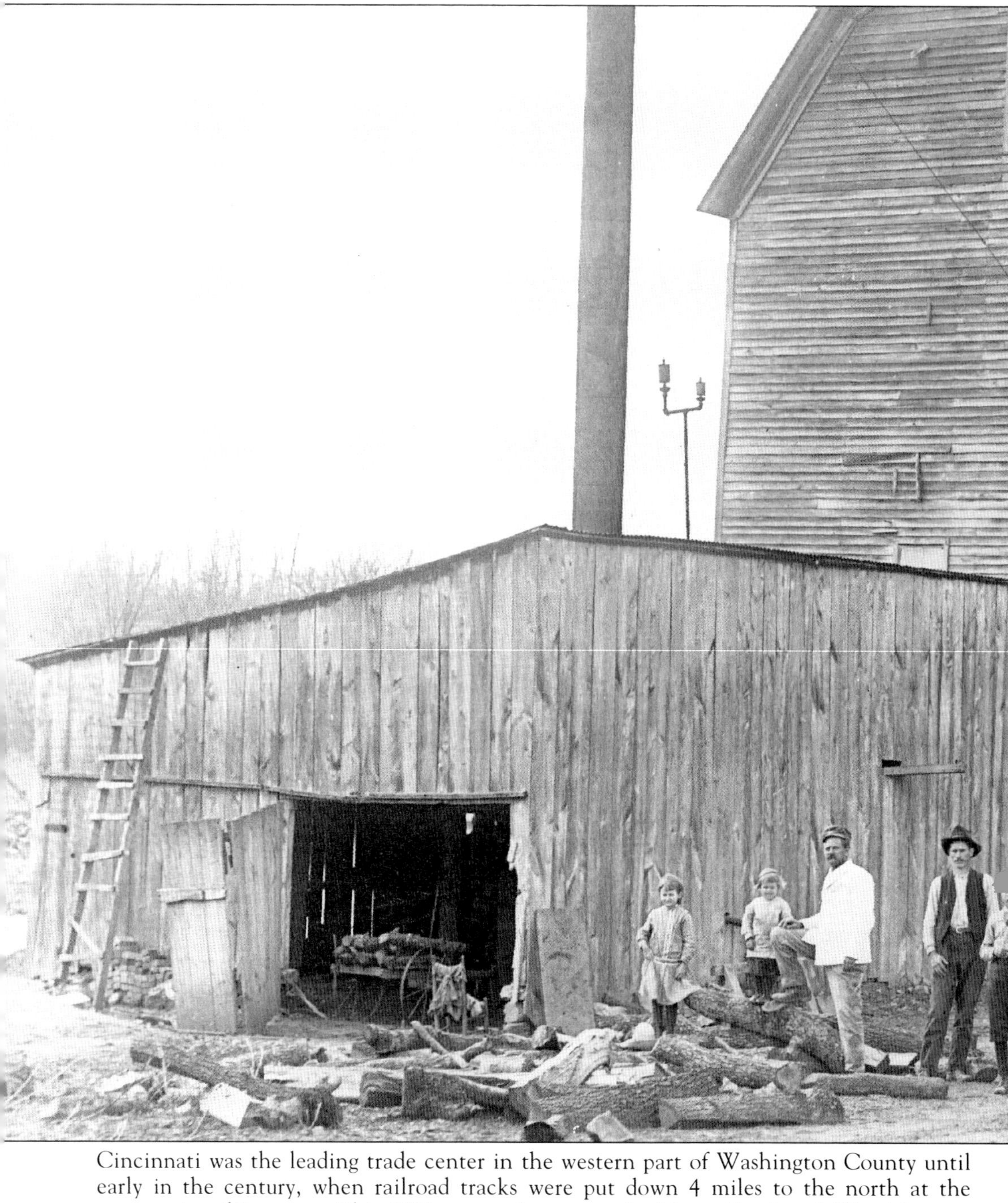

Cincinnati was the leading trade center in the western part of Washington County until early in the century, when railroad tracks were put down 4 miles to the north at the community of Summers. This 1912 postcard captures the Moore Brothers Mill, with some

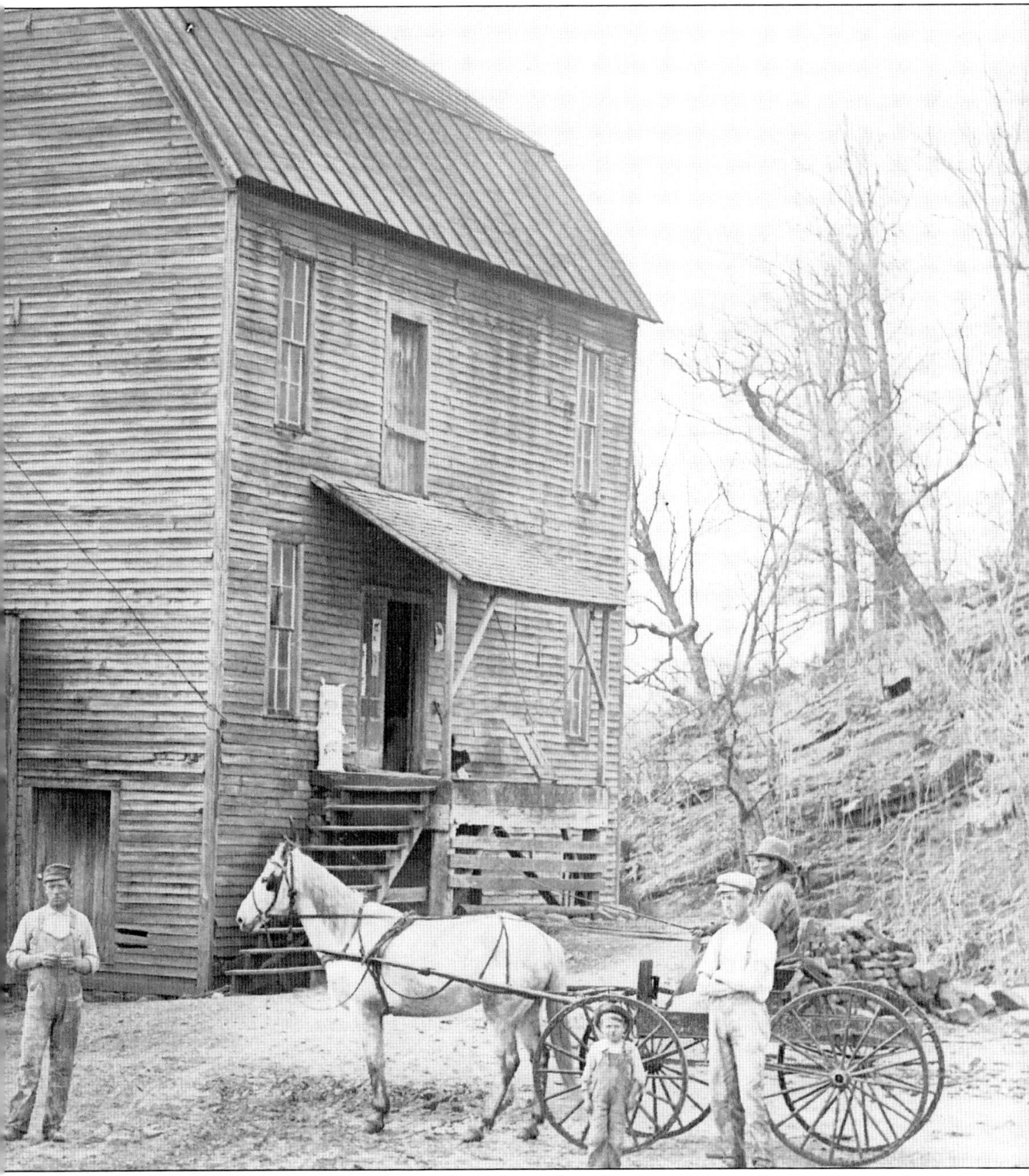

of the owners' children posed in front of a pile of logs being cut into firewood, on what appears to have been a winter day. The mill, likely spring powered, would have converted corn into flour and meal.

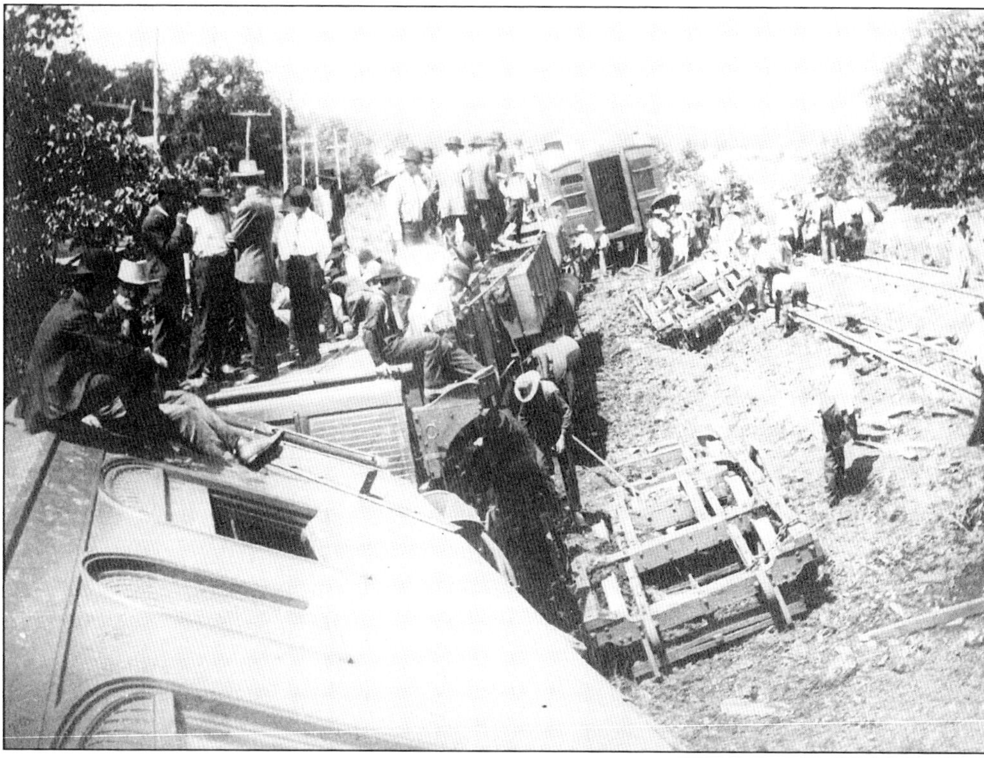

In the 1907 photo above, the hazards of passenger train travel filled the camera's lens in Johnson, a small community northeast of Fayetteville. The cars have separated from the wheels after toppling off the tracks. "Rubberneckers" of the era had turned out in force, some sitting on the overturned passenger car. Perhaps train wrecks were on the mind of the man who received the card seen below. Mailed to Frederic Bowen of the Washington County town of Harris (the same "Uncle Fred" who mailed postcards at the time of Woodrow Wilson's election, seen on page 45), this card sought to sell him the "Classiest Speedster on the Market," produced by the Velie Motor Vehicle Company in 1911. The "Model 'H' 1 Racytype Roadster" came with a 40-gallon gasoline tank, a 12-gallon oil tank, and port holes through the sides of the hood. "Guaranteed top speed, 65 miles per hour." Unknown is whether Bowen was tempted to purchase the sporty $2,000 vehicle.

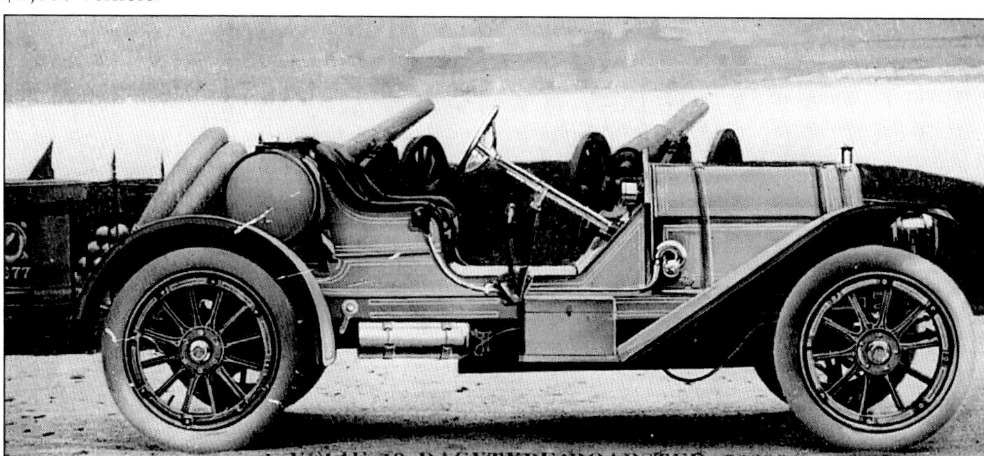

Three

BENTON COUNTY

BENTONVILLE AND ROGERS

Both Benton County and the county seat of Bentonville were named to honor U.S. Senator Thomas Hart Benton of Missouri. Benton, a veteran of the War of 1812 against the British, went to the senate in 1820 and was instrumental in helping the Arkansas Territory achieve statehood in 1836. The resolve of the county's namesake might well be found in remarks he made on the floor of the Senate in 1850: "Mr. President, Sir, I never quarrel, Sir, but sometimes I fight, Sir, and when I fight, Sir, a funeral follows, Sir." Bentonville and Rogers would become the largest towns in the county, but also prominent in postcard history would be a host of small villages and resorts tied to the numerous springs and waterways that coursed through the rolling hills.

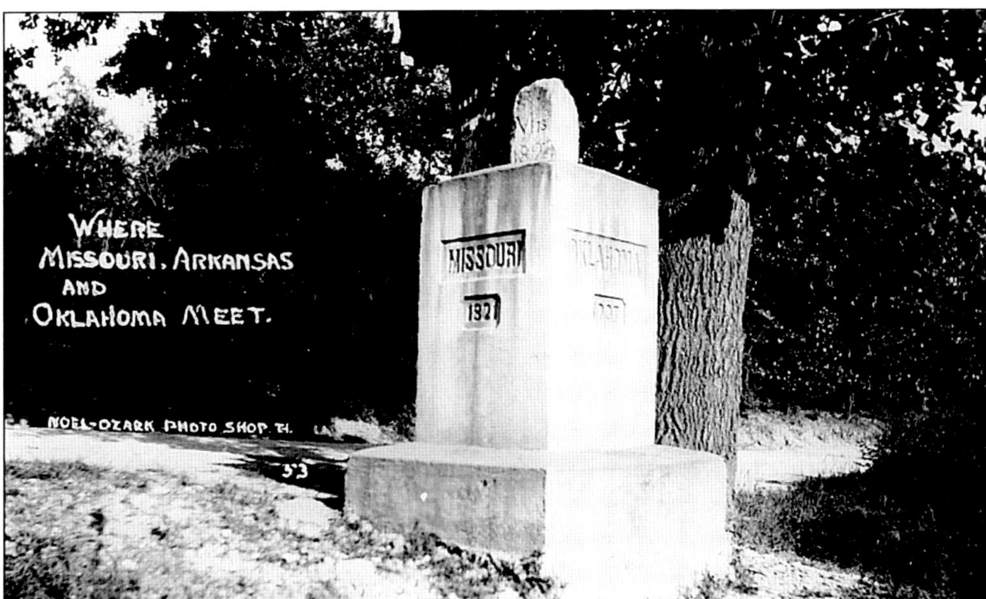

Benton County hugs the far northwestern corner of Arkansas, touching Missouri to the north and Oklahoma to the west. This concrete marker designates the meeting point of the three state lines; on the top of the monument is the survey marker from 1823. The marker site may still be reached today, off Oklahoma Highway 20. (c. 1930.)

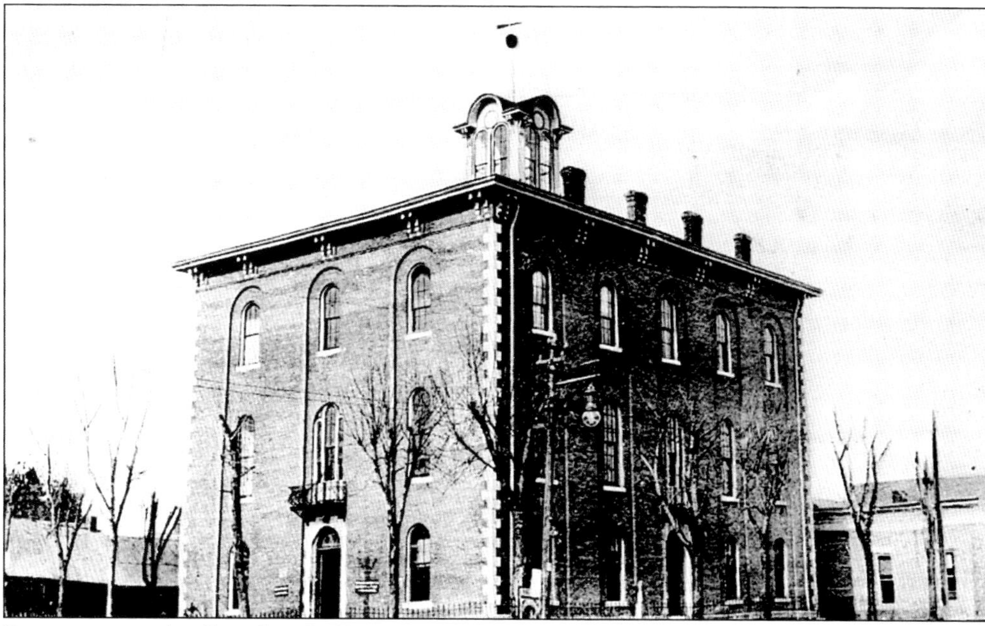

By printing and selling bonds, Benton County erected this three-story courthouse in 1874, replacing one destroyed during the Civil War. The county jail was on the third floor, giving the prisoners a good view of the town. The 1909 message on the card read, "I have 2 court house views for you. I like historical or monument views now. For the rest of my collection, If [sic] I can get anymore C.H. views you shall have them." The card was exchanged with a fellow collector in New Jersey. The courthouse was replaced in 1928.

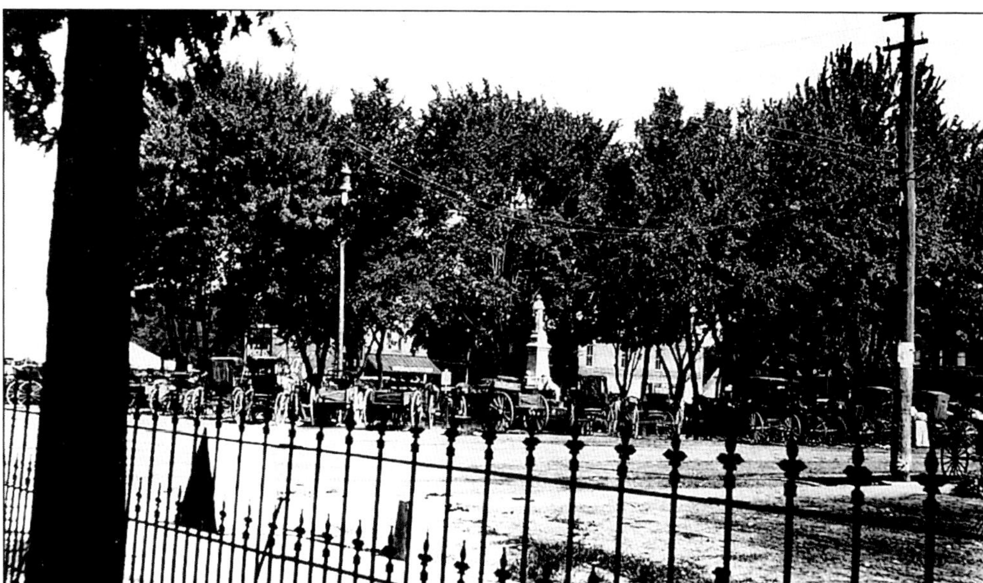

The courthouse lawn opened up onto the street across from a city park in the center of Bentonville's town square. "We are anxious to know how you are improving," reads the 1909 message on a card showing every parking space filled around the square with wagons and buggies. In the center of the square is the town's Confederate monument.

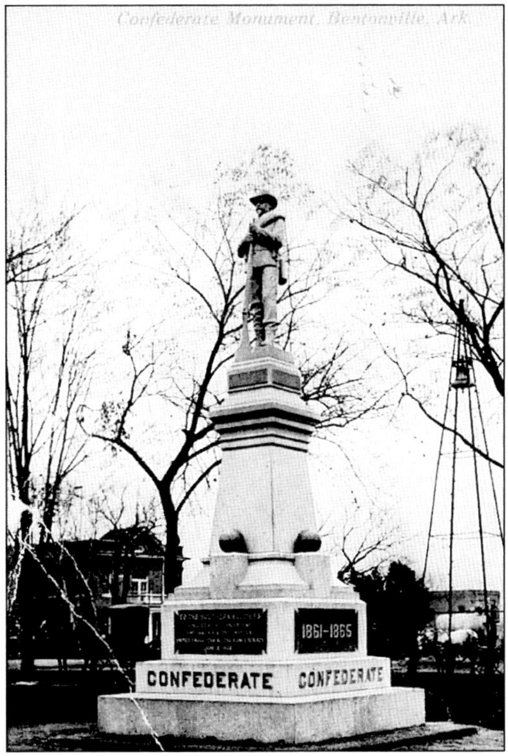

Strains of "Dixie" filled the air on August 8, 1908, when the James H. Berry Chapter of the United Daughters of the Confederacy unveiled this monument to the men who had fought for the South some 50 years before. Surviving veterans, stooped with age, paraded into the square to see the monument, engraved with: "Their Names Are Borne on Honor's Shield. Their Record Is With God. They Fought For Home and Fatherland." The sender of the card in 1919 wrote to his aunt in Norman, Oklahoma, that he had arrived in Arkansas, and "I traded my car for a pair of mules." (Card *c.* 1911.)

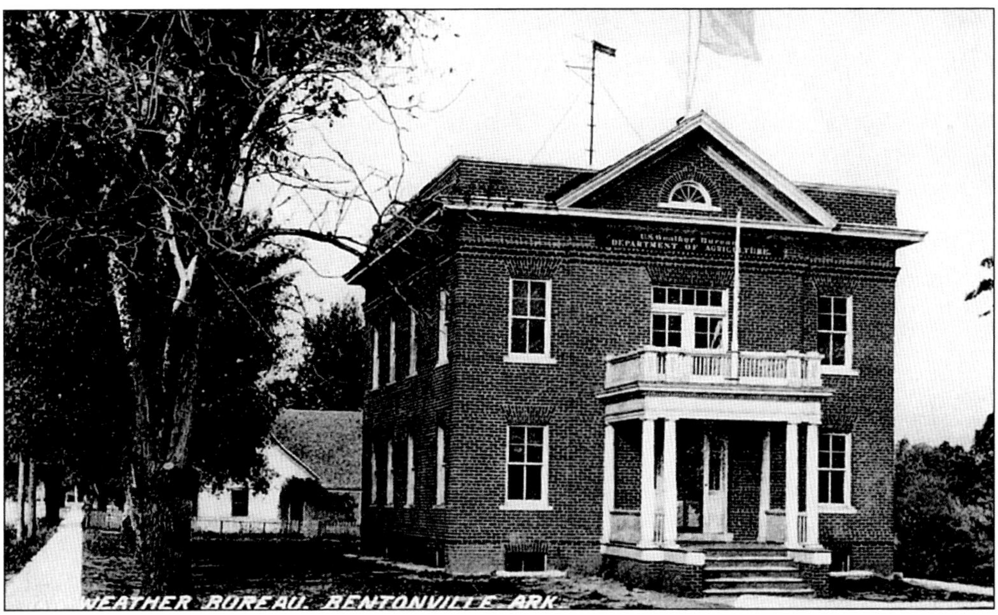

In 1906, Bentonville became the smallest town in the nation to have what was labeled a "First Order Weather Bureau." The resource was obtained through the work of the Horticultural Society and Senator James Berry of Bentonville. Union Army veteran Capt. Orin Parker was given charge of the Bureau, deemed vital to the many fruit growers of the area whose incomes depended on the hard-to-predict Arkansas weather. The building was torn down in 1934 to make way for a new post office.

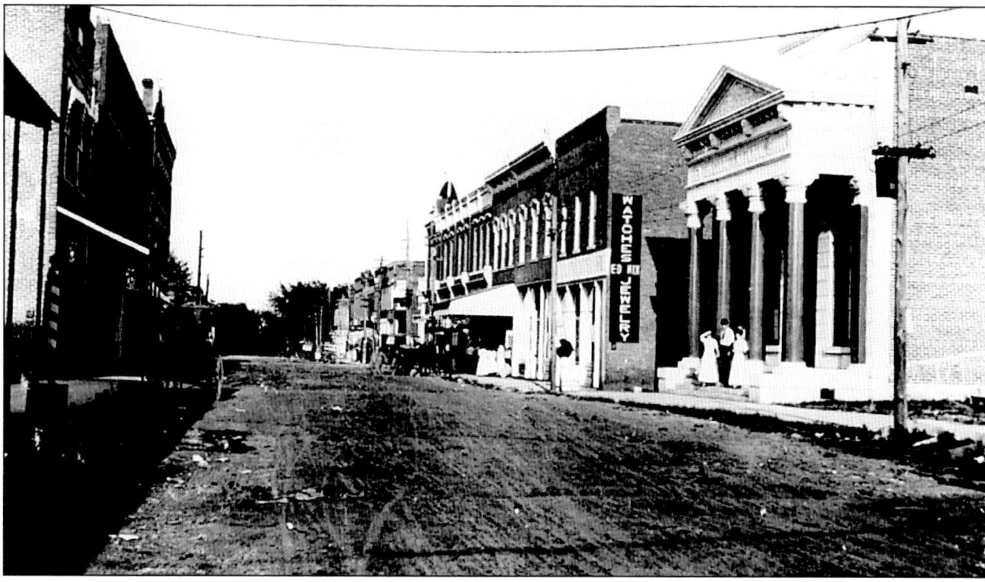

Spring Street was almost empty when this c. 1905 photo was made, though the street was marked with wagon wheel tracks, trash, and horse droppings. A striped barber pole is seen to the left; across the street are Ed Nix's Watch and Jewelry shop and the columned Benton County National Bank. A man and two women, perhaps employees, posed on the bank steps; up the sidewalk stands a cluster of shop patrons.

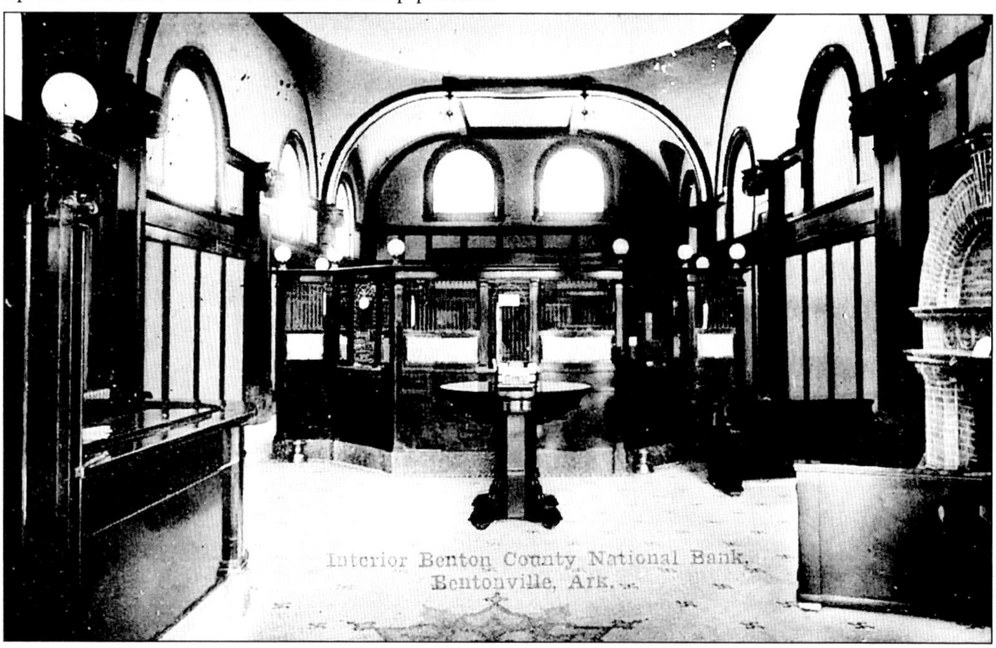

Customers doing business with the Benton County National Bank would have found several tellers behind cashier's cages, and a table in the center of the lobby on which to fill out deposit tickets. To the right is something very less likely to be found in a modern bank lobby, a handsome brick fireplace to warm customers on cold winter days. The bank consolidated with Bentonville's First National Bank in 1930; shortly afterwards it failed, a victim of the Great Depression. (c. 1910.)

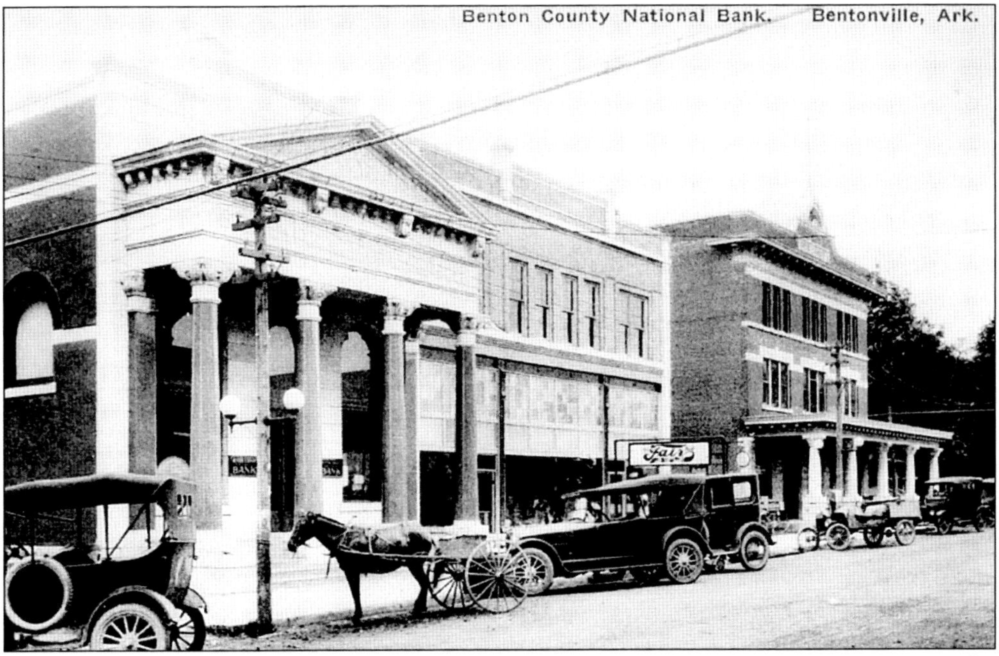

The Benton County National Bank is seen here, some ten years after the street view on the previous page, and progress is apparent. While a two-wheeled horse-drawn cart is parked at the curb, it now shares the street with a growing number of automobiles. Down the street, in front of the Hotel Massey, one vehicle is little more than a frame with an engine on four wheels. (c. 1915.)

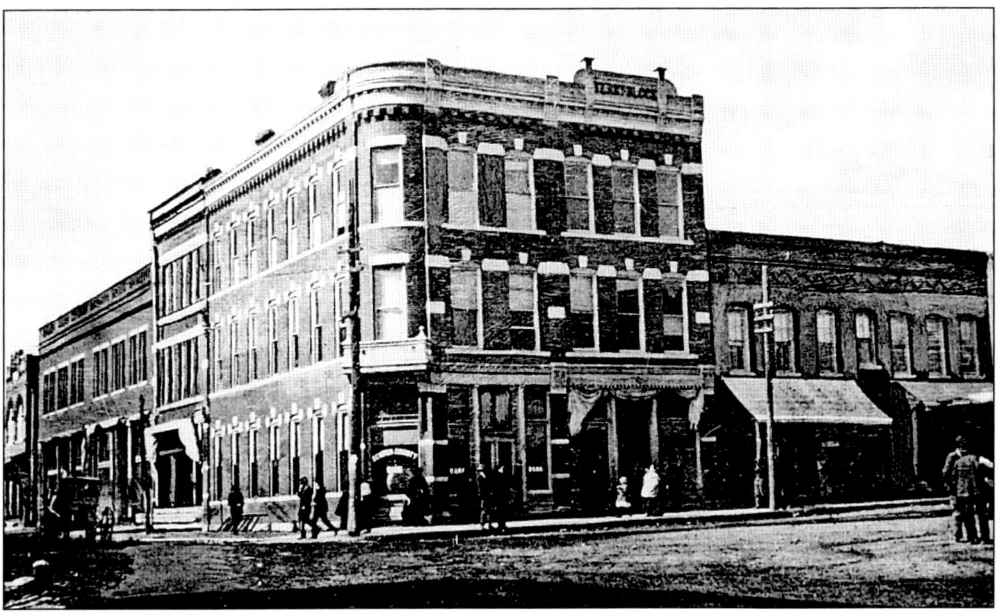

Among the Benton County National Bank's chief competitors was the Benton County Bank, located in a prominent ground floor corner location in the Terry Block Building. At the turn of the century the bank had been the richest in the county. "I will be home just as soon as I get the fence done," reads the message sent to Preston, Kansas, by a traveling fence installer. (c. 1914.)

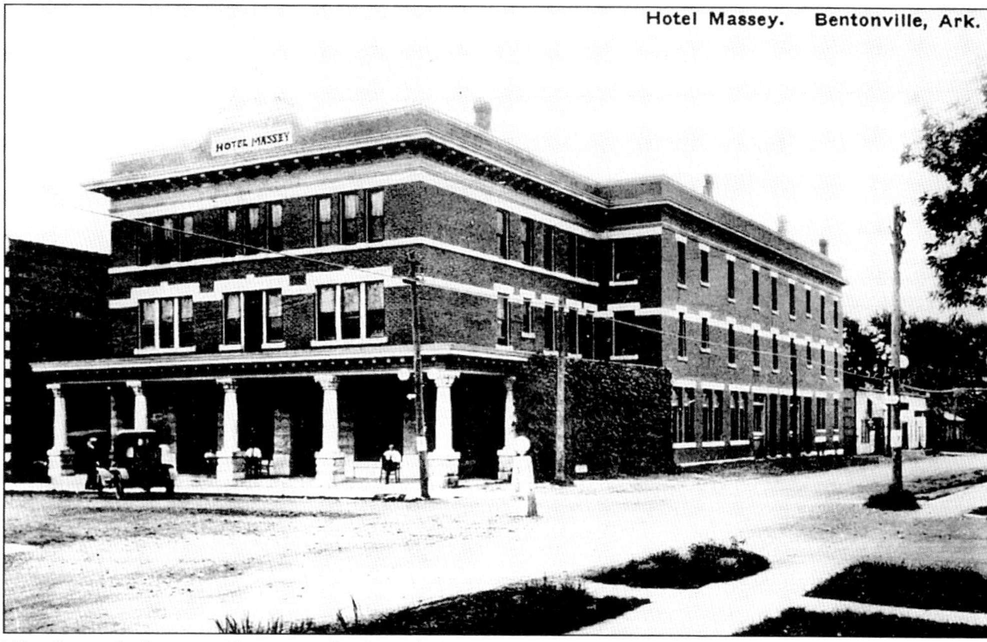

The finest lodging in Bentonville for a half-century was the Hotel Massey, in the heart of the business district. The hotel opened in 1910 and operated until 1961, after which it operated for several years under the name Town House Hotel. Damaged by fire in 1975, the hotel was bought by the Walton family, who restored it and donated it to the city for use as a library. The building is on the National Register of Historic Places.

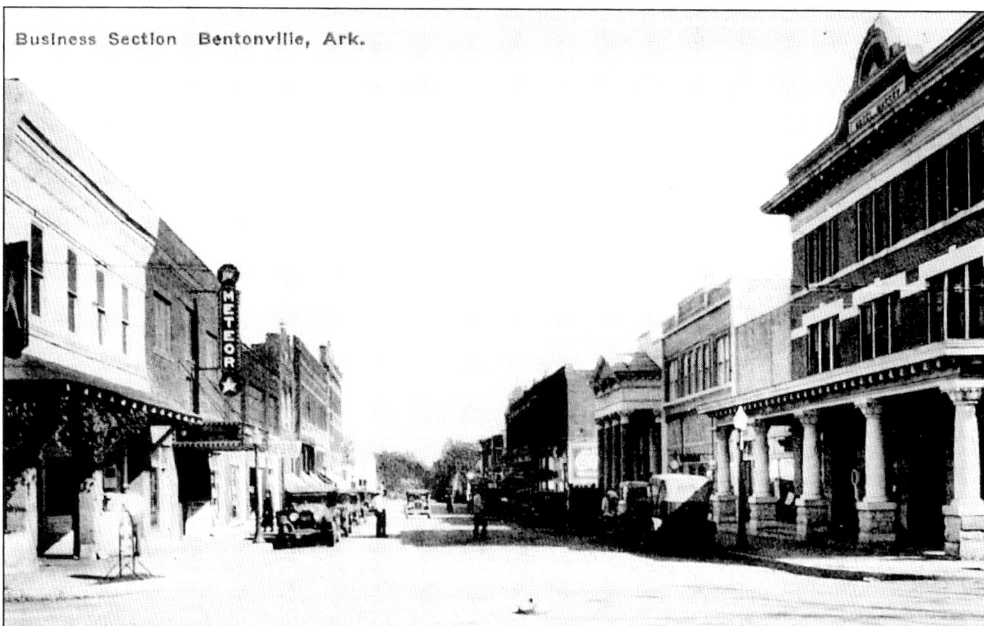

The Hotel Massey's location in the heart of the business section of Bentonville is readily apparent in this c. 1920 card. Hotel guests could have stepped down the block to the Benton County National Bank, its columned facade visible next to the Coca-Cola sign, visited several stores, or walked across the street to take in a silent movie at the Meteor Theater.

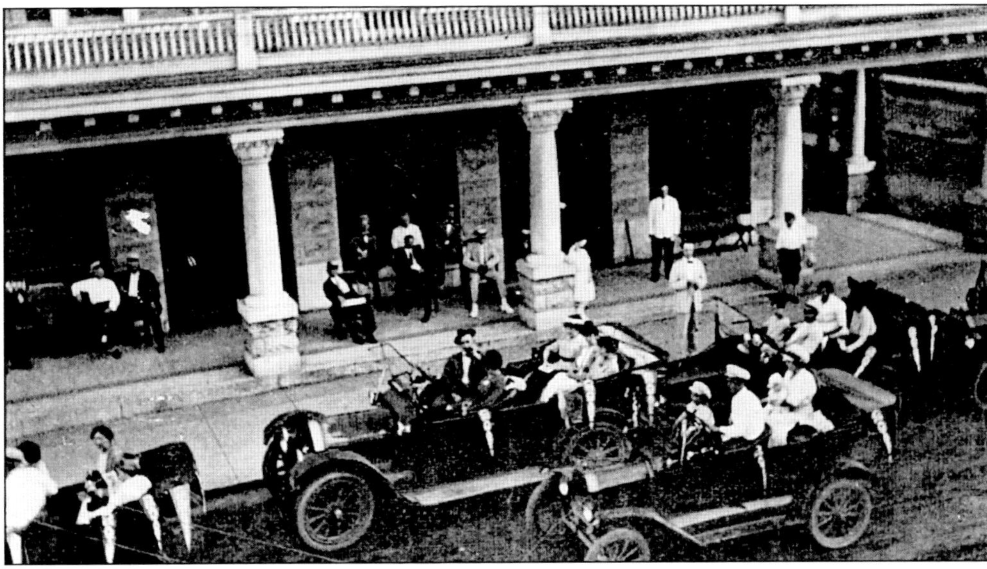

A parade had formed outside the Hotel Massey around 1915, an event that had drawn spectators to the front porch of the hotel. The open-topped cars sported similar pennants and carried men, women, and children, all seemingly dressed in their finest, for a now-unknown occasion. The first automobile agency had opened in Bentonville in 1912, when a Ford touring car like these cost $600. The first gas station was the Benton County Hardware Company, which buried a 500-gallon tank in an alley beside the store, filling it with gasoline brought from Rogers in 50-gallon drums.

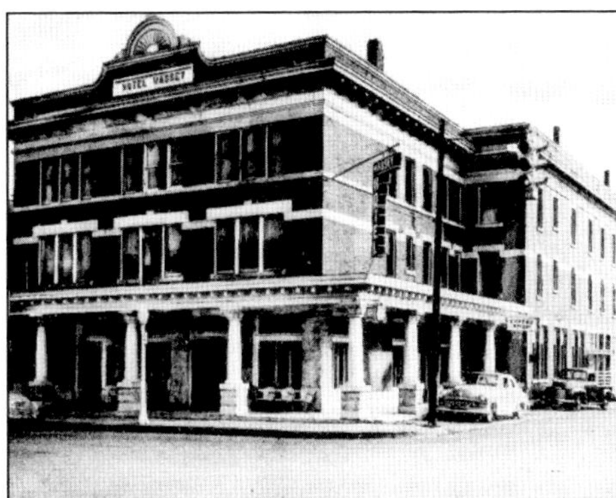

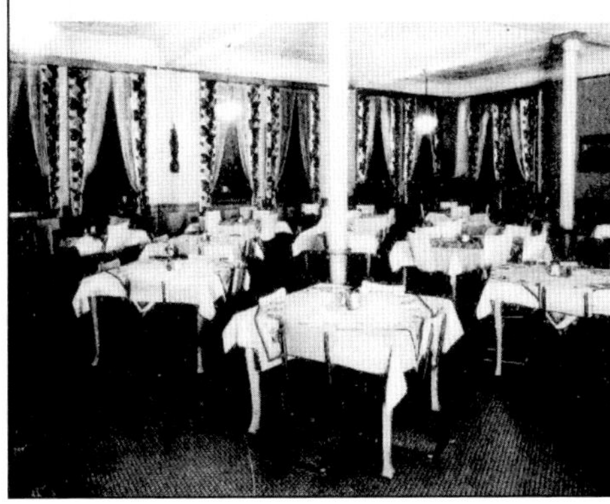

The Hotel Massey was still doing business in 1953, advertising on the back of this card that it was "a home away from home." The entrance to the hotel coffee shop is seen at the right side of the building, between the car and the truck parked at the curb. The day of small-town hotels like the Massey was fading fast. In years to come, motels on the highways outside of town would take away customers, and chain restaurants would pull diners away from the hotel coffee shops and local cafes.

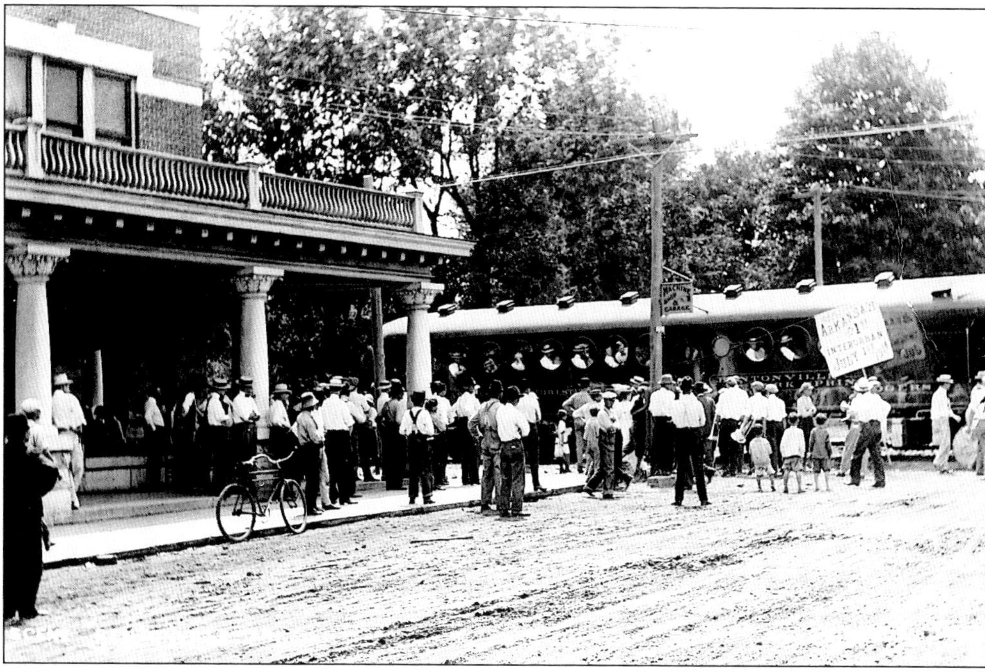

"We are sending birthday greetings with the new inter-urban car," reads the message on a photo outside the Hotel Massey, showing the inauguration of an inter-urban rail service that ran between Bentonville and Rogers. The big red, 92-foot long coach made several runs a day, hauling passenger and mail between the two Benton County towns. The rail car could carry up to 130 persons, and would stop anywhere along the route to pick up passengers at 15¢ a fare. A popular stop was the Park Springs resort, located outside of Bentonville on the way to Rogers. The growing popularity of the automobile led to declining patronage, and in 1916, after only two years of operation, the Frisco Railroad ordered the inter-urban off its tracks for non-payment of lease money. Northwest Arkansas' experiment with mass transit was over.

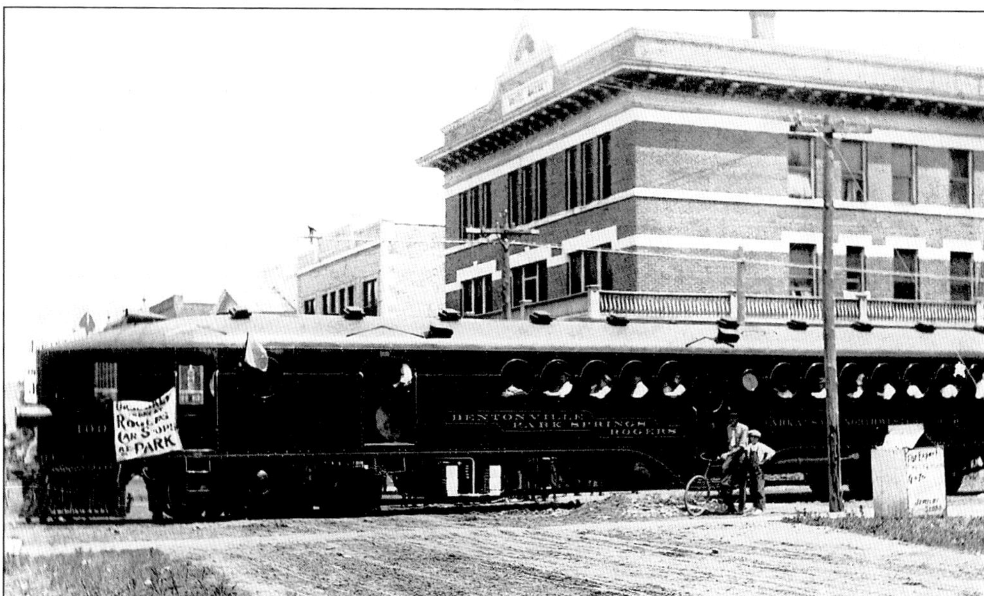

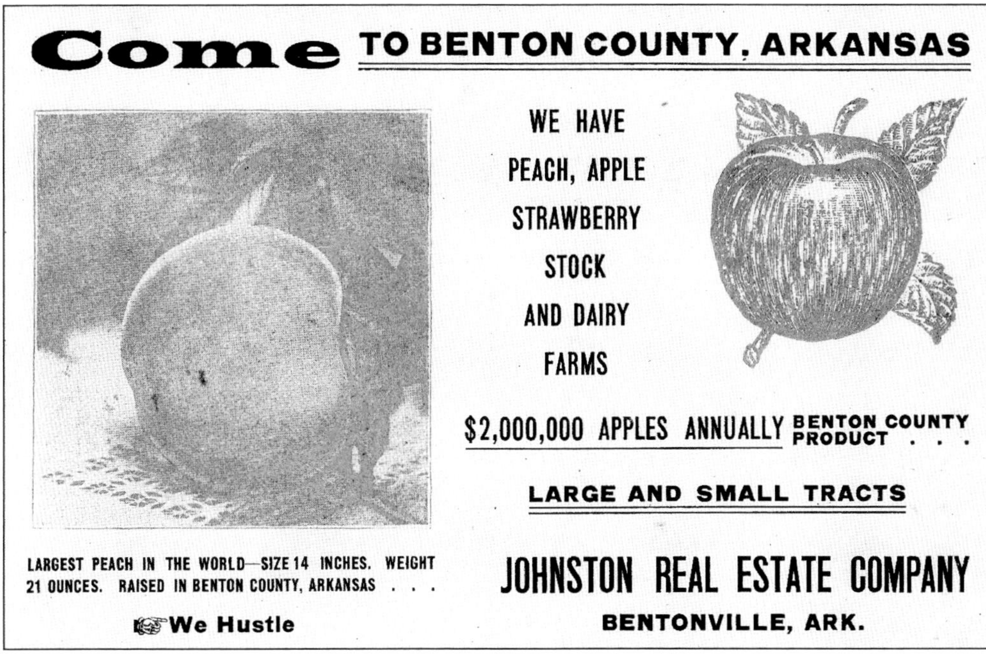

During the first two decades of the century, Benton County produced some of the most bountiful crops of fruit, especially apples, in the nation. Benton County apples won all the major prizes at the 1904 World's Fair in St. Louis, and in 1915 the region shipped 5 million bushels of apples, with an average selling price of $1 per bushel. The card above used bountiful fruit to attract real estate customers in 1911. The card's sender penciled on the reverse side: "I have eat apples till I am sick. I was through the saw mill and the distillery and seen lots of things." The card below, from Bentonville, depicts what is billed as the world's largest apple brandy distillery. The business would have supplied a market for excess apples and those culled from shipments of eating apples.

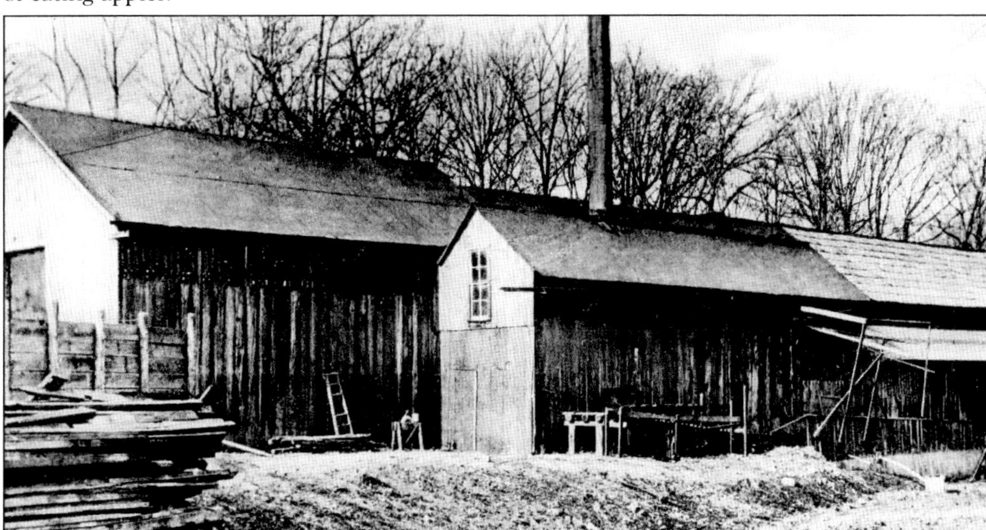

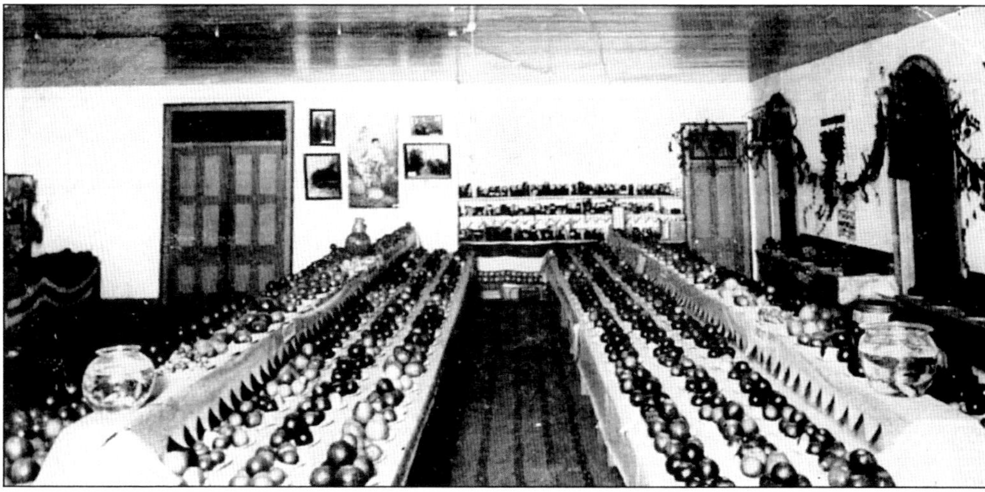

At county fair time in Bentonville, displays of fruit stretched out showing the many varieties produced, such as these apples laid out on tables around 1910. The apple boom would fade away in the 1920s as hungry insects became immune to the increasingly heavy sprays applied to the trees, most of which withered and died over a period of a few years.

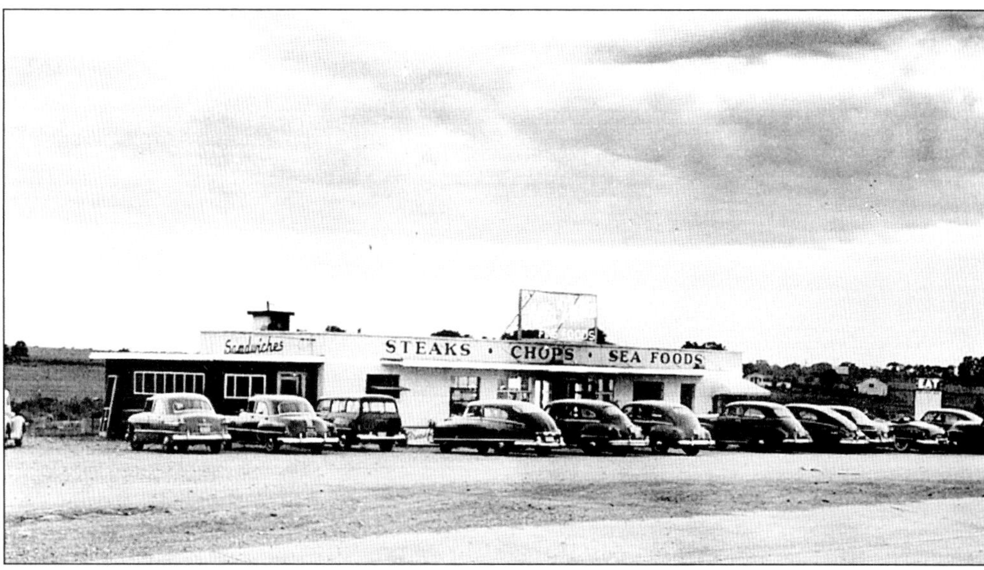

The decline of apple production in Benton County led to the development of another cash crop that is today hugely important to northwest Arkansas—poultry. A fair amount of chicken was consumed at the Neta Villa Restaurant and Drive-In, located 2 miles south of Bentonville. The ad on the back of the card reads, "Specializing in Benton-Quality Chicken, Nest-O-Chick, 1/2 Fried Chicken, Hot Buttered Rolls and Honey, Steaks, Chops and Mexican Foods." (*c.* 1950.)

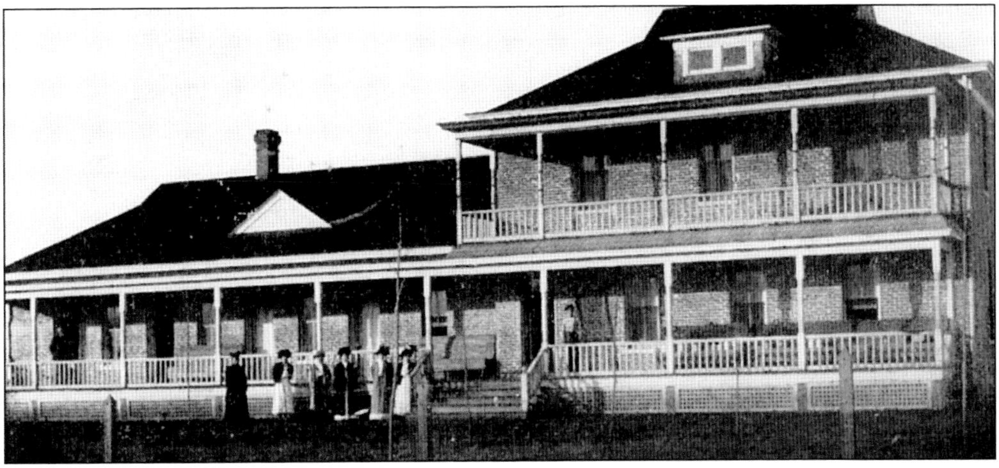

The poor and destitute of Benton County had few options, in an era before the advent of government welfare programs such as subsidized housing and food stamps. The last refuge for such families was sometimes the Benton County Poor Farm at Bentonville. Imagine life within this rambling building, and the conversations that would have occurred on the long porch. The Poor Farm's name was changed to the "County Home" in the 1920s; it was located on Highway 102 West. It was torn down in the 1950s, and the site today is occupied by the County Extension Service building. (c. 1909.)

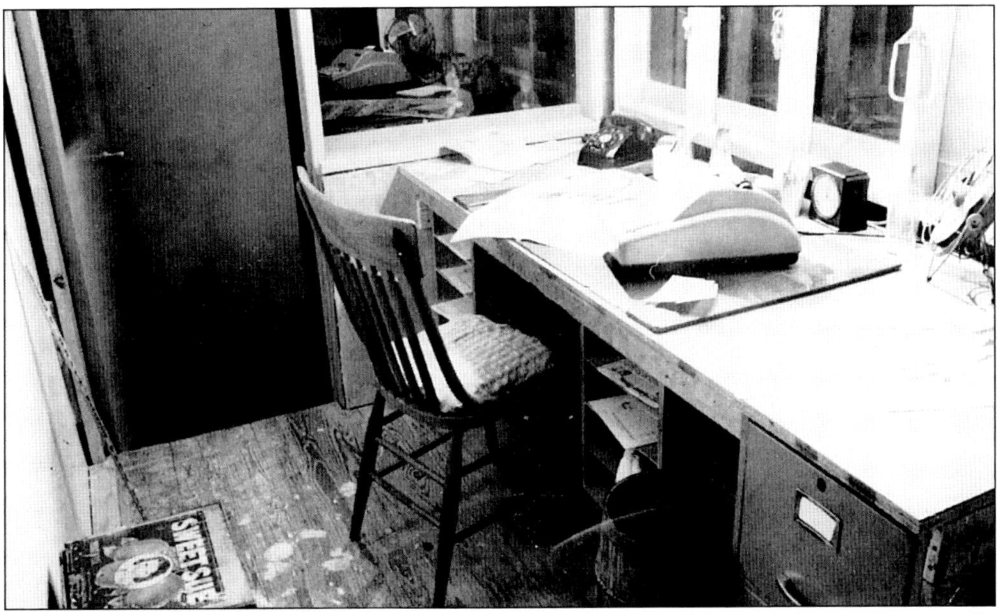

In unique contrast to the Benton County Poor Farm is the story of the most famous Bentonville resident, Sam Walton. When Walton lost the lease on his Five and Dime store in Newport, Arkansas, he relocated to Bentonville in the early 1950s. He opened Walton's 5 & 10-Cent Store in downtown Bentonville, a store he supervised from this humble office. The little 5 & 10 Store would be the seed from which grew Wal-Mart, today the leading retailer in the world. The phenomenal growth of Wal-Mart made Sam Walton a billionaire many times over. Today Bentonville is the world headquarters for Wal-Mart, and this 5 & 10 Store office is part of the Wal-Mart Visitors Center there. The sweet potato crate shelf and fruit-basket waste can attest to Walton's frugality.

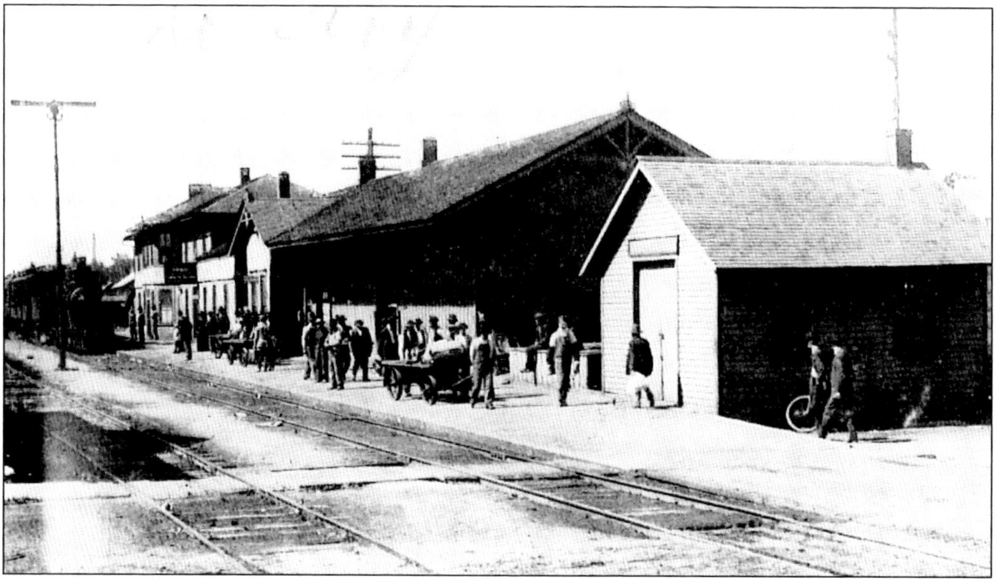

Rogers owes its existence and its name to the Frisco Railroad, which chose to lay its tracks across the town site in 1881. The General Manager of the Frisco, Capt. C.W. Rogers, gave his name to the new town. The depot shown here, located between Elm and Poplar streets, served the Frisco Line into the early 20th century. Among the items shipped from here in 1907 were 190 train cars of green apples. The depot, freight station, and adjoining Fred Harvey Dining Room were all destroyed by fire in 1914. (c. 1905.)

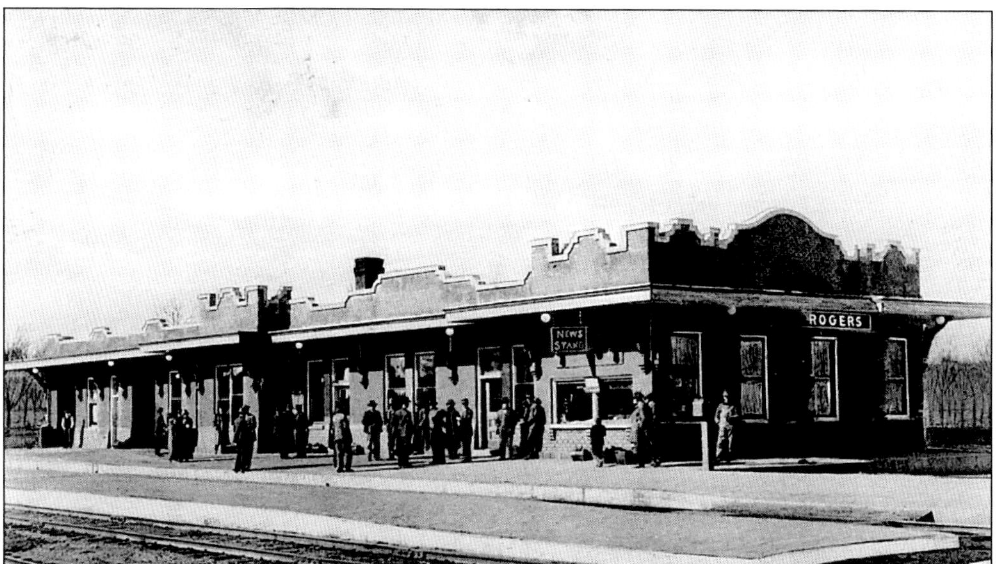

Built to replace the depot lost in the 1914 fire, this Frisco Depot would be a landmark for more than 60 years, before being torn down in 1975; the passenger trains had stopped running years before. The 1915 message on this card states "Tom is with threshing machine."

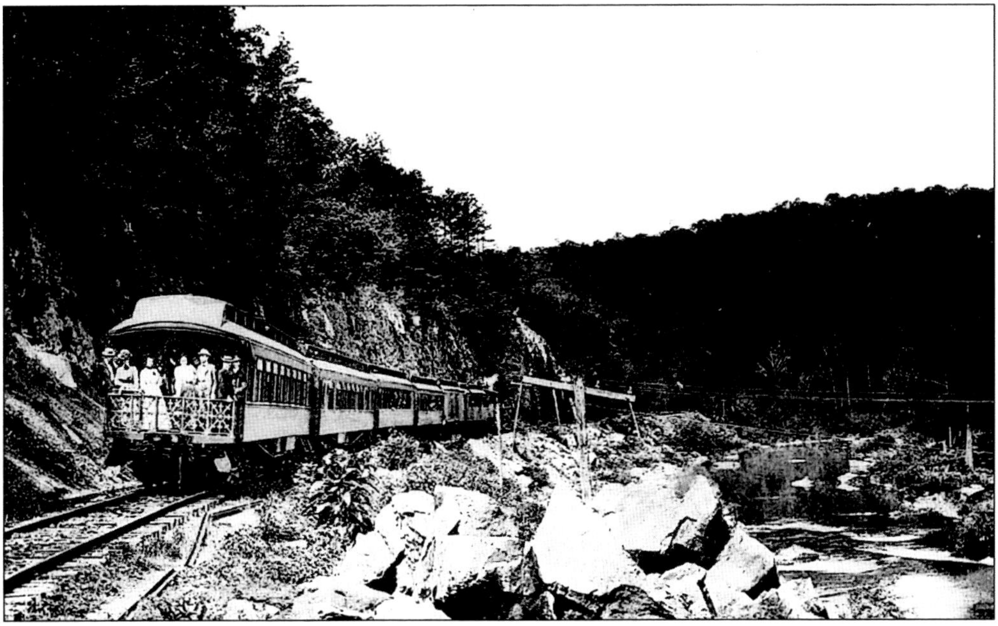

Most visitors came and left Rogers by train. Enjoying such scenery as this, on the Frisco route south of Rogers, was an added bonus to the ticketed passengers. Very likely the train was stopped for some reason while the photographer stood on one of the creekside boulders to take this c. 1910 photo.

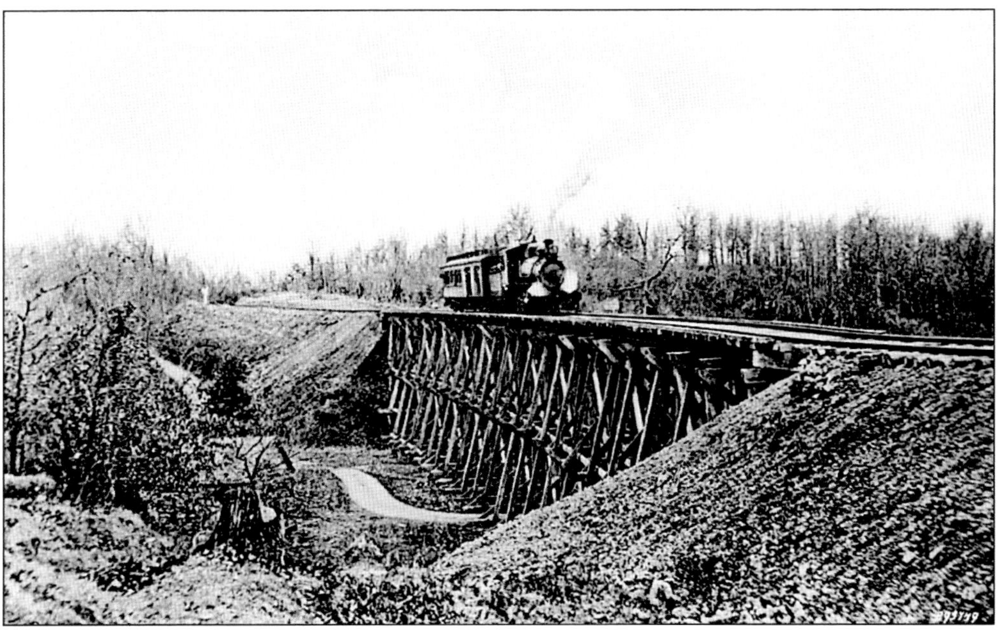

The Arkansas, Oklahoma, & Western Railroad, usually called the A.O. &W, built a line into Rogers in 1906, crossing this wooden trestle en route. In 1910 the line became the Kansas City and Memphis Railroad, adopting as its symbol large red apples painted on the boxcars, in recognition of the importance of the fruit to the economy.

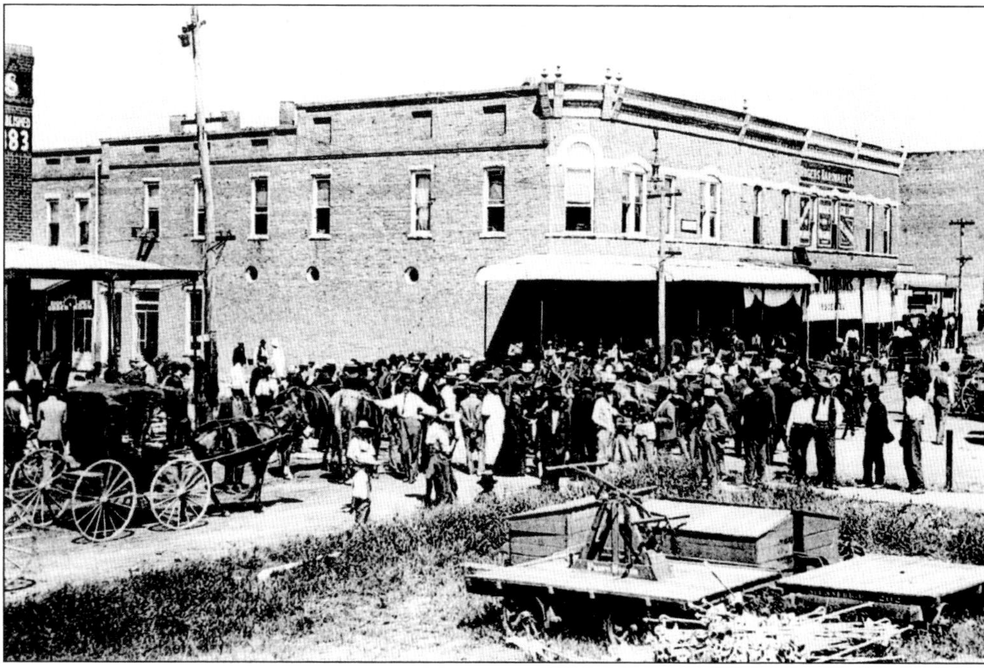

Saturday would have been the busiest day of the week for the merchants along Walnut Street, as farm families poured into town to shop and visit. The card, printed in Germany for Carnahan and Bradford's Drug Store in Rogers, describes the scene as "sales day." Indeed, most customers seen here appear to be headed for Rogers' Hardware Company to the right. Of note are the railroad handcars parked in the grass.

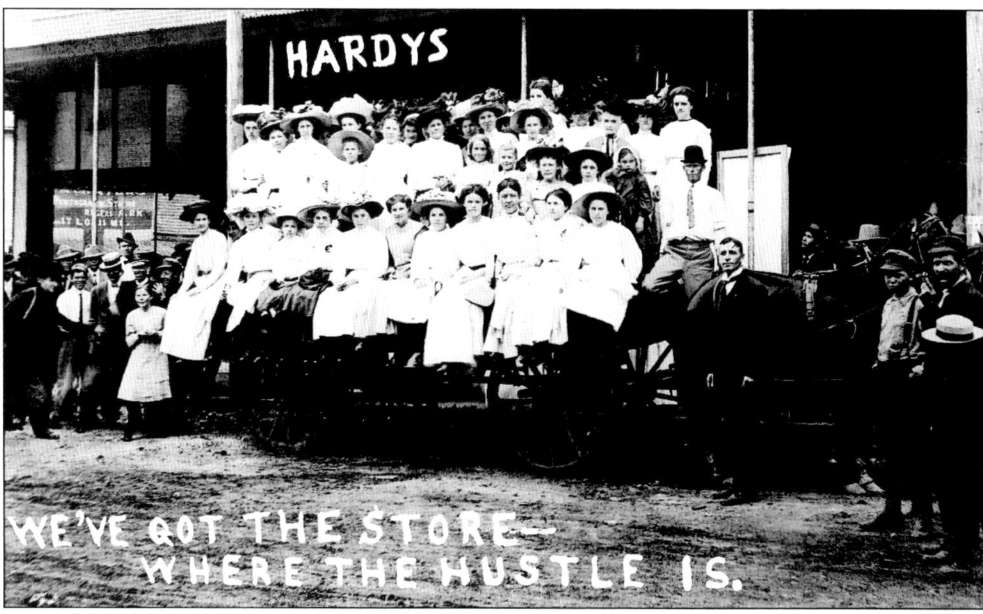

Marketing slogans have long been a part of the retailing business in the nation, and such was the case with Hardy Brother's Meat Market on South First Street in Rogers around 1910. "We've Got the Store Where the Hustle Is," proclaimed a card showing a wagonload of women parked in front of the store.

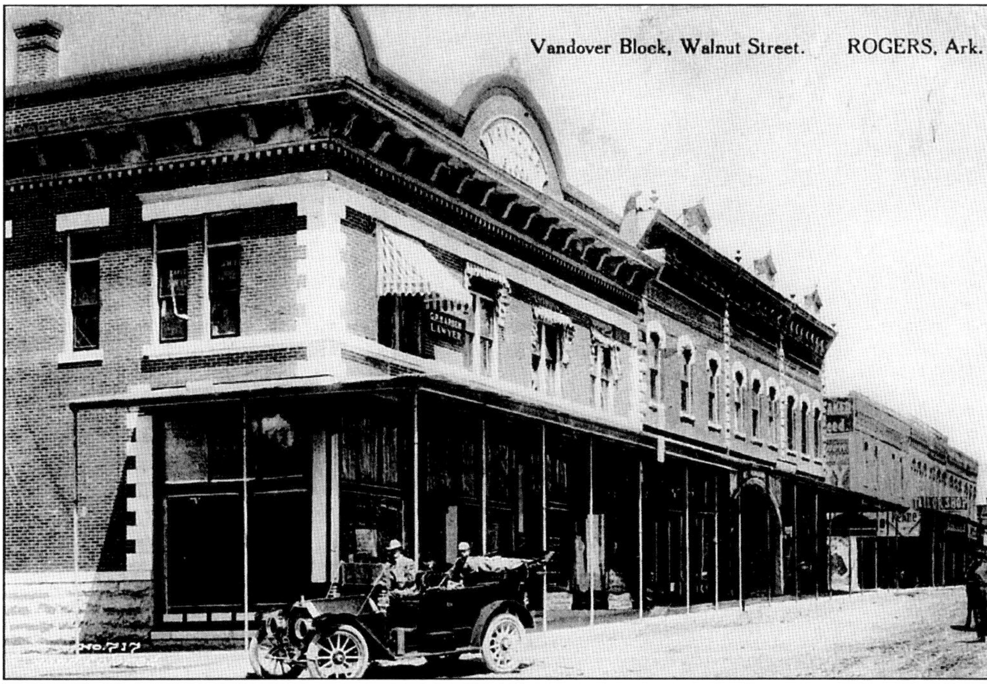

The Vandover Building in Rogers was home to the second-floor law offices of G.P. Harben. The building was owned by J.M. Vandover, a prominent local businessman who, as a sergeant in the service of the Confederacy, had been wounded at the battle of Pea Ridge. Vandover died in 1916, the year after this card was mailed.

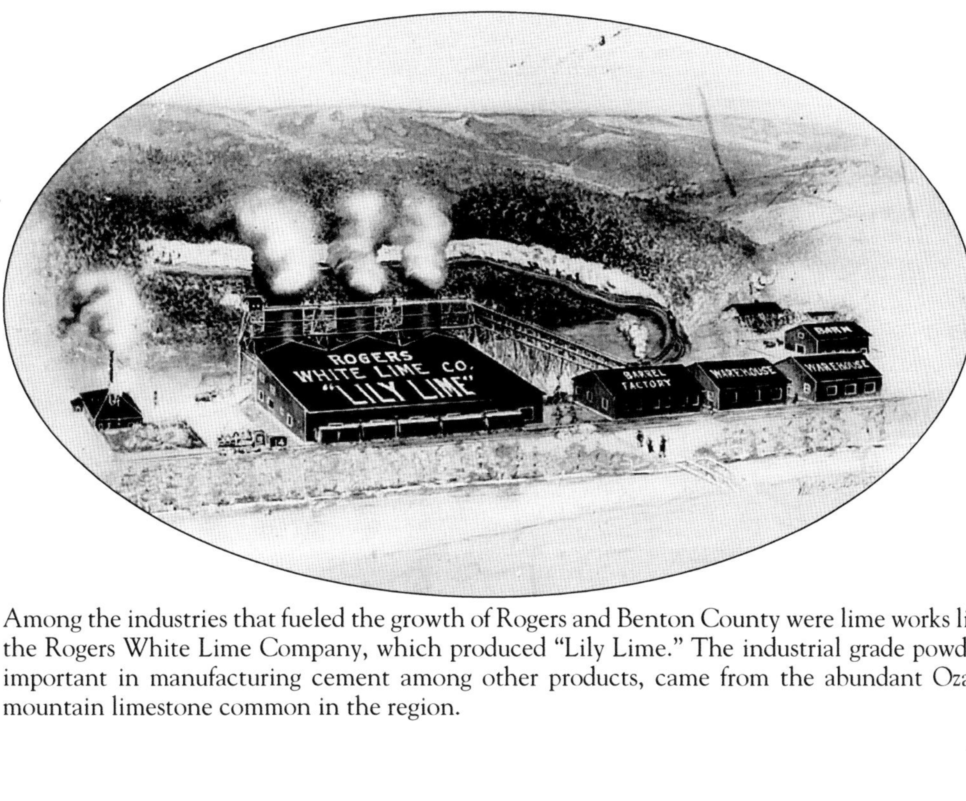

Among the industries that fueled the growth of Rogers and Benton County were lime works like the Rogers White Lime Company, which produced "Lily Lime." The industrial grade powder, important in manufacturing cement among other products, came from the abundant Ozark mountain limestone common in the region.

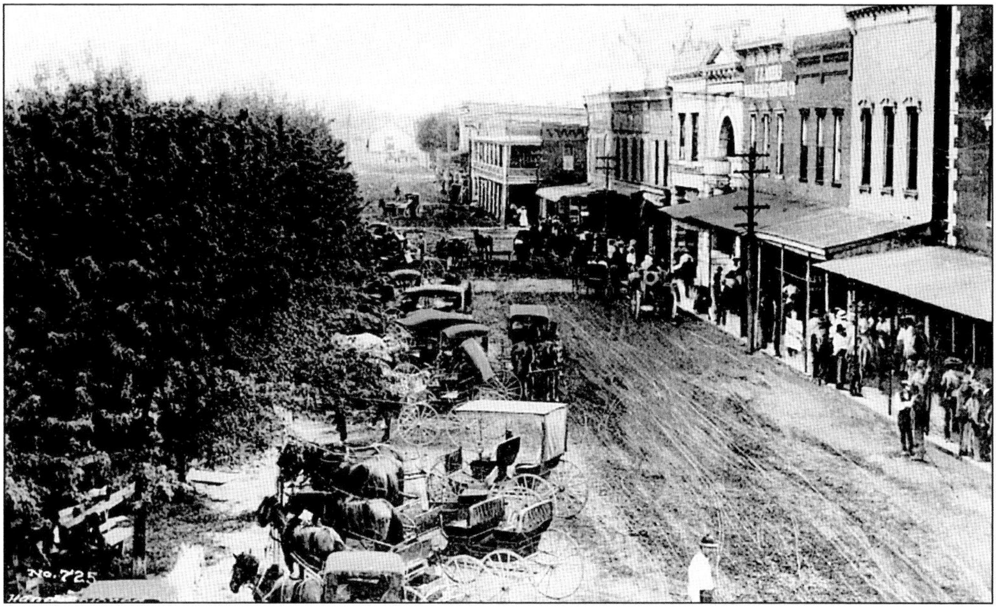

"Snowing here tonight, no spring in sight yet. New passenger station stands where you can see the house at the end of street, card was made before the depot was built" were the words written March 19, 1915. The card of downtown Rogers was mailed from train #5 of the Monett & Paris Railroad, according to the card's postmark. In the center of the block in this view is seen the Bank of Rogers, also depicted on the card below.

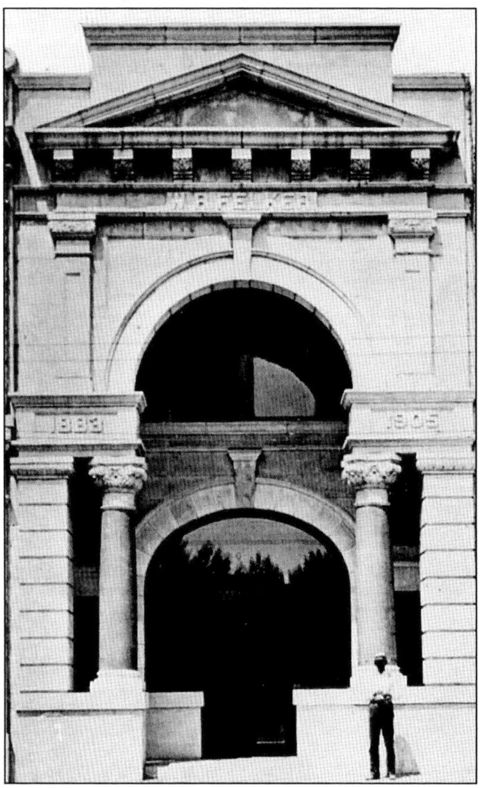

This impressive building for the Bank of Rogers was erected in 1905. The first few years of the bank's history, customers would have parked their wagons or horses across the street under the trees prior to visiting the bank, as seen in the card above. The front of the building bears the name of W.R. Felker, the president of the Arkansas, Oklahoma, & Western Railroad. The restored building today houses an architectural firm.

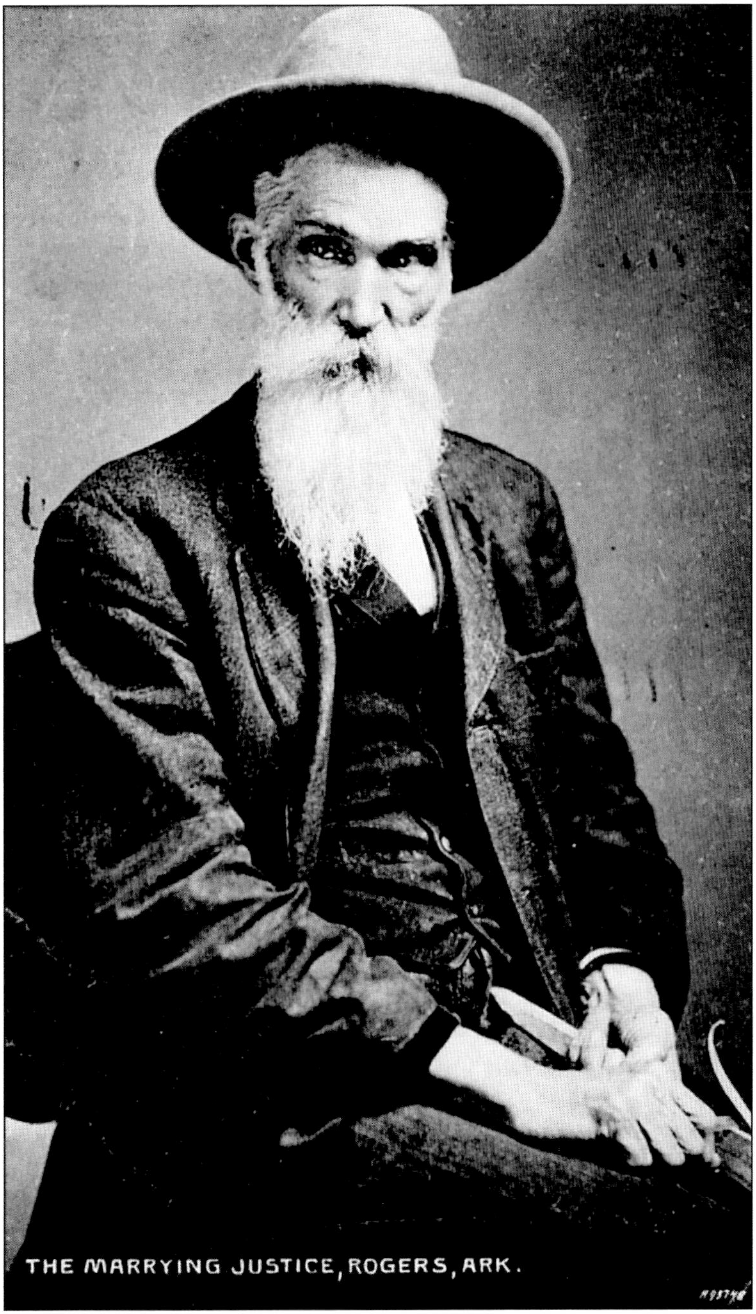

"How is this for a character study?" reads the card sent to Massachusetts. The "marrying justice," presumably a justice of the peace, appeared on this postcard carving a piece of wood. His name is not recorded, but we expect that nuptial couples who stood before him never forgot the intense eyes that would have met theirs over the long white beard. Perhaps one of these couples was described in a local 1908 newspaper, as quoted from *History of Benton County* by J. Dickson Black: "Now that we are married," he said, "We are one, and I must insist that this be the last time that you appear in public in a low-necked gown." "We may be one," she replied, "But you are only half of us, and I shall dress my half as I please." (*c.* 1910.)

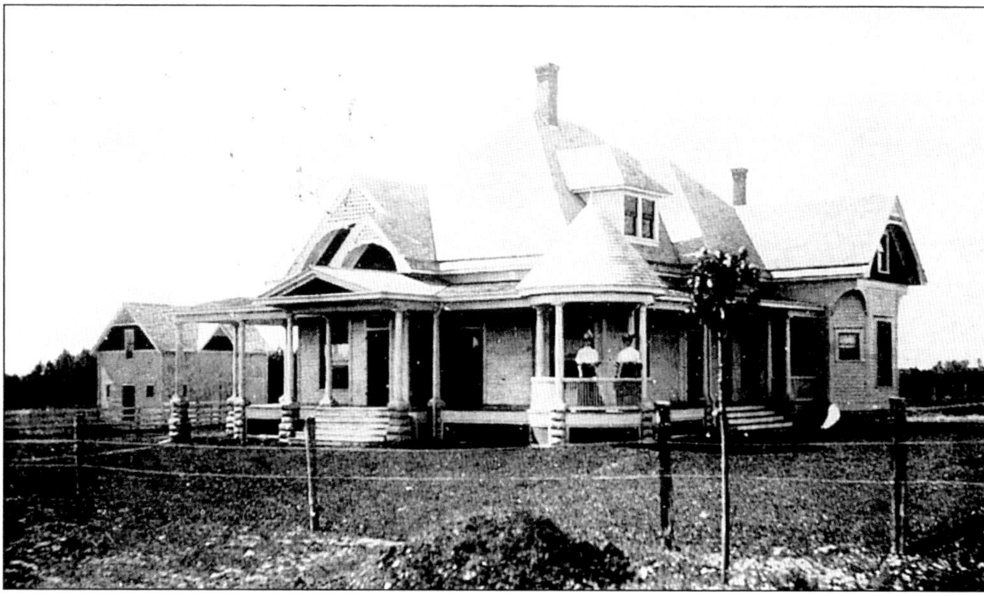

The economy of Benton County generated profits that allowed some to construct large homes, such as the residence of J.L. Chapin, seen in the card above. The 1908 message read, "John asleep, he is the best little fellow you ever saw, is going to be walking soon. Boys are playing cards, come over and help." Chapin was the president of the Farmers State Bank at Rogers from 1910 to 1916. The hilltop home in the card below was the summer residence of attorney George Mansfield, member of a noted firm that earned $750,000 representing the displaced Cherokee Indians. Mansfield apparently lived most of the year in California, summering in Benton County. The log and stone home was built in 1905 for $10,000. Water was piped in from the spring at the base of the hill. Mansfield's wife's poor health necessitated a permanent move to California sometime around 1908, and the home was sold.

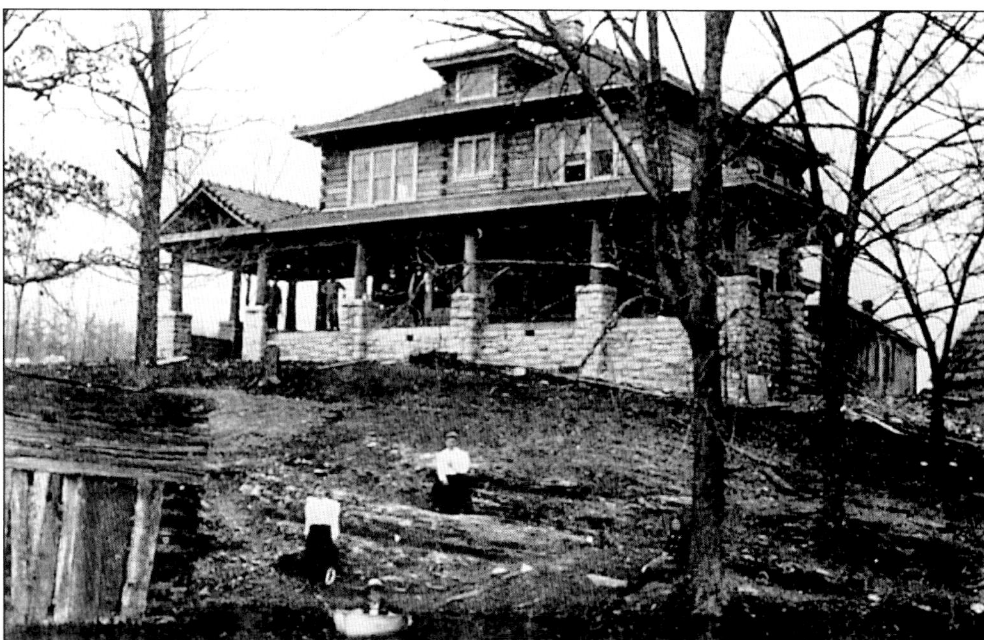

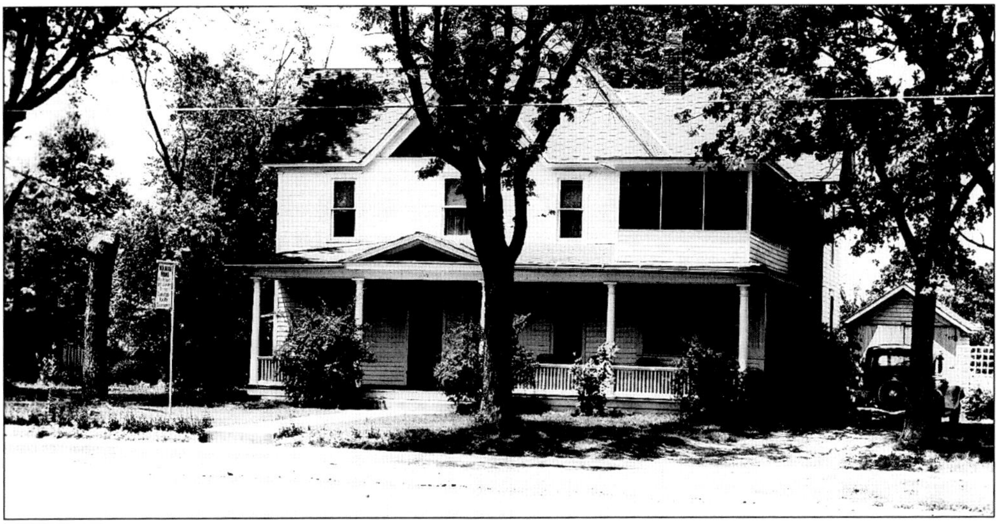

In 1908 a young lady named Betty Blake married a vaudeville performer at her family's home, seen here at 307. E. Walnut. The groom was Will Rogers, who would become one of the best-loved American personalities of the century, before his 1935 death in an Alaskan plane crash. Of Arkansas, Rogers once said, "Arkansas voted last Tuesday against Evolution and Republicans. They don't want anything taught about either in their schools." The home is gone today, and the site is a parking lot with a plaque marking the historic location.

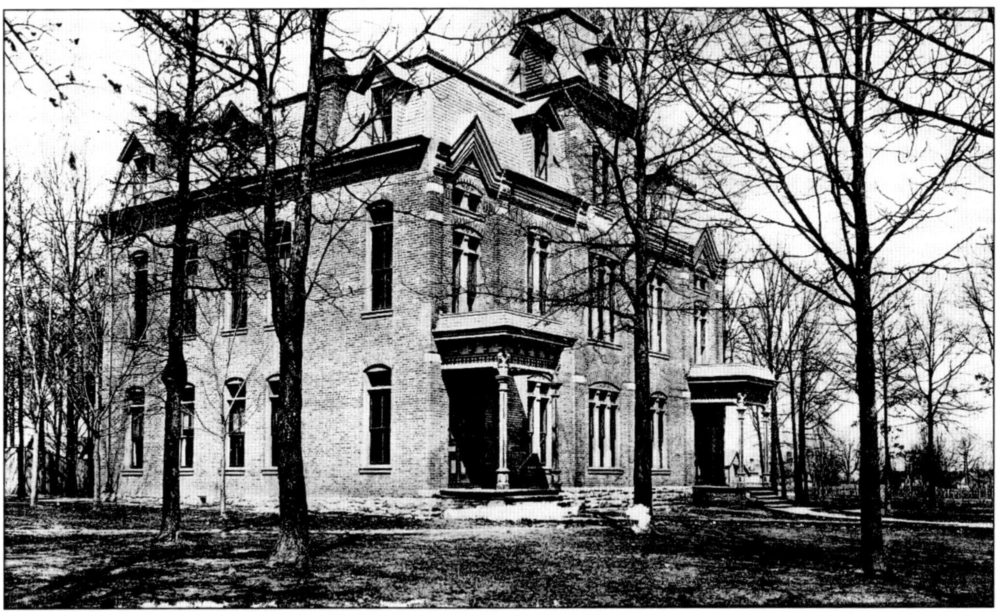

The first school in the city was the Rogers Academy, erected in 1883 at a cost of $1,451, money raised by local citizens of the newly formed community. Lacking any additional funds, the city was fortunate to have the American Missionary Society of the Congregational Church agree to run the school and to cover costs. Tuition at the school ranged from $3 to $10 per 3-month quarter, depending on the student's grade level. Rules for students included no tobacco use and mandatory church attendance on Sunday. Financial setbacks led to the closing of the school in 1914; the Rogers Public School District acquired the property, but the historic buildings are gone today. (*c.* 1905.)

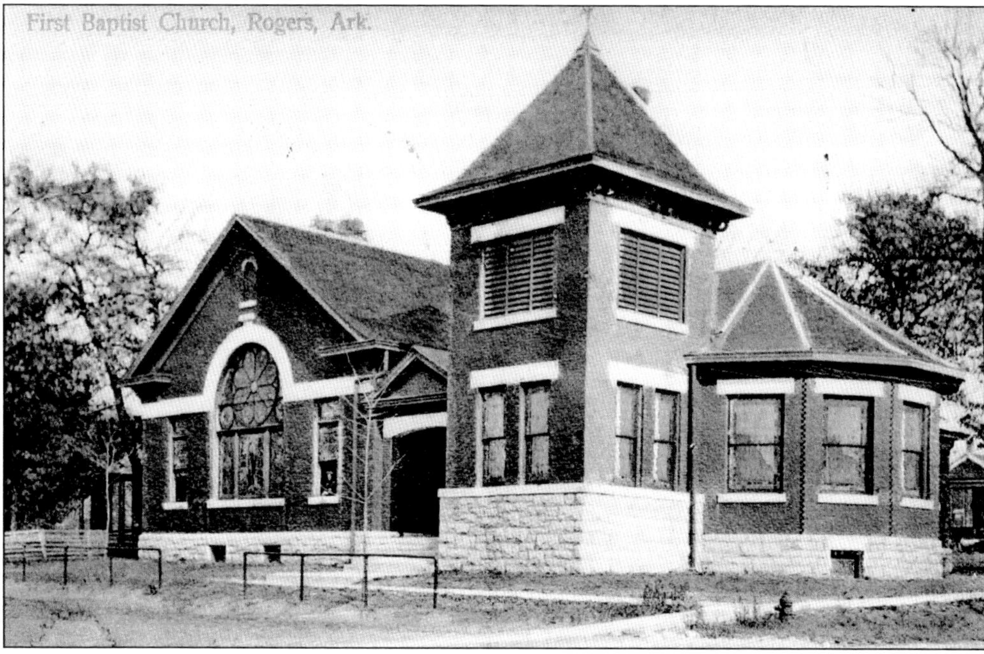

Although modest in size, the town of Rogers was home to churches of most denominations by the early part of the century. On the reverse side of the card of the First Baptist Church in 1909 were the words, "Hope you are much better at this writing, you have had lots of trouble, seems to me. Write soon. Aren't the new hats beautiful?" The card below exhibited the striking interior of the Methodist Episcopal Church. The curved pews were set beneath stained glass and an arched ceiling; the floor sloped down to the altar, where the minister would have talked of the scriptures interwoven with the events of 1910.

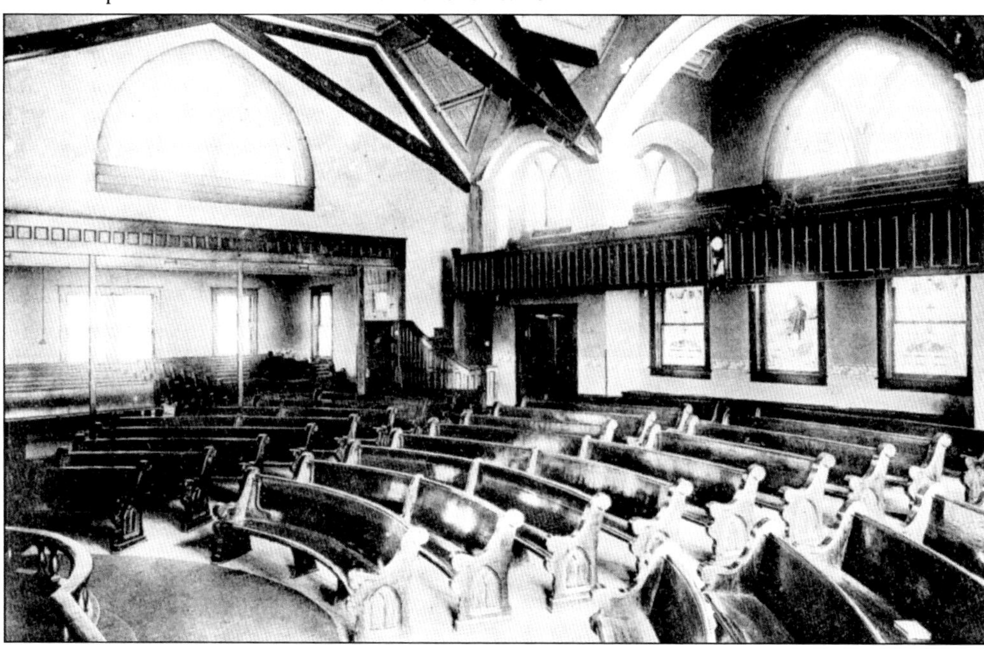

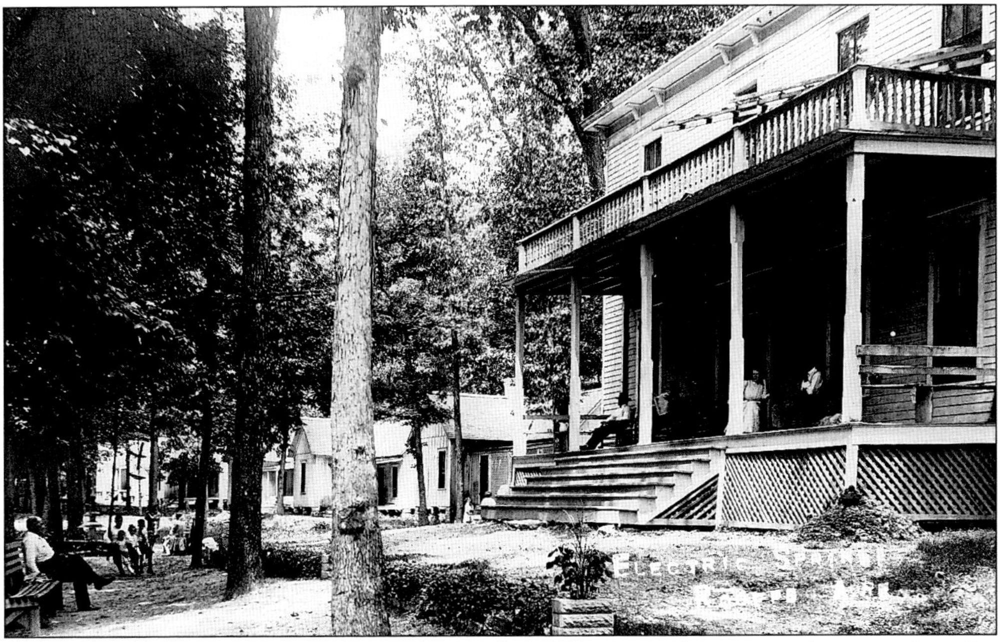

Electric Springs was located at the northeast edge of Rogers, and was a popular resort from the 1880s into the first few years of the 20th century. The spring, which was considered to have curative properties for a variety of ailments, gave rise to a hotel and a sanitarium building. Seen in the *c.* 1905 card above is some of the lodging that housed visitors who came to drink the water and to walk the shady trails. The card below was mailed on the Fourth of July, 1909; it shows a family drinking the water and filling a pitcher set on the ground between the ladies on the far right. "Say I had some time in the Moose Hall to-day, there sure is a fine hall here" were the words from a visiting member of the fraternal organization. The resort is gone today, and the area is now residential.

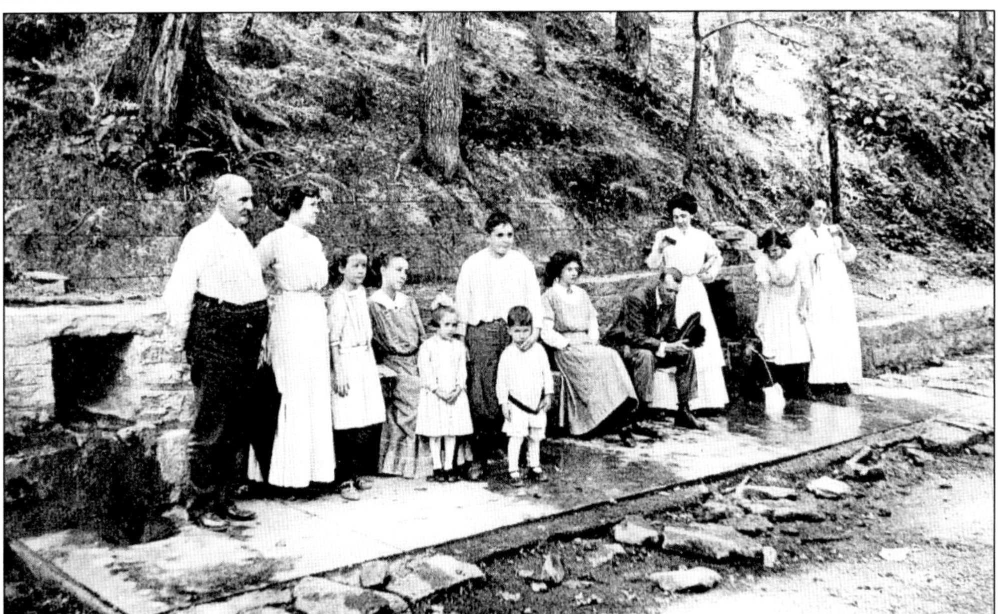

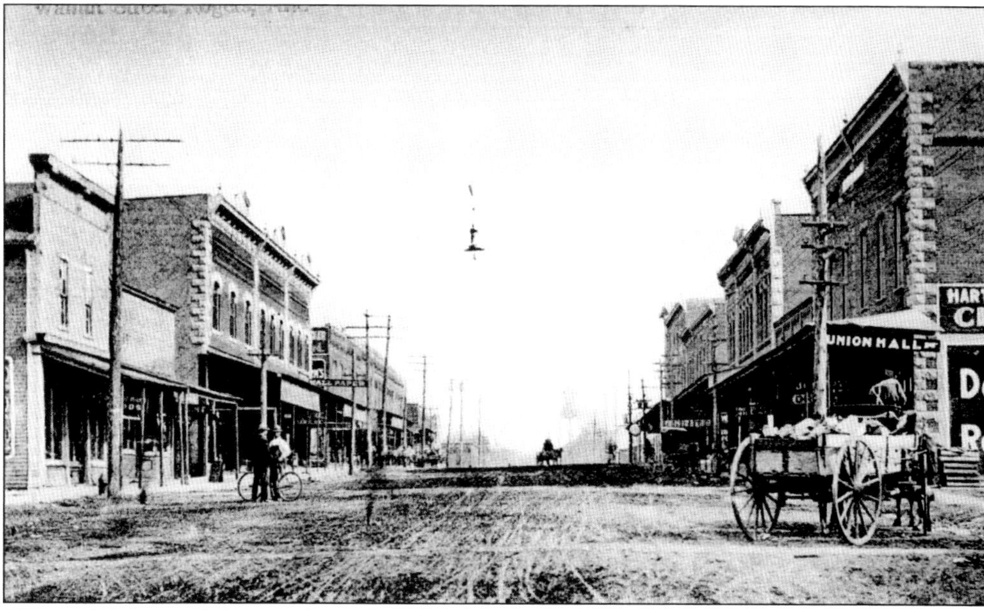

The card above and the two that follow present a tour through the passage of time, showing the same block of Rogers' Walnut Street across a span of more than half a century. "With bushels of love and kisses," this *c.* 1905 card was sent, bringing a scene of a wagon turning towards the Union Hall; a sign for Hart, Schaffner, and Marx suits is painted on the brick wall. Across the rutted dirt street, two men talk over a bicycle. At the far right end of the street is seen the 100,000-gallon elevated water tower, erected in 1900.

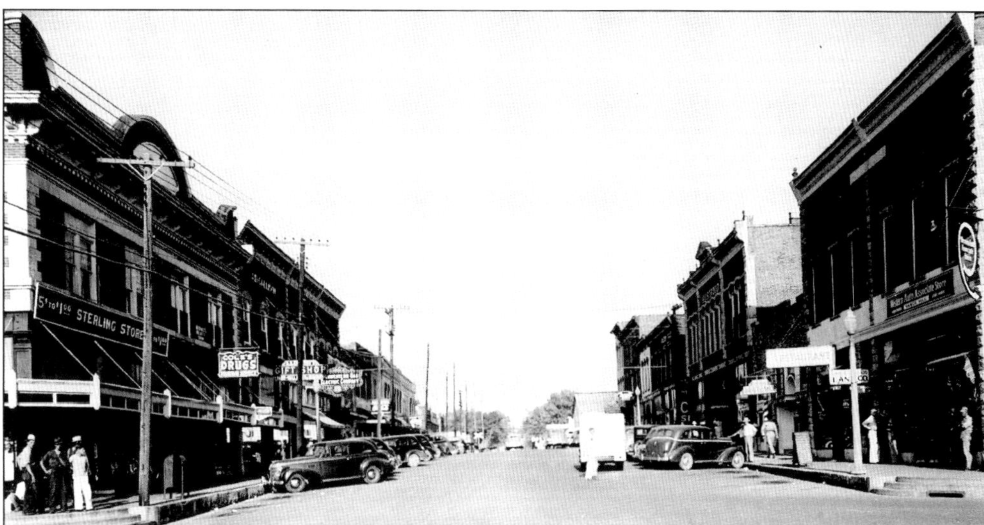

In this *c.* 1945 view of the same block of Walnut Street, most of the 1905-era buildings remain from the photo above, although a larger building now stands at the far left, housing Sterling's 5-cent to $1.00 Store and Cole's Drug Store. Across the street, now paved with bricks, Western Auto and a restaurant occupy the building that had housed the clothing store in 1905. The water tower is still visible in this view.

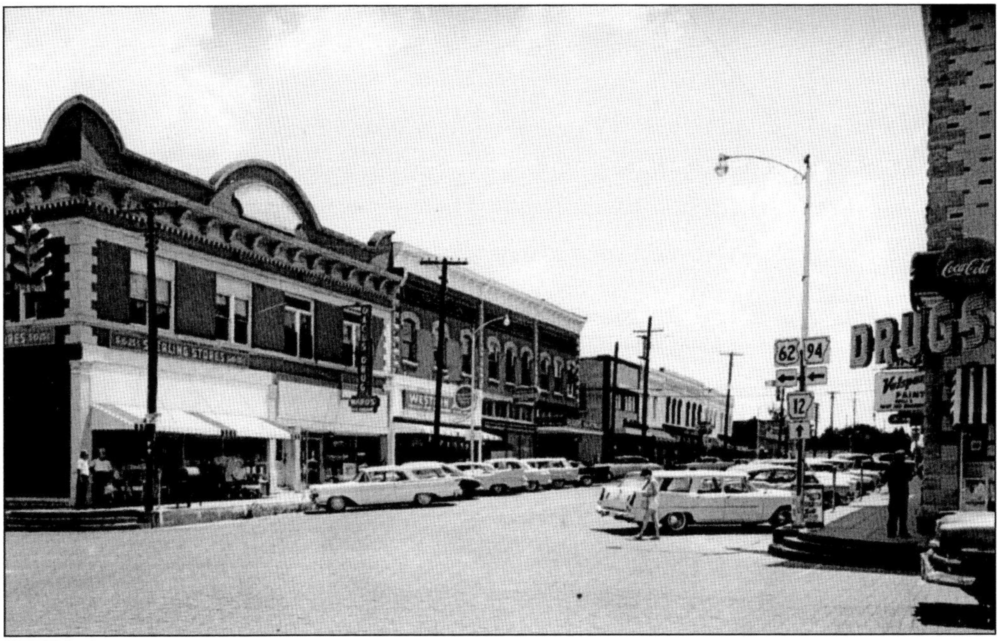

In this c. 1960 view of Walnut Street, the now-blacktopped street still finds Sterling's Store on the left corner, beside the renamed Dacus Drug Store. Western Auto has moved across the street, into the middle of the block on the left. The building on the left corner that had housed the clothing store in 1905, and Western Auto in 1945, was home to a drugstore and a paint store at the time this view was taken. Today most of these buildings still stand, but the businesses have mostly been displaced by shopping centers on the outskirts of the city. The restored Walnut Street is today a proud participant in the Main Street Arkansas Program.

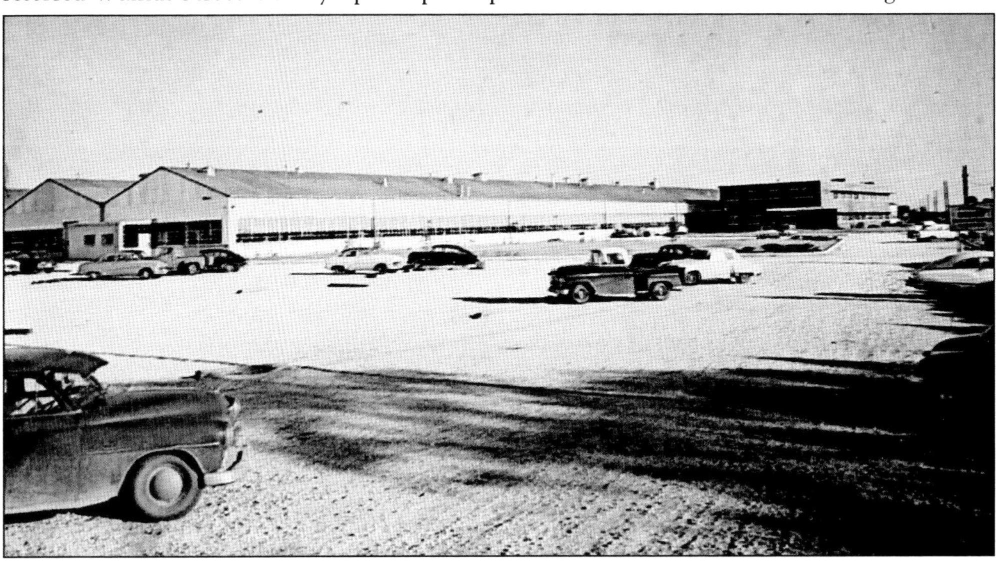

The Rogers economy got a major boost towards diversification in the 1950s, when the Daisy Air Rifle Company moved its manufacturing plant from the northeastern United States to this site. The air rifles were first manufactured as a promotional item by the Plymouth Iron Wind Mill Company of Michigan in the 1880s; if a farmer bought a windmill he got a free air rifle. A museum of guns opened next to the Rogers plant, offering another tourist draw to the area.

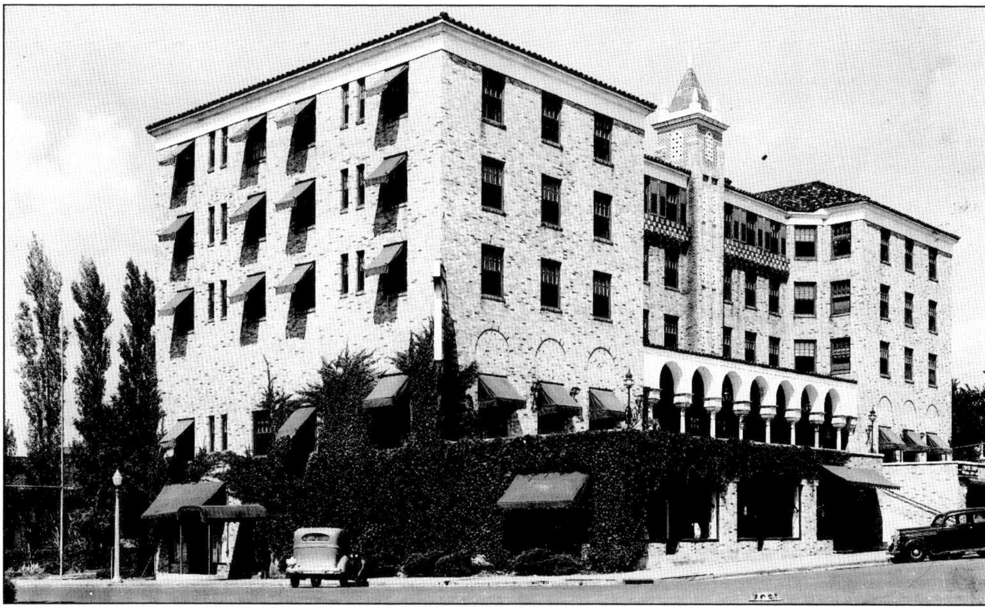

The place to stay in Rogers for many years was the Moorish-styled Harris Hotel, which was erected in the 1930s. One hotel guest wrote on a card, "This hotel is wonderful, each bath room has tub, glass & tile fittings, most beautiful." The Harris was advertised as the "Palace of the Ozarks"; on some postcards it claimed to be located within 500 miles of 19 million people. (*c.* 1940.)

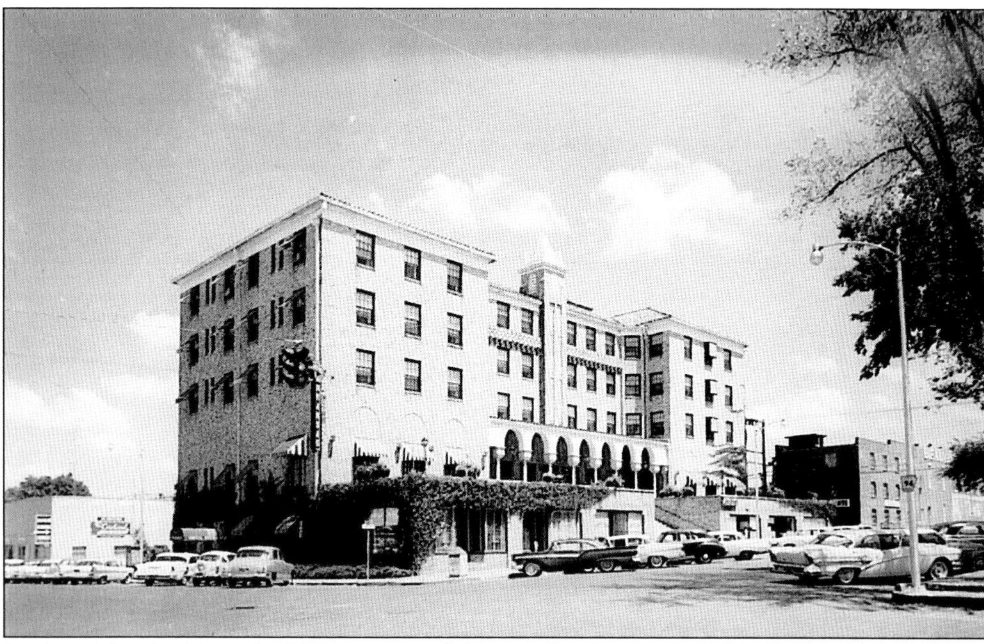

By the 1950s the Harris had been renamed the Hotel Arkansas, as it tried to compete with the growing number of highway motels that the motoring public began to find more convenient. The back of the card invites guests to spend carefree days in air-conditioned comfort. The building still stands today but no longer serves as a hotel. It closed for that purpose in 1963, and is today operated as a retirement home. (*c.* 1957.)

Four

BENTON COUNTY
VILLAGES, RESORTS, AND AN ECCENTRIC CHARACTER

In the early years of the century, as Bentonville and Rogers developed into first-class cities, the rest of Benton County was developing around agriculture and tourism, the latter produced by resorts that grew up around numerous springs and the White River. The combination of tourism and robust agricultural industries led to a very large production of postcards, leaving a rich legacy of a region that is today beset with, for better or worse, some of the most rapid development in the nation.

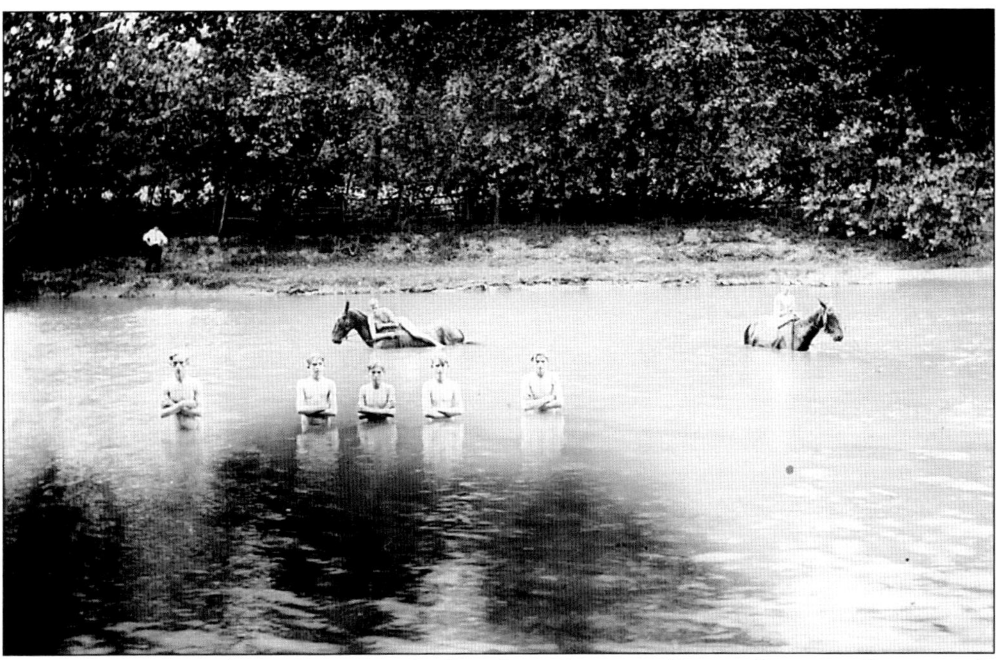

The White River and its tributary creeks flow through eastern Benton County, offering ample recreational opportunities. In this c. 1910 card, the photographer captured seven young men "skinny dipping" with what appear to be two mules. These boys, all likely born before the turn of the century, would be most surprised to find this photo in a book almost a century later.

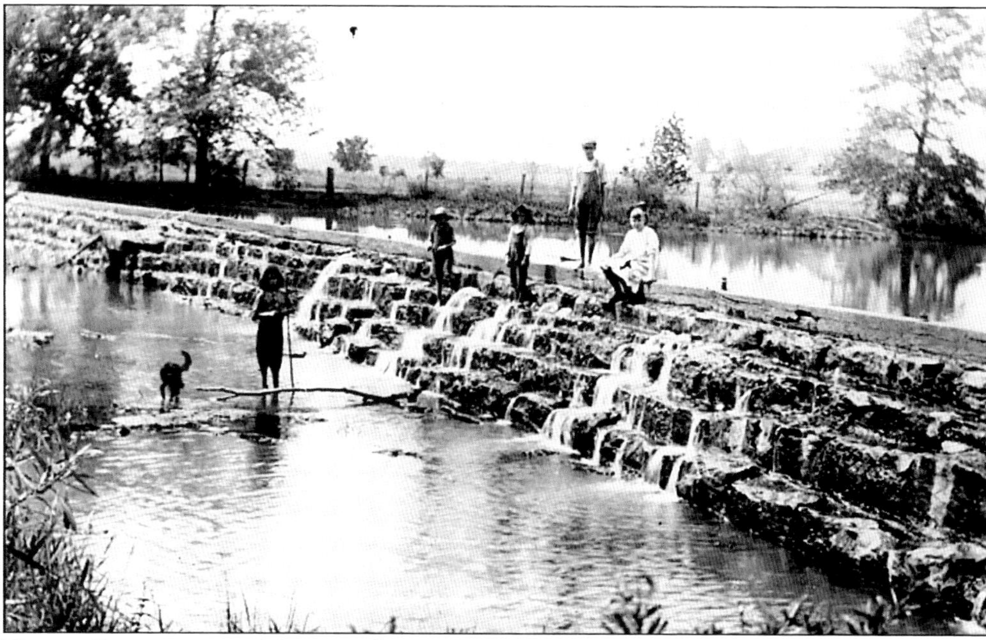

The small community of Osage Mills was formed in 1852, but lost its post office in 1906 and faded away, not even appearing today on most maps. A dam of cut stone formed a pool on a creek, proving a delight to five barefoot children and their dog around 1900. The names of the children are penned on the card: Bennie, Glenn, Albert, Orphia, and Claude.

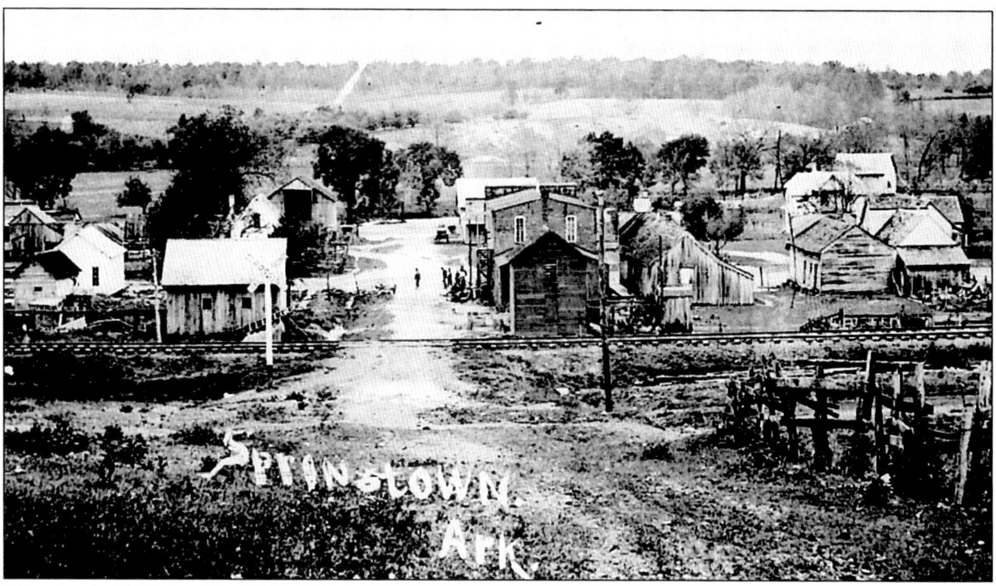

"Don't think I am lost. Just blew in here this AM and thought I would let you know I was thinking of you" were the 1909 words from the village of Springtown. The town was formed in the 1860s, some 18 miles southeast of Bentonville; it prospered until around 1915, when it began to fade, losing momentum to other towns of the county. Today the still very small town lays in close proximity to the developing Northwest Arkansas Regional Airport, and is perhaps now poised for future growth.

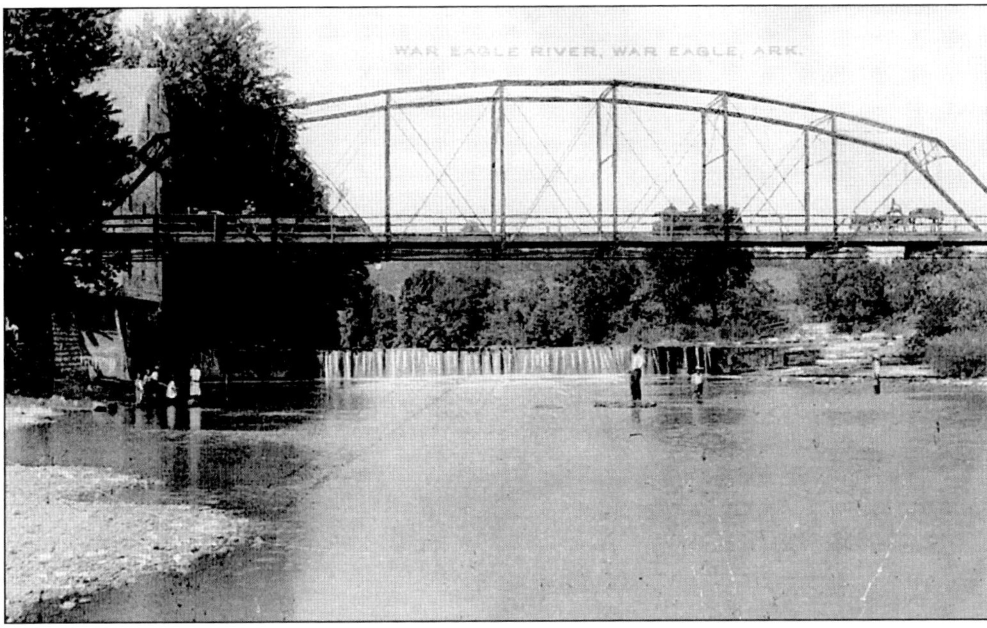

The first gristmill was erected at this site on the War Eagle River in 1835; it washed away in a flood in 1848 but was quickly rebuilt. That mill was burned by the retreating Confederate Army in 1862. Ironically a larger, four-story mill and a rock dam were built in 1872 by former Confederate Capt. J.A.C. Blackthorne. For some 50 years the landmark, seen just to the left of the bridge, did a thriving business converting grain to flour, until it was destroyed by a fire in 1924. Today the bridge still stands, as does a rebuilt functioning mill that draws many tourists. (c. 1910.)

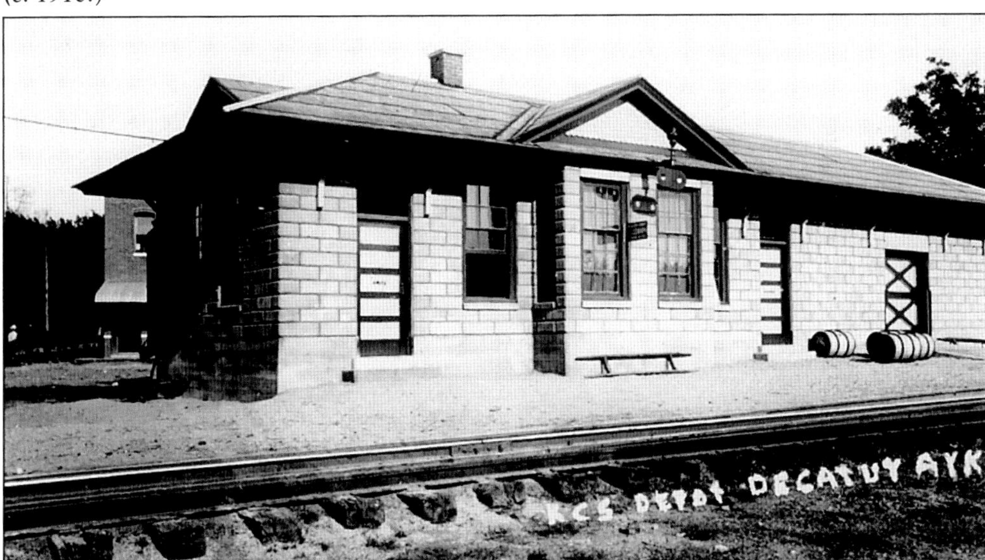

Decatur, located west of Bentonville, was formed in the 1880s. Decatur got a major economic boost in 1893 with the coming of the Kansas City, Pittsburgh, and Gulf Railroad, which put its tracks through the small village. The railroad eventually became the Kansas City Southern Railroad, which would build this sturdy depot so vital to shipping the bumper crops of apples produced around Decatur each year. (c. 1910.)

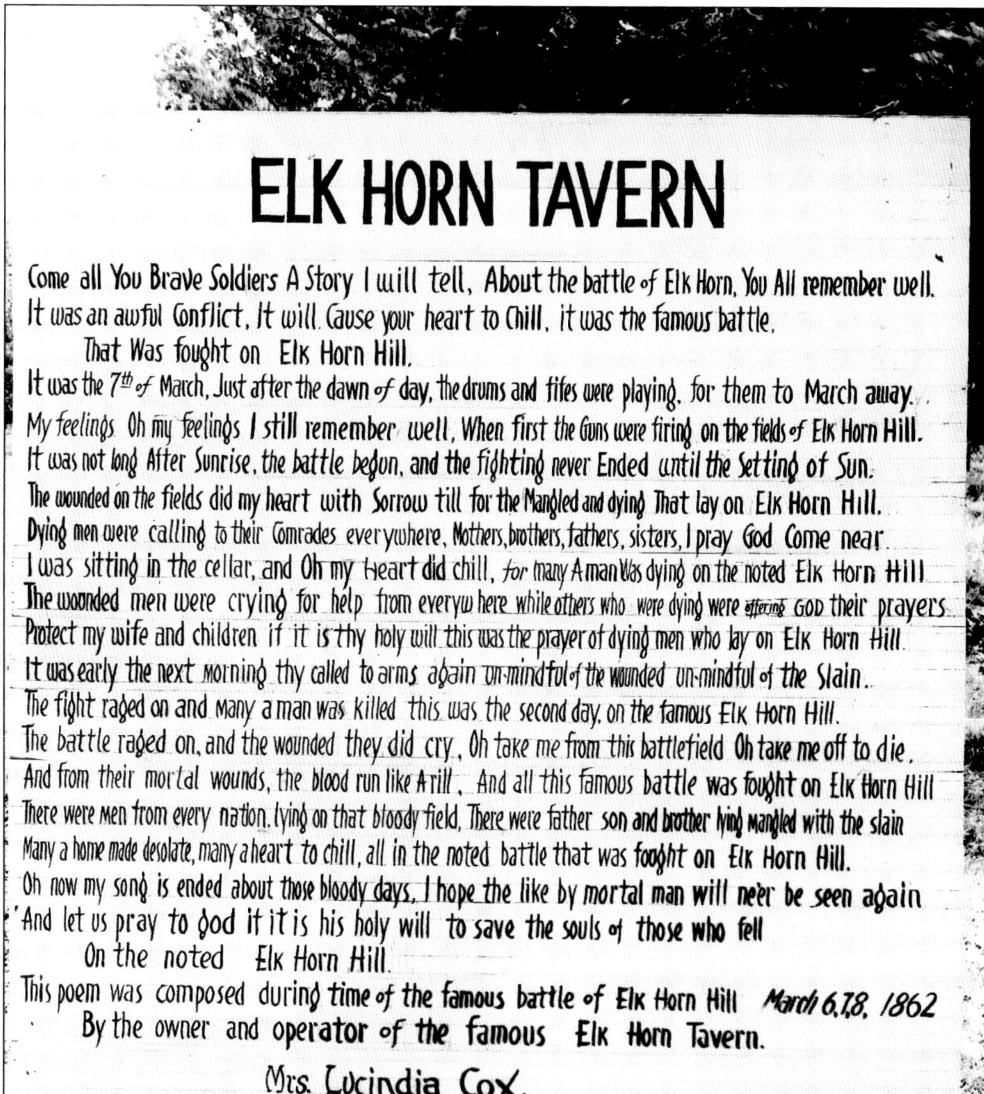

Over a three-day period in March of 1862, the Union and Confederate Armies collided at what is alternatively referred to in history as the Battle of Pea Ridge, or Elk Horn Tavern, the site of some of the bloodiest fighting. Some historians have labeled the battle the "Gettysburg of the West," for if the Confederacy had won they might have taken St. Louis and Missouri, thus preventing the vital Union capture of the Mississippi River the next year. A series of tactical blunders on the part of Confederate commanders gave the Union a victory, and perhaps sealed the loss of the war with the North. The sign in this 1930 card displays a poem written at the time of the battle by Lucindia Cox, which told the story in verse. "I hope the like by mortal man will ne'er be seen again, and let us pray to God it is his holy will to save the souls of those who fell on the noted Elk Horn Hill."

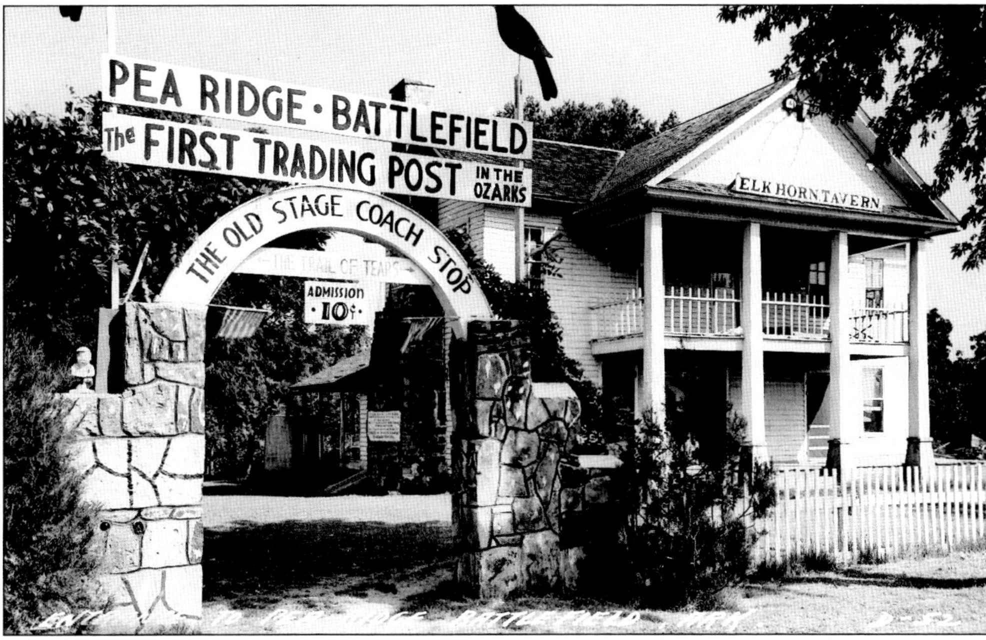

By the early 1930s the site of the Pea Ridge battle, where more than a thousand men died, had become a tourist attraction. The above photo shows the famous tavern, considerably altered since the war, for which admission could be gained for 10¢. A sign over the gate also promotes the Trail of Tears, denoting the forced march of the Cherokees in the 1830s when they were forcibly moved from the Southeastern U.S. to the Oklahoma Territory, passing through Benton County along the way. In the card below a group of tourists posed next to a cabin referred to as the "Castle." One of the signs on the building reads, "Built in 1851 by Hezekiah Lasater. Stood on the firing line of the battle of Pea Ridge March 1862. Bullets have all been removed from logs by souvenir hunters." Today the site is known as the Pea Ridge National Battlefield, and is under the care of the National Park Service.

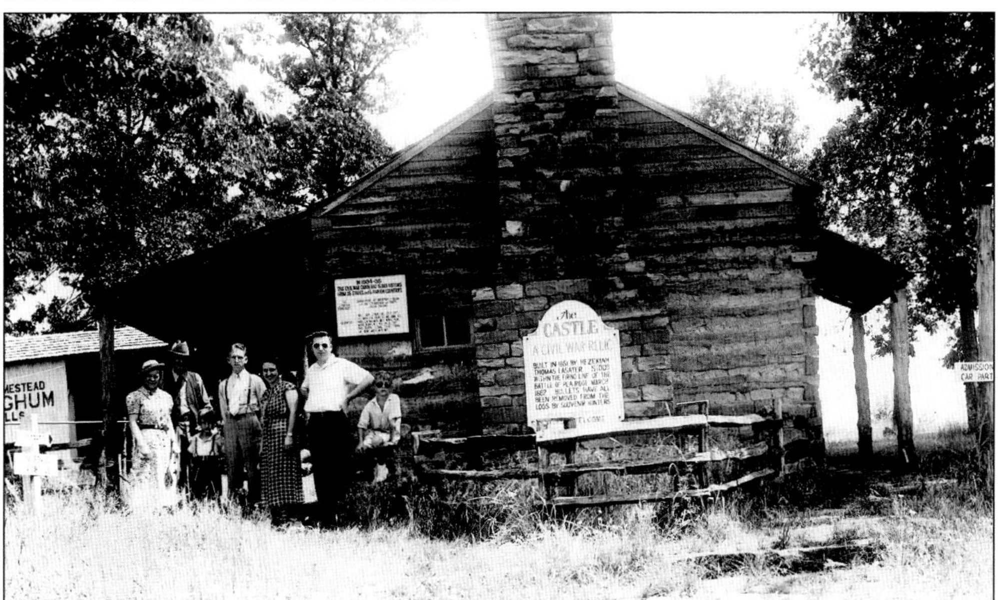

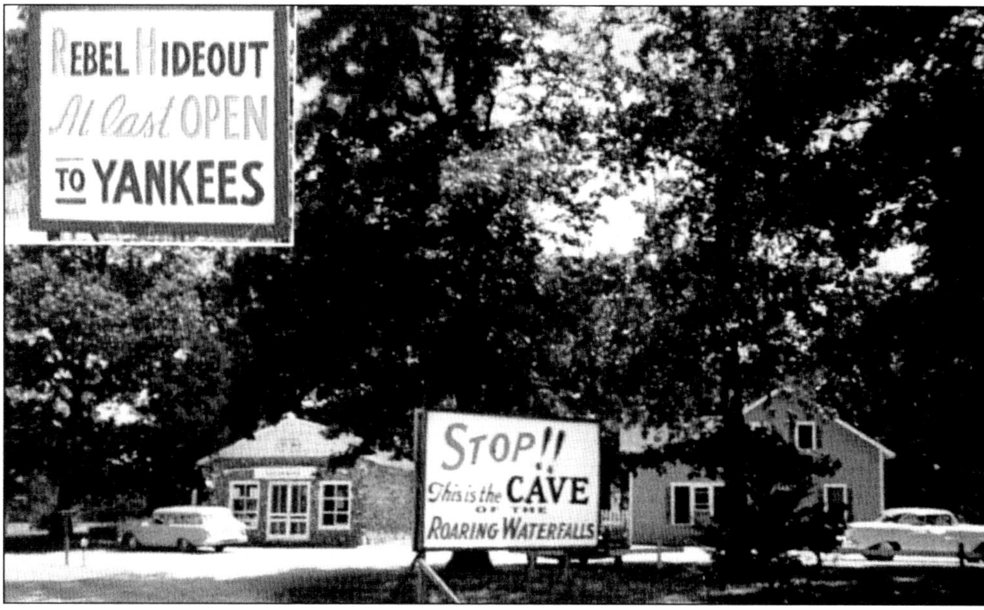

Caves proved a popular tourist draw in Benton County, and one entrepreneur combined the draw with a Civil War theme. The "Civil War Cave," located about 4 miles from Bentonville, was reputed to have been used during the war. One of the signs along the road to the cave read, "Rebel Hideout at last OPEN to YANKEES." An underground roaring waterfall was also part of the tour. The cave is still open to visitors today. (*c.* 1955.)

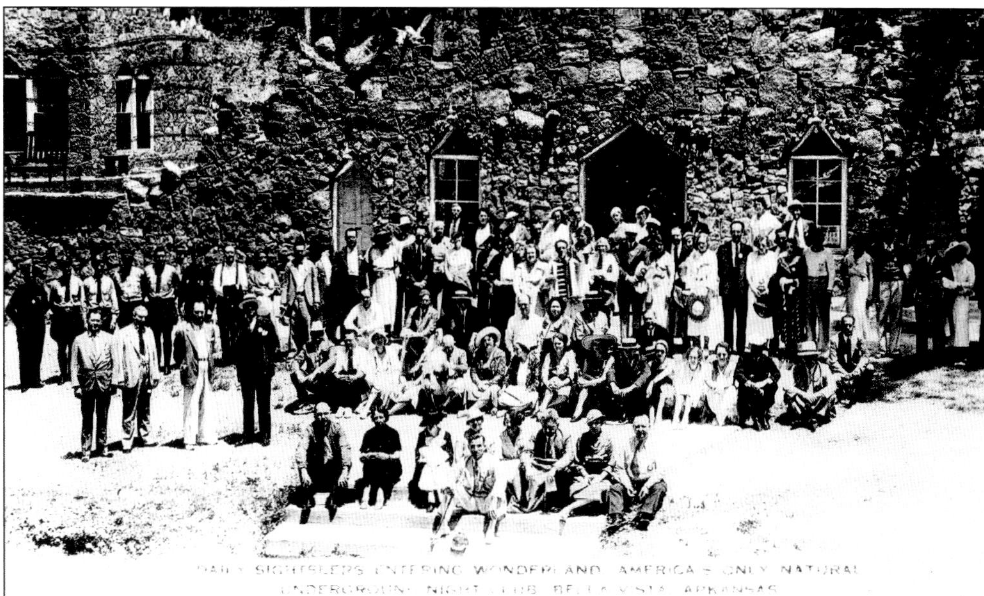

"We just left the place on the card. We went through it. It was rather spooky & Lucille & I were glad to get out again. This is an underground cave. They do have a nightclub too." At Bella Vista, the travelers pictured above had just concluded a 1936 visit to one of the most unusual attractions in the nation. The cave's owner had visited a Paris cabaret housed in an underground cave in 1930, and he came back to Benton County inspired to open his own Arkansas version of the French wonder.

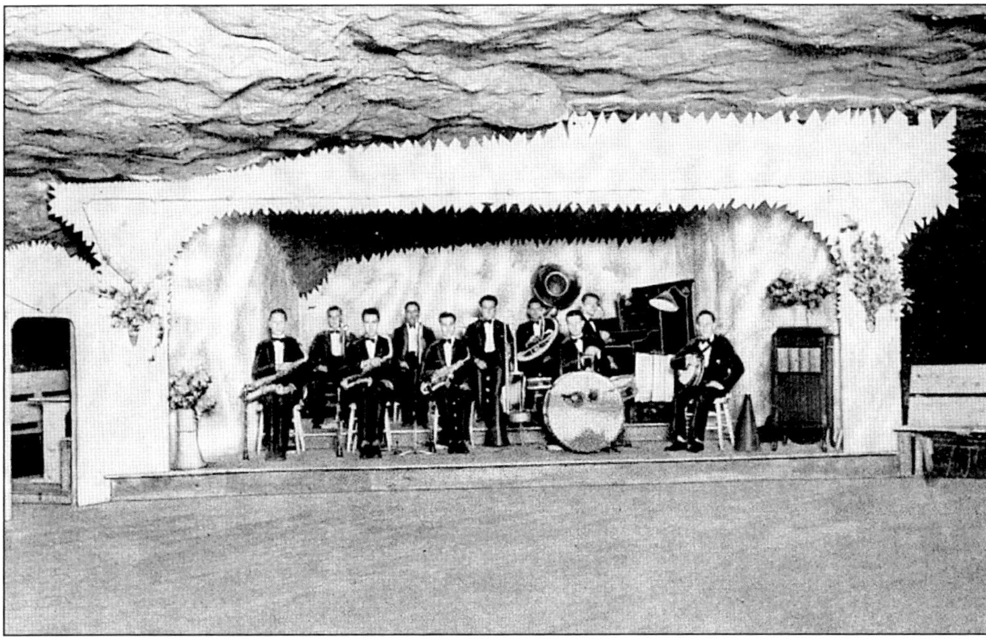

When the Wonderland Cave nightclub opened in 1930 to a crowd of 800 people, it had as a draw such performers as Cab Calloway lined up to entertain the patrons who flocked to the year-round 62-degree cave. These two *c.* 1935 cards show a performing band and the dance floor, with dining tables to the left in the lower view. Over the years Wonderland Cave was featured in *Ripley's Believe It or Not* and in a host of national magazines. At one point during the 1940s, a brief session of the Arkansas Legislature was convened in the cave. The popularity of the attraction waned over the years, and by 1980 it was closed, when cracks detected in the ceiling raised safety concerns.

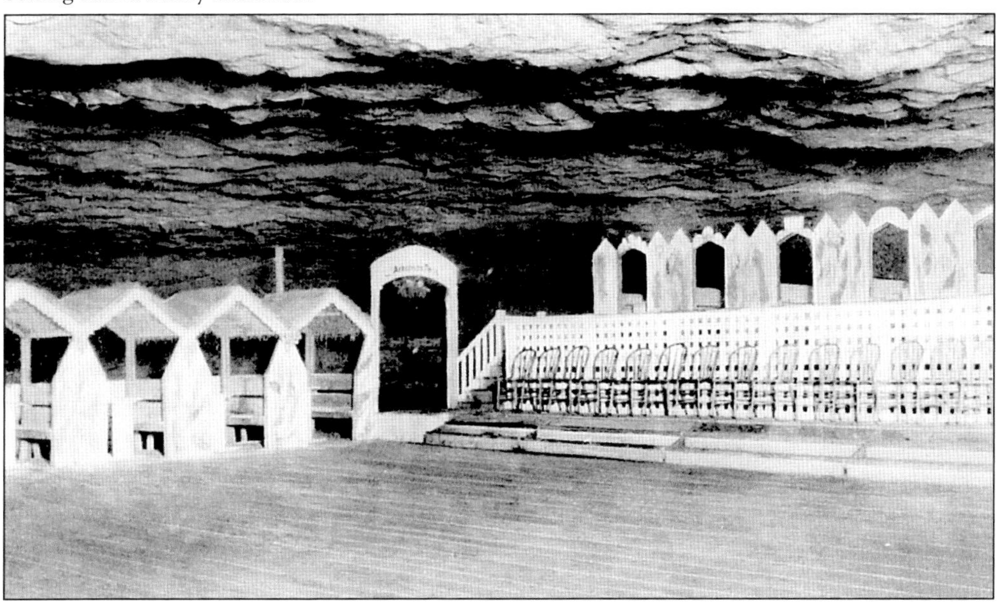

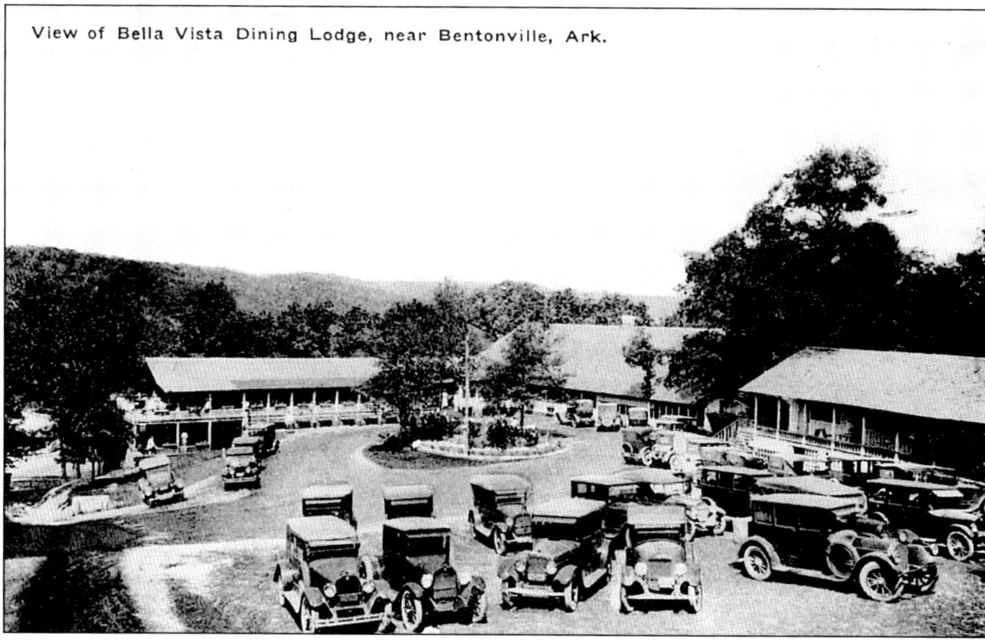

Bella Vista was born as a private, for-profit resort enterprise, founded in 1916 by Dr. Cotton Smith, 5 miles from Bentonville. The eventual array of attractions included a dining lodge (seen above c. 1935), dance pavilion, a lake, and first-class hotels, all of which served to draw people from across the entire region. In a step unusual for Arkansas resorts of the day, a number of people bought lots and built summer cabins, like the one shown below in August of 1923. The arrangement catered to the motoring public of modest means, who would have a retreat away from the city but near all the amenities offered by the Bella Vista development. The Cooper Communities Corp. acquired Bella Vista in the 1960s, and today the area is an upscale retirement community laced with golf courses, drawing retirees from across the nation to spend their golden years in Northwest Arkansas.

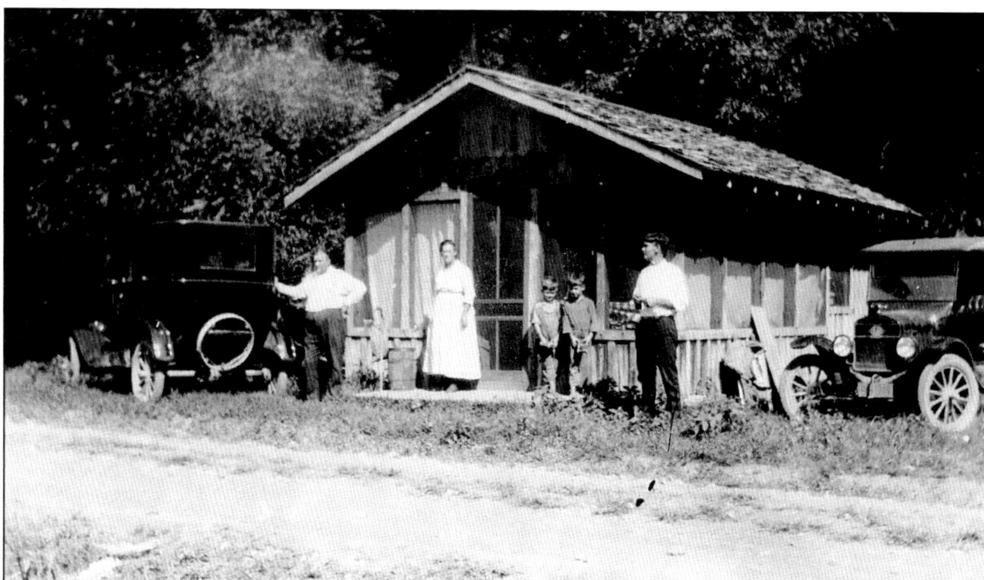

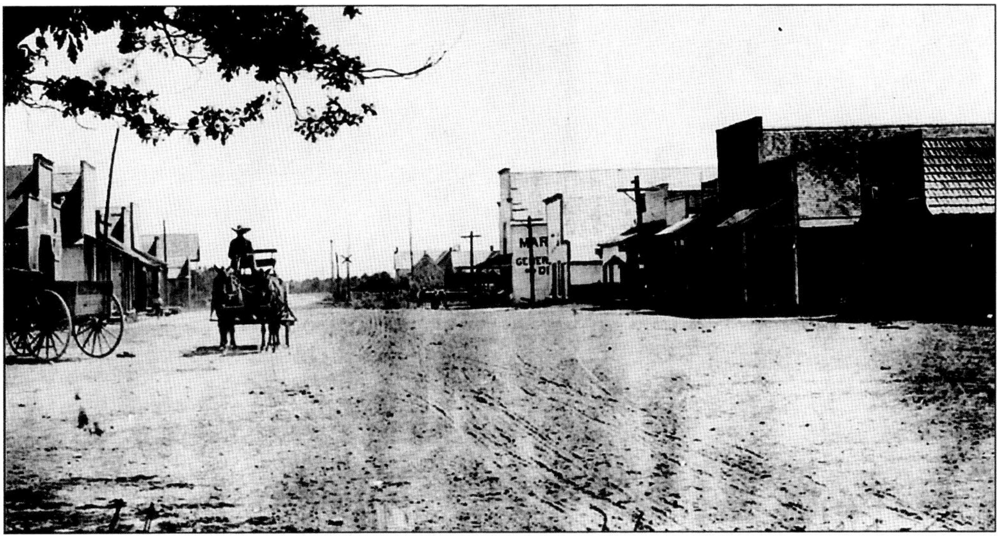

Hiawasse was launched as a town in 1898 with the coming of the railroad tracks across the site. In the Cherokee language hiawasse was said to mean "meadow," or in other accounts "sunny spot"; the tribe brought the word west when they were forced from their tribal lands in Georgia in the 1830s. Like so much of Benton County, the prosperity of the town was built on apples; the railroad allowed the tiny town to become a major shipping center for the fruit. The apple crops began to fail by 1920 and the town's growth was brought to a halt. The card's 1910 message, sent to Kansas by a woman named Bertha, reads, "I am a way down in the jungles of Ark." Today Hiawasse is an unincorporated community of around 300 people.

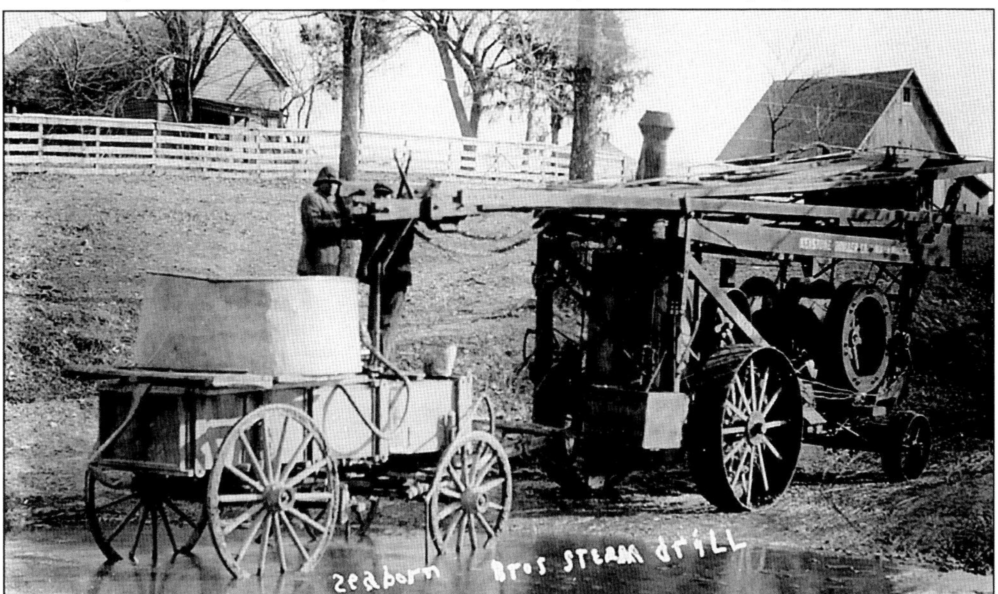

The photo for this postcard was taken on a farm road somewhere in Benton County around 1910, and pictures a portable steam-powered well drilling rig. Water boiled in the large tub would have powered the drill. The man on the wagon wrote on the back of the card, "We have drilled in solid limestone from 30 to 85 feet in dirt as high as 150 and 175 feet." Farmers would have been dependent on the wells the man dug to serve their remote homes and livestock.

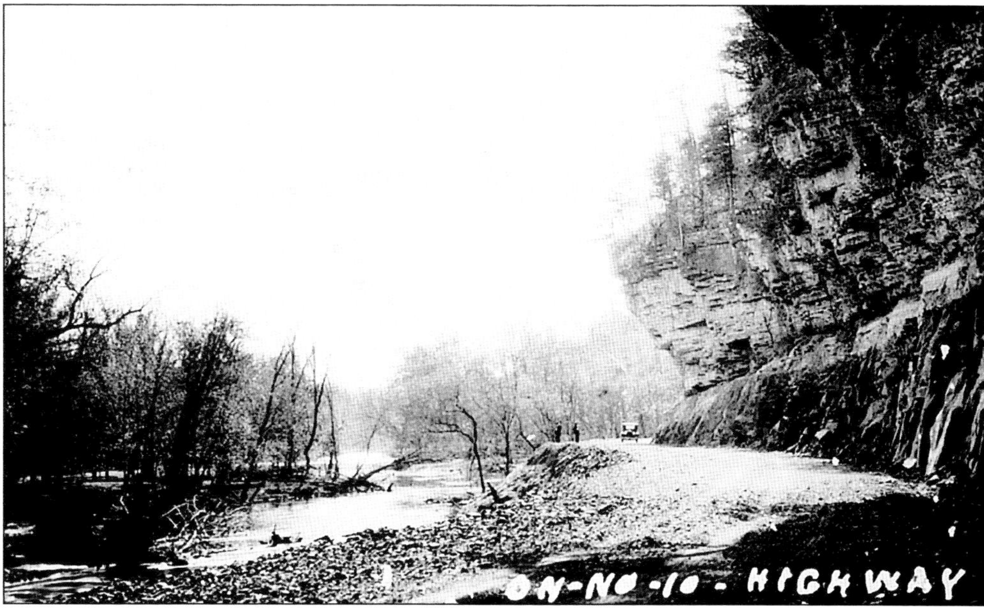

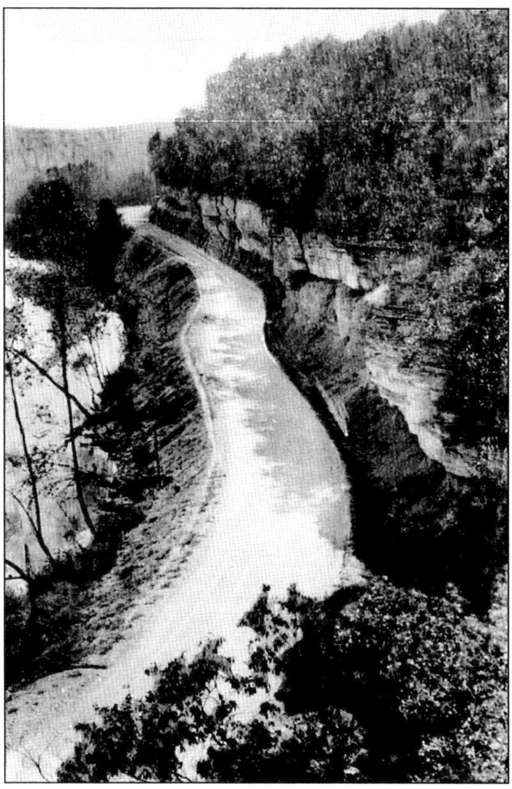

The roads of Benton County were rough and rocky for the early years of the 20th century, and as a result most commerce moved by the extensive network of rail lines. In the photo above, postmarked at Monte Ne in 1929, a car is seen coming around the bend, below a bluff on a road that would have often been washed out by the adjacent stream. In the photo to the left is seen Highway 71, north of Bentonville around 1920. What would become a major, paved U.S. highway within a few years was then a gravel road cut from a bluff above a stream bed. Better roads would rapidly become a priority for Arkansas, as there were already in excess of 100,000 automobiles registered in the state; half of these were Fords.

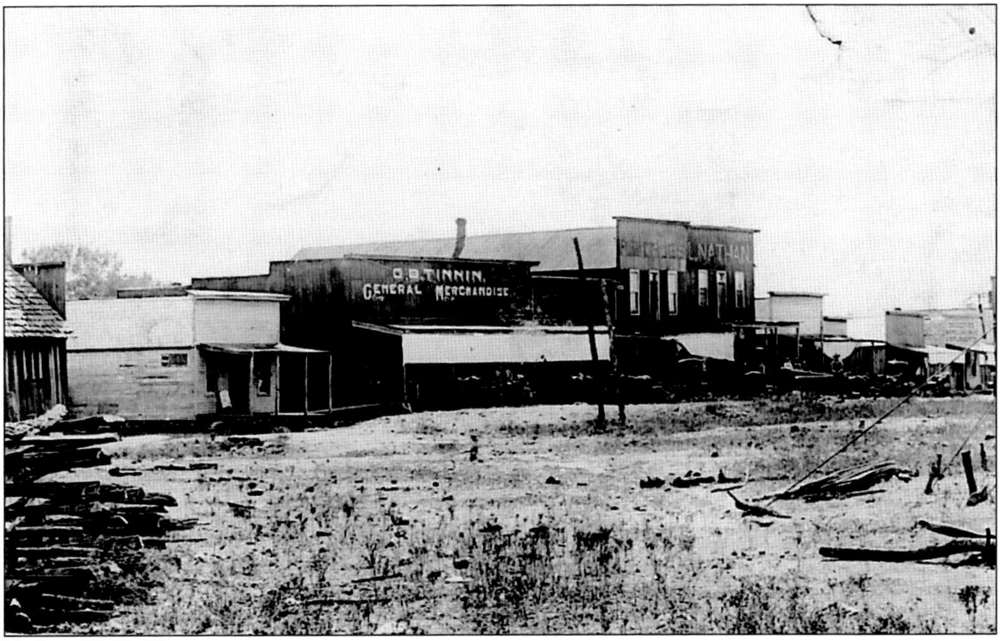

Maysville is among the oldest communities in Benton County, and is located hard against the Oklahoma state line. The first store was opened in town in 1839 by an Englishman who primarily traded with the Indians. In this *c.* 1900 photo, a rough rail fence is seen to the left; the business block is composed of wooden store buildings. The center building houses O.B. Tinnin General Merchandise, before which are parked wagons and buggies in the dirt, weed-infested street.

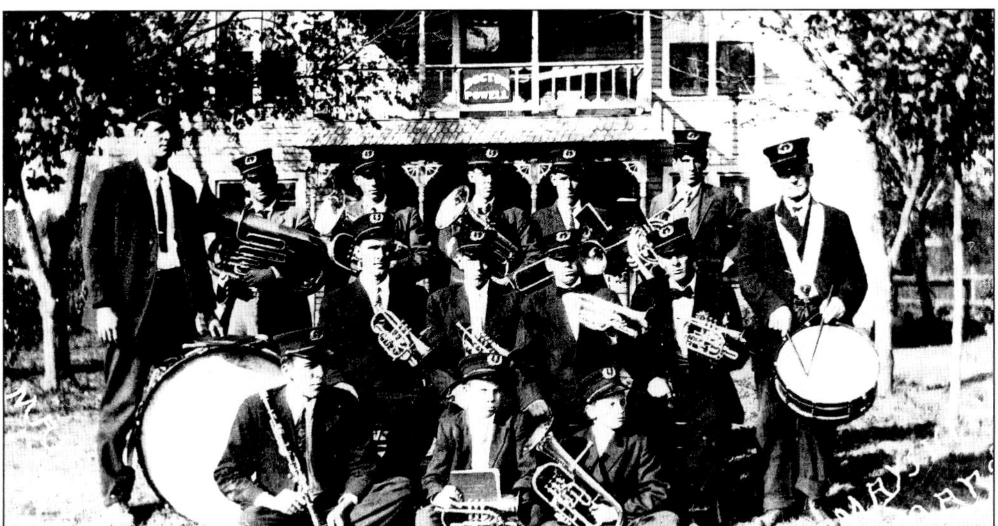

Maysville was, as it remains today, a very small town of some 200 people, but it did record some culture on postcards. The Maysville Town Band posed in uniforms with their instruments in front of Dr. Powell's office around 1910. The band would have been prominent on the Fourth of July and other special occasions. The town was named for Martin Mays, an early 1830s settler.

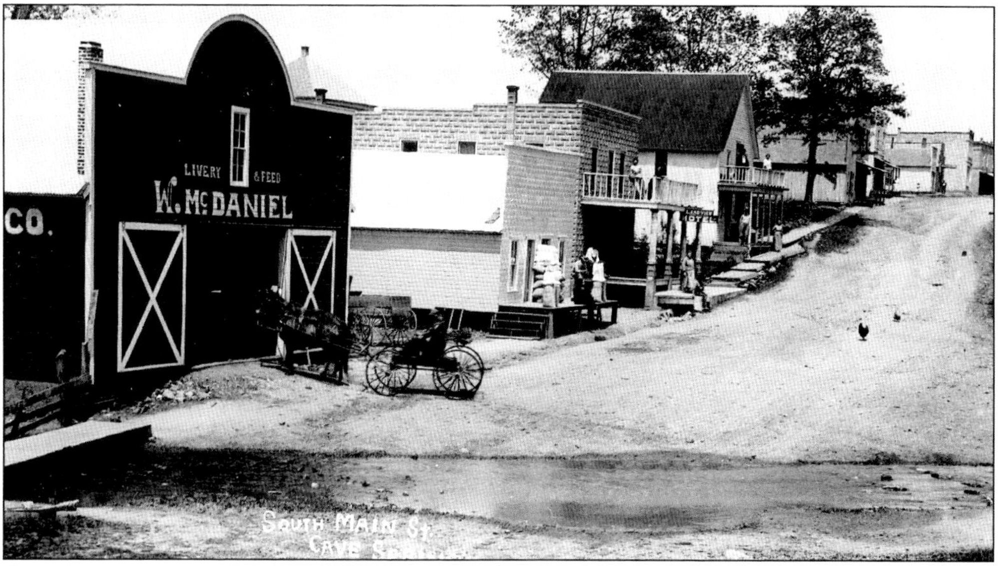

Cave Springs was, at the turn of the century, a classic rural community with the necessary livery and feed store owned by Mr. McDaniel, seen on the left in this card. A horse and buggy are parked at the door, much as would be waiting automobiles at a dealership service department today. Just beyond the livery is the feed store, with its elevated front dock to allow easier loading of heavy sacks into the wagons of customers. Next to the feed store is the Lake View Hotel, so named for the lake formed by a dam at the cave spring. Marching down the center of the street is a mother hen, followed by her chicks. (*c.* 1900.)

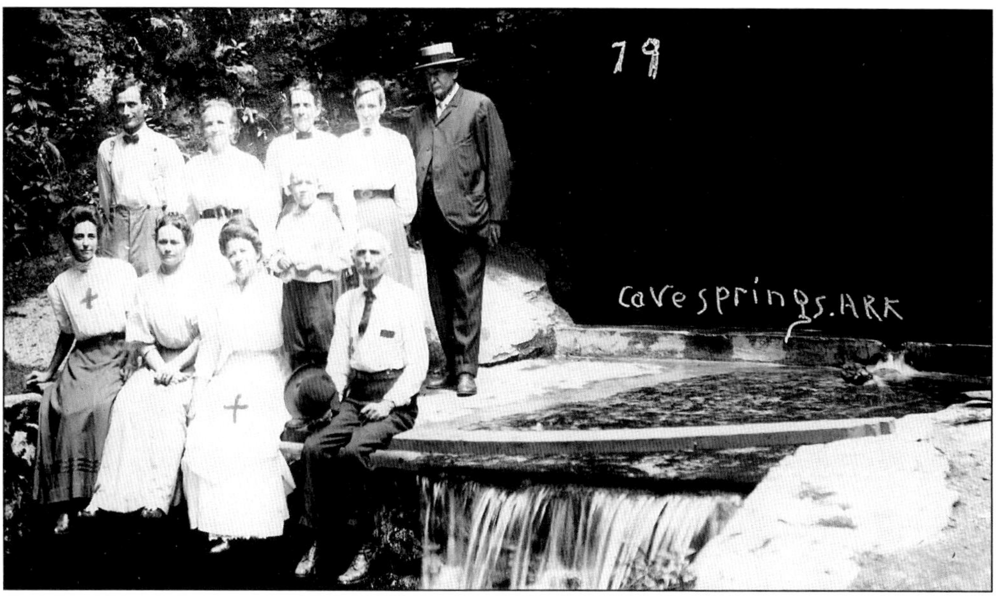

The town of Cave Springs was named Cannon until early in the century, when the name was changed to match the area's best-known feature. The cold water spring that came gushing from a cave drew large numbers of people to picnic and enjoy the natural wonder. This card of the spring was mailed on Christmas Day, 1910, with the message, "Old Santa was good to me this year. Can you find me on the other side? This is one of our main springs, don't you think it beautiful?" Ethel had marked herself and her sister in the picture with a "T."

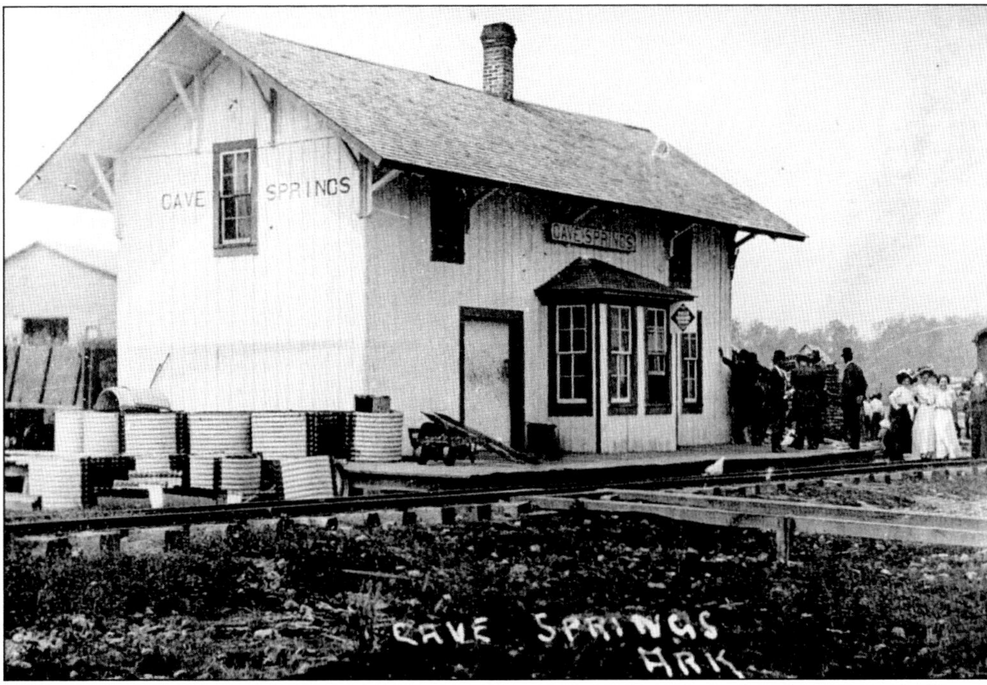

Cave Springs boomed for a period early in the century after the railroad came and allowed efficient shipment of the Benton County mainstay crop of apples. The two-story depot was unusual for such a small town; a shipment of drainage pipes can be seen unloaded at the end of the building, likely for track work on the line. The tracks were taken up in 1917 and sold for scrap; the apple crop faded and the town remained a small village that today is home to around 500 people.

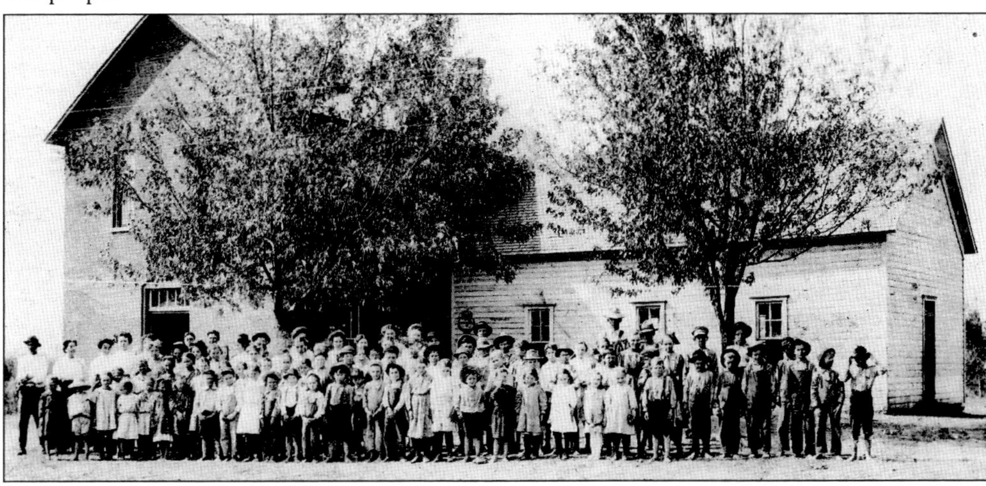

Lowell, located in southern Benton County, was one of a number of towns that sprang up when the Frisco Railroad laid tracks through the northwestern corner of the state. It was known for a time as Bloomington. In this c. 1915 card, the new two-story brick school to the left was the backdrop for a pose by what was likely the entire student body. All the boys were wearing hats, though the young man at the far right was having trouble keeping his on. Many of the students were barefoot. In the center, just over the children's heads, is an iron bell that would have summoned them in from recess.

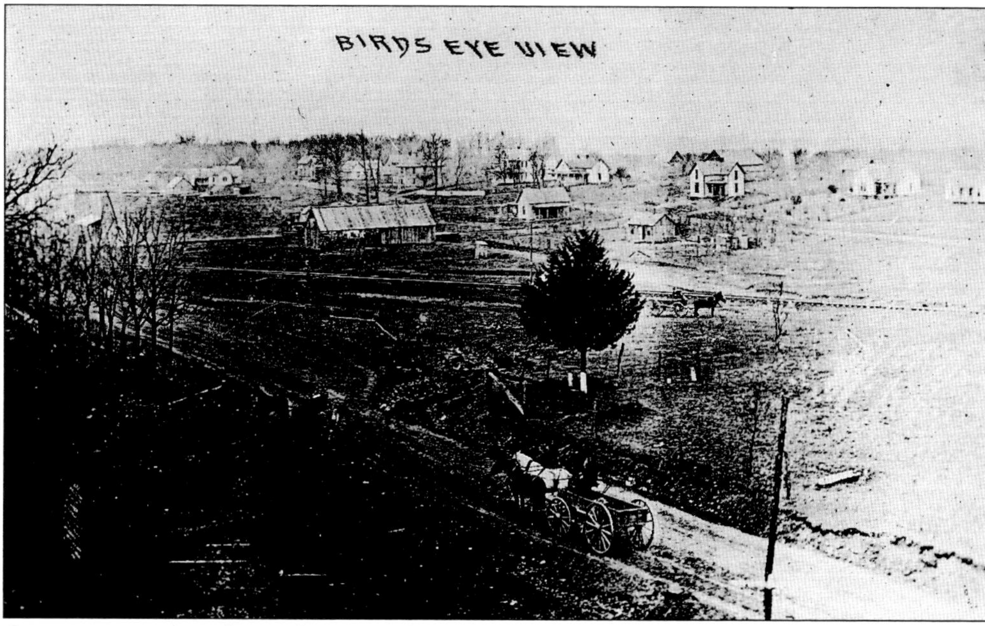

Centerton was platted near the geographical center of Benton County, hence its name. As with much of rural Benton County, the railroad and the apple crop sustained the small town. There were, at one time, four apple evaporators in the town, which was home to 300 people by 1915. The familiar pattern of small-town Benton county was repeated in Centerton—the railroad pulled out, the apples failed, and the town never grew. In the *c.* 1910 card above, a rutted wagon road is seen leading into Centerton; newly constructed homes are visible in the distance. In the card below, also *c.* 1910, a farmer and his young son were photographed feeding their large herd of pigs. The hogs would have provided both food for the family and cash for necessities, when the surplus animals were sold.

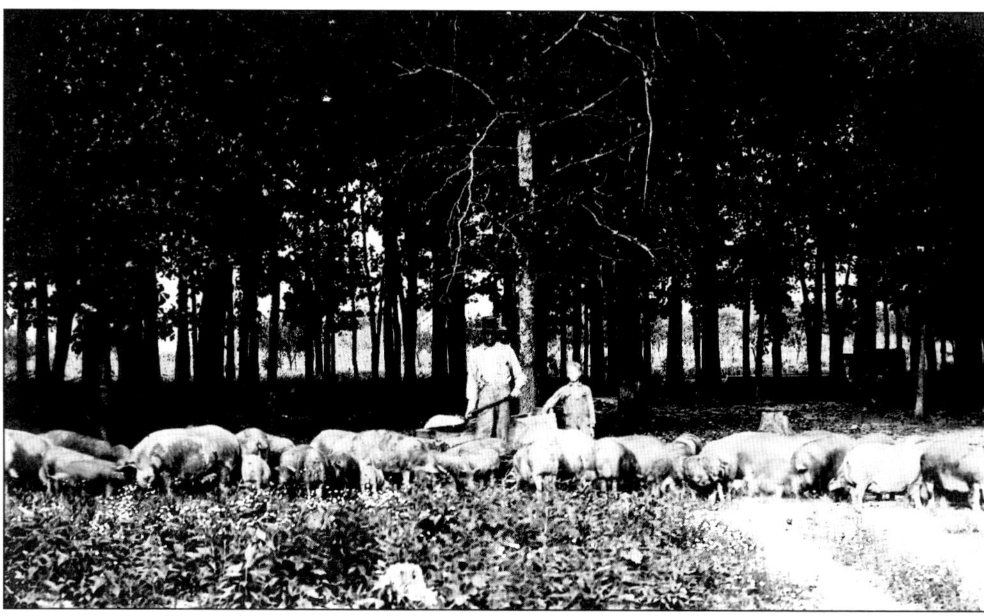

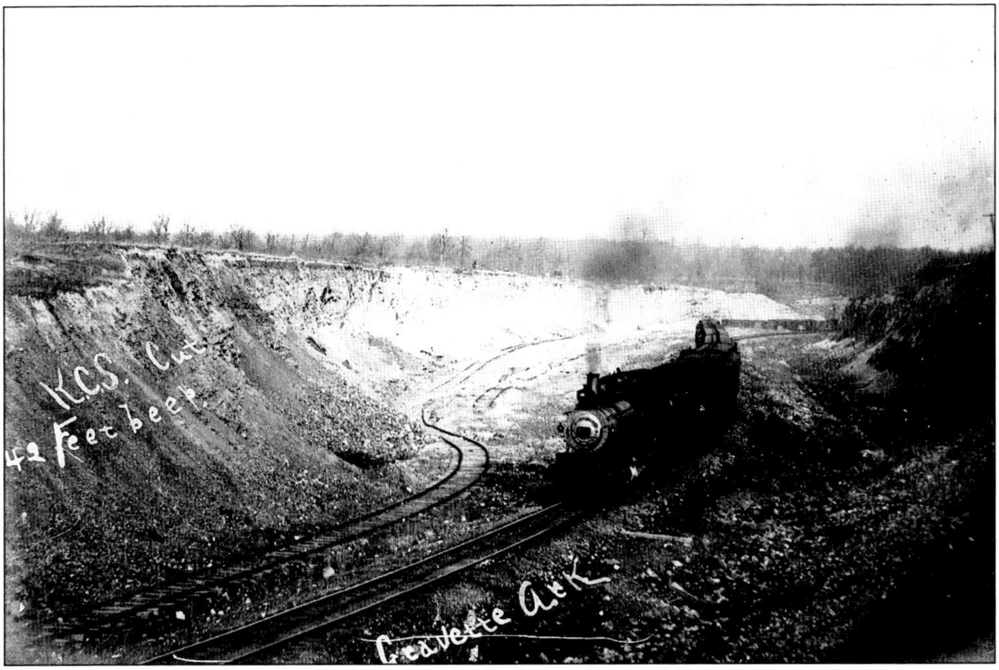

The railroad's approach to the town of Gravette was made possible by a 42-foot deep grade cut, seen in the card above with a train steaming through, in 1908. The railroad, conceived in 1890, would eventually connect Kansas City with New Orleans. In the process, it would foster vital economic links down the western side of Arkansas, particularly by connecting to smaller rail lines in Benton and Washington Counties. In the card below, the same rail cut is seen around 1920; trees have grown up along the rim, and a wagon driven along the edge of the tracks is visible, perhaps on a mission to inspect the rail bed for problems.

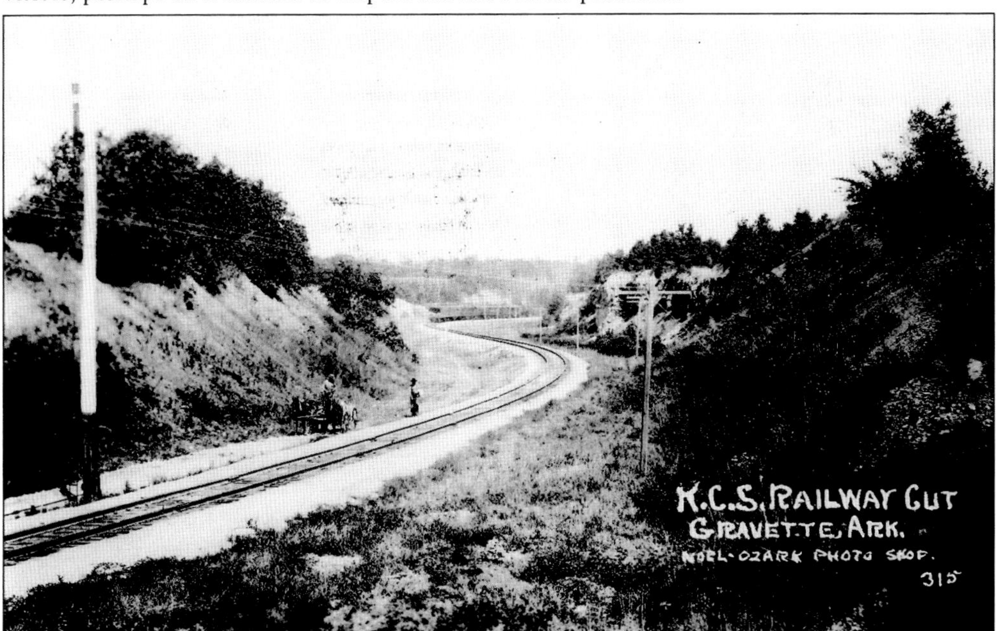

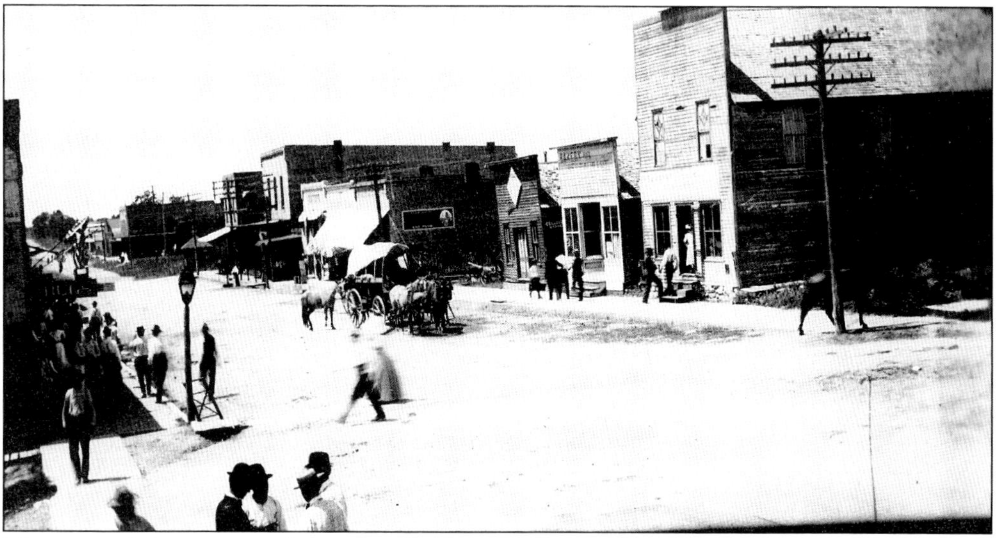

The town of Gravette was born when E.T. Gravett moved his Chalk Valley Distillery, which made corn whiskey, from the nearby community of Nebo to a location adjacent to the tracks of two railroads. With the distillery relocated, the rest of the town of Nebo soon followed. Gravett gave the new settlement his own name, restoring the "e" which he had dropped earlier, reportedly over a family dispute. In this *c.* 1900 view a covered wagon with a cow tied behind makes its way down Main Street. Men are gathered near the drugstore in the foreground, while patrons approach the dining room across the street.

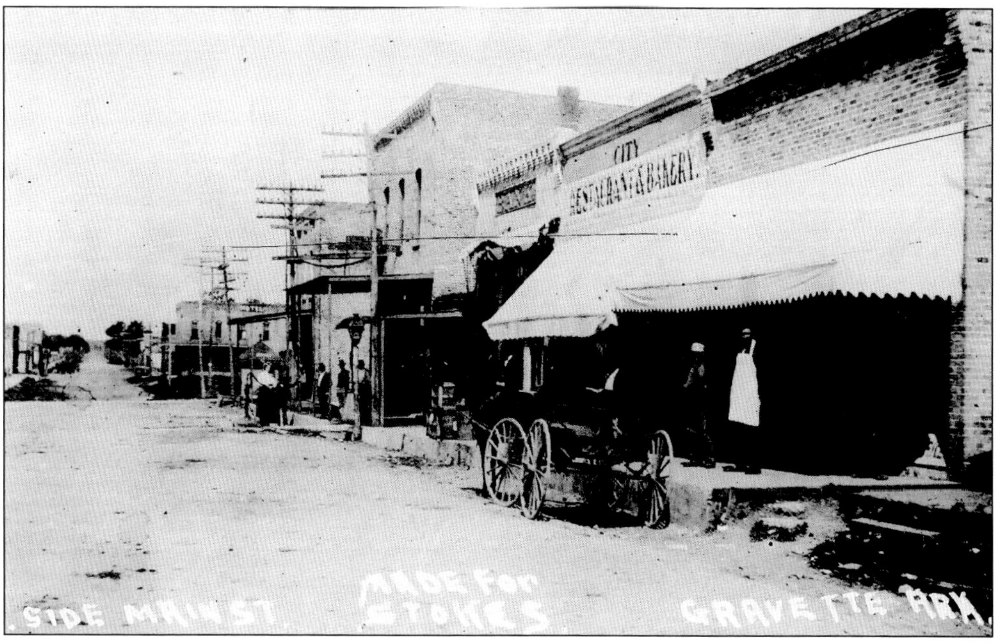

"This is a view of one of our streets" are the words from Gravette on the reverse of this *c.* 1908 card. The buckboard wagon is parked in front of the City Restaurant and Bakery, and a meat market is seen in the foreground. The man in the white apron was most likely the butcher, while the man with his hands in his overalls was perhaps a customer. Both men's attention was on the photographer.

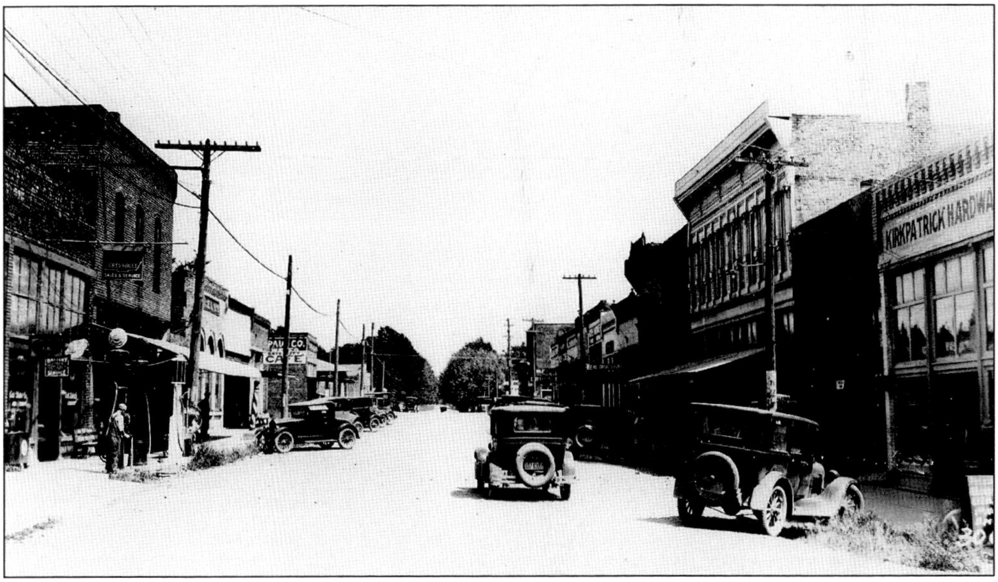

By 1930 Gravette was well acquainted with the automobile, as is evident in a view looking the opposite direction down Main Street from the card above. A Chevrolet dealership is seen to the left, with gravity-fed gasoline pumps positioned on the sidewalk; a bank, barbershop, and the Gate City Cafe are just beyond. On the right side, weeds fill the edges of the still dirt street; Kirkpatrick Hardware is seen, along with the Ozark Photo Shop in the right foreground.

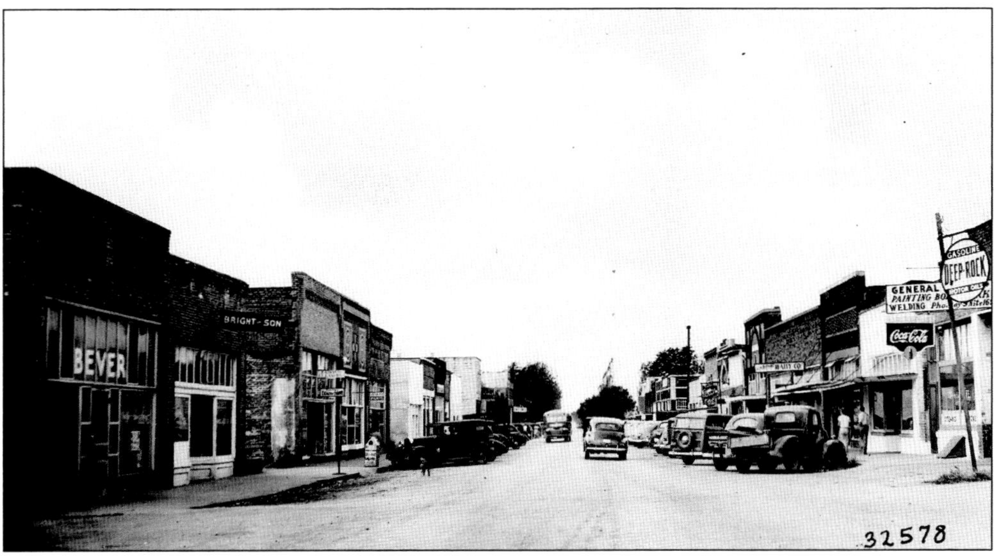

With this card, in conjunction with the previous three, a time-travel experience is offered of small-town Main Street America. From the covered wagon in 1900, to a 1908 buckboard, to Depression-era cars on a dirt street, to this c. 1945 view, much has changed. A passenger bus approaches in the distance, and a "Woody" station wagon is parked among the vehicles to the right. In the timespan of these four cards have occurred two world wars and the Great Depression.

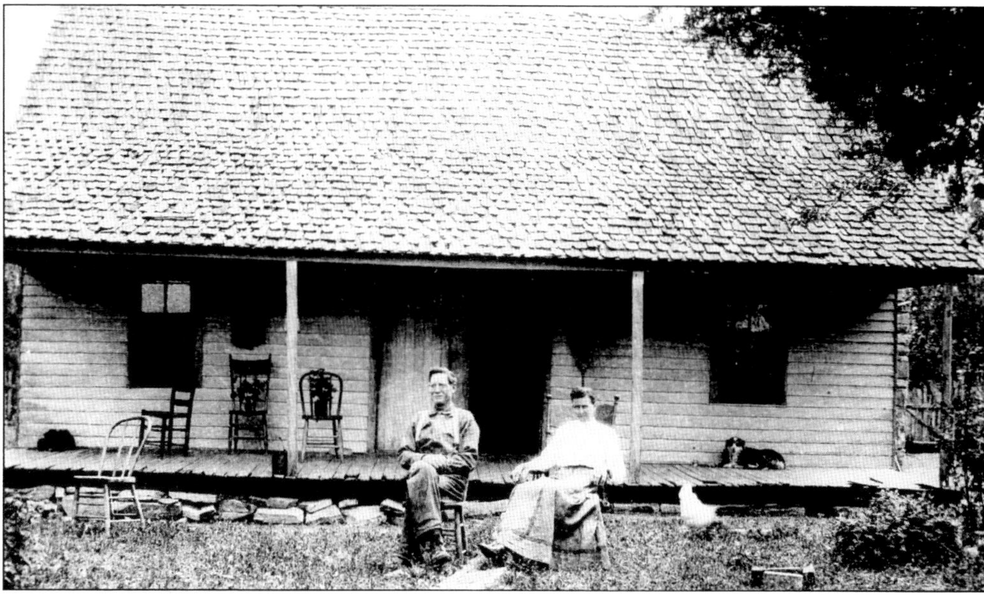

George Foster and his wife are seen in the yard of their Gravette home, perhaps listening to the whistle of a passing Kansas City Southern locomotive, perhaps discussing the changes in their town. The house was typical of modest-income homes in the era, with wooden shake shingles, a porch supported by field stone, chickens in the yard, and a dog on the porch. The kitchen chairs had been brought outside, suggesting that visitors were present, perhaps including the one with a camera in hand. (c. 1915.)

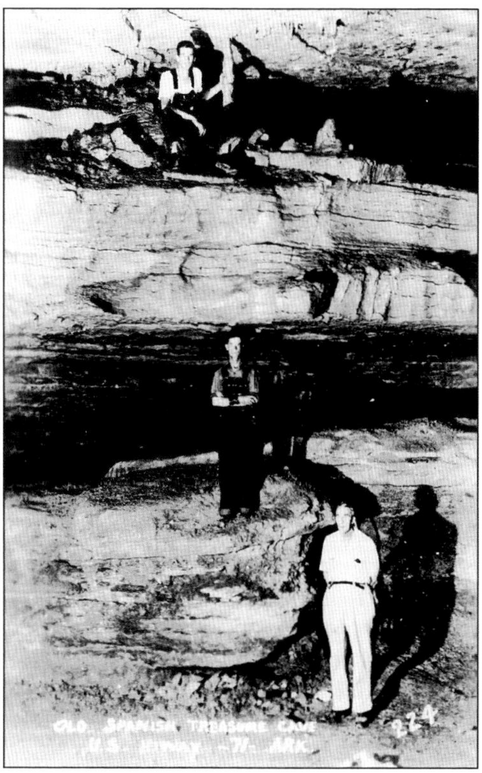

Just south of Gravette was the "Old Spanish Treasure Cave," which offered a tour of the site where a legendary early Spanish explorer had buried treasure. There was little to substantiate the legend, but tourists came for a pleasant visit to the cool cavern and perhaps send home a postcard like this one. (c. 1940.)

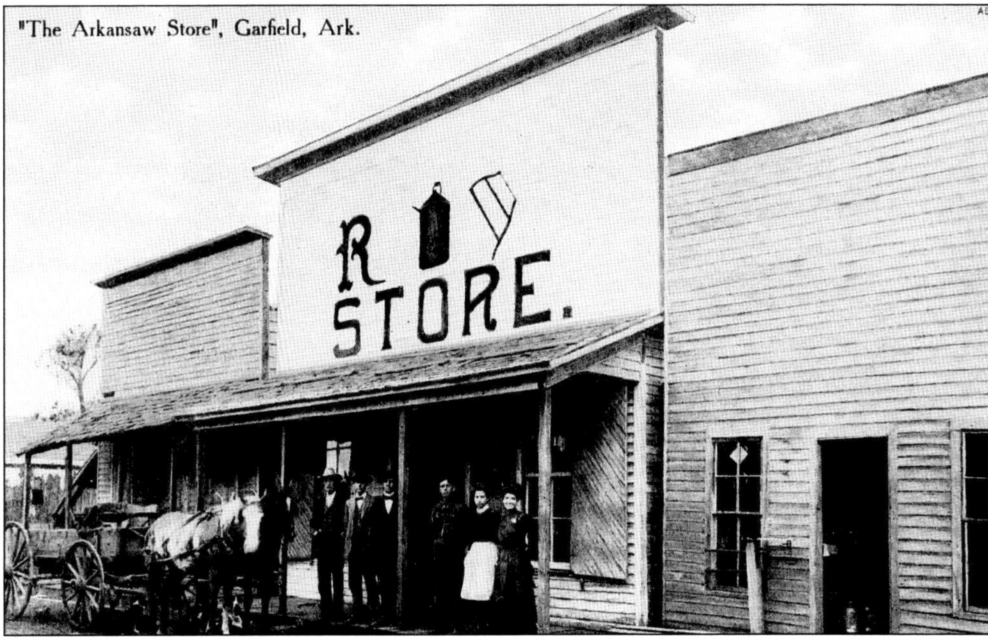

Garfield had its start around 1880, very likely named for President James Garfield. The most-photographed building in town was the "Arkansaw Store," with its distinctive sign spelling out the name in pictograph using an "R," an oil can, and a saw. The store reportedly carried everything from diamonds to buggy harnesses, and presumably also a supply of postcards. The store has been gone for many years. (*c.* 1910.)

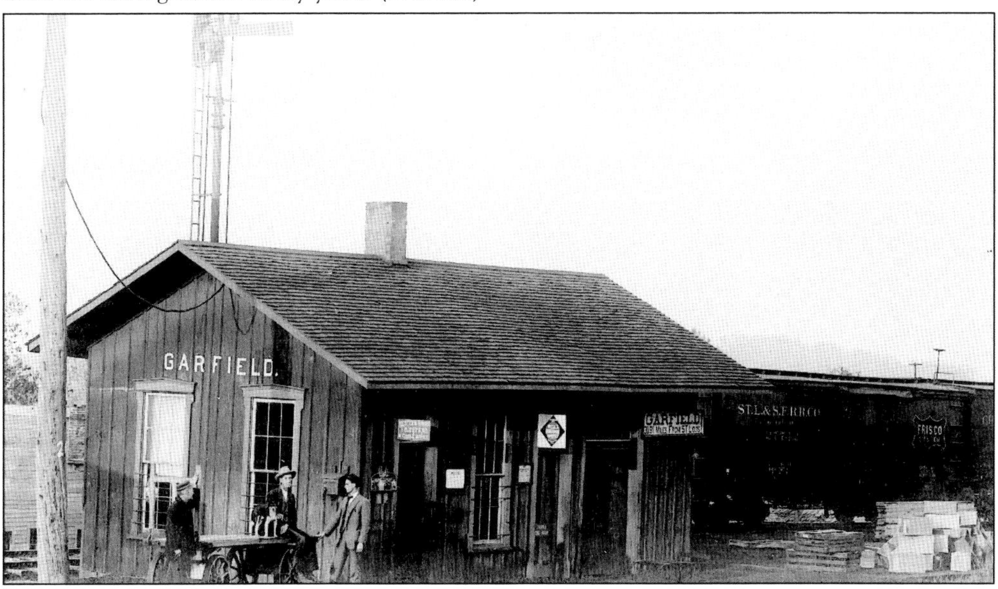

Garfield, like so many small Benton County towns, owed its relative prosperity to the railroad, in this case the Frisco Line, which built the small depot. At the left, men are lounging around a baggage cart, upon which stands a sturdy little dog. A sign affixed to the building says "Garfield 319 miles from St. Louis." Note the man high on the pole, apparently adjusting the signal for a soon-to-be passing train. The Frisco would have shipped tons of fruit, timber, and lime powder from a local plant. (*c.* 1910.)

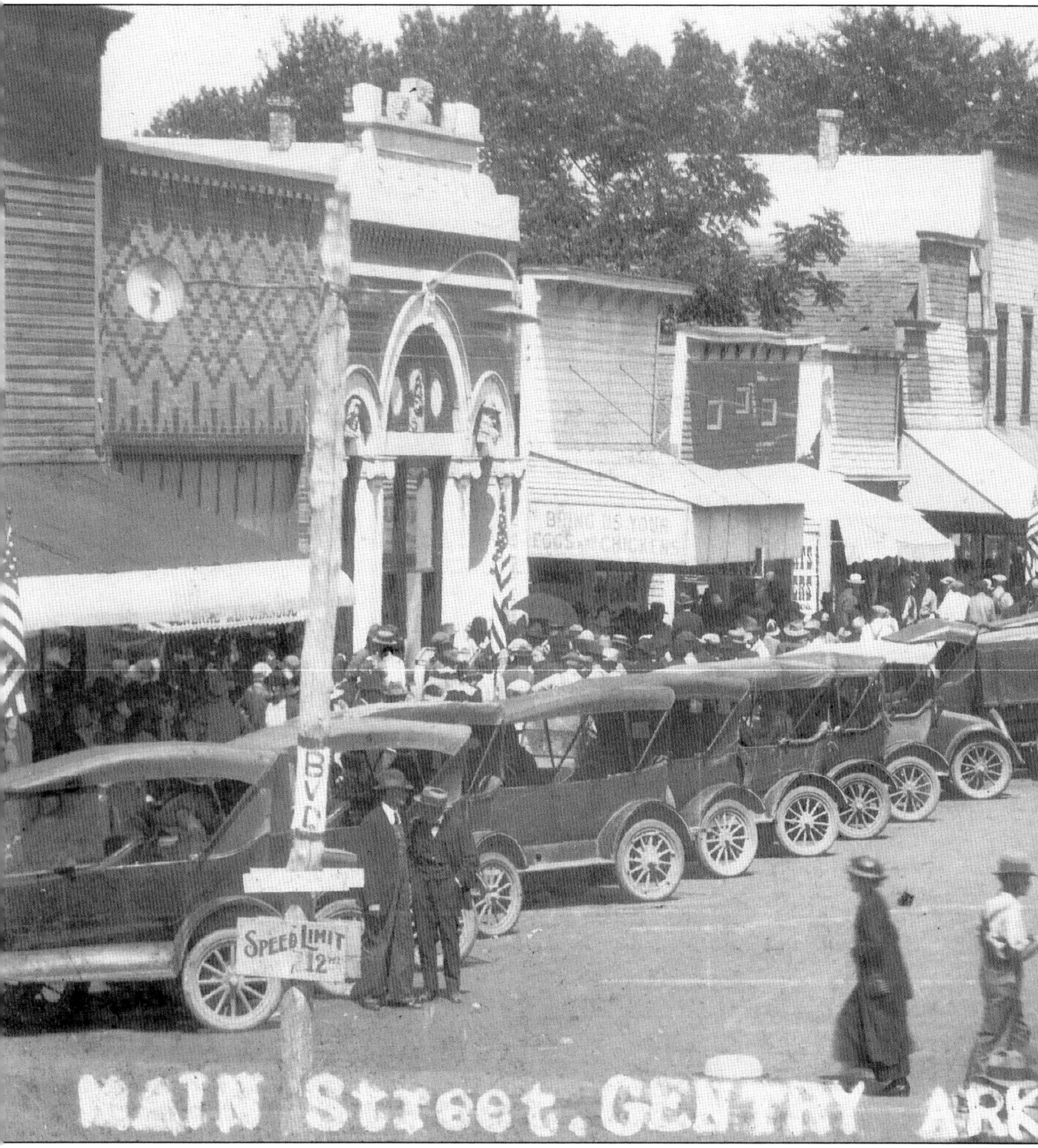

"After living here a while, the life is not so simple, as you see these are not ox teams nor wagons. The fare is not so bad as you will observe the lady in white, who is crossing the street, she is not especially thin. I make haste to say that it is not me. Altho both C.F. and myself are now what is termed 'stout.' " These words were carried on a *c.* 1918 postcard of Gentry's Main Street. Originally founded in 1893, Gentry had prospered, as evidenced by the profusion of canvas-

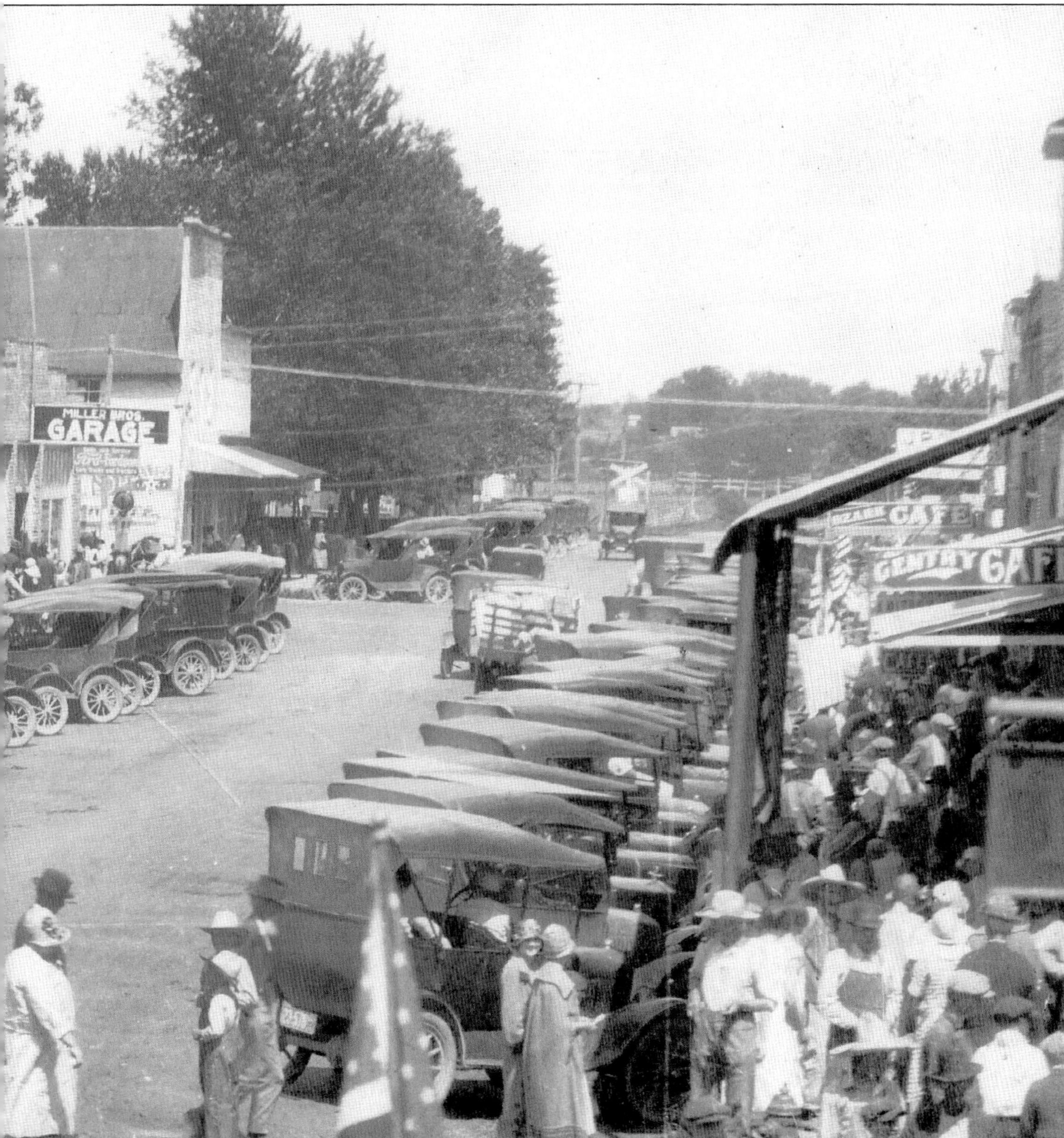

topped black cars. The presence of American flags in this crowded shopping district suggests possibly an impending Fourth of July parade. The sign in the middle of the street to the left reads, "Speed Limit 12 MPH." To the right are the Gentry Cafe and the Ozark Cafe; in the distant left is Miller Brothers Garage. An awning at the left advises, "Bring us your eggs and chickens." Today the frame buildings are gone but several of the other buildings remain.

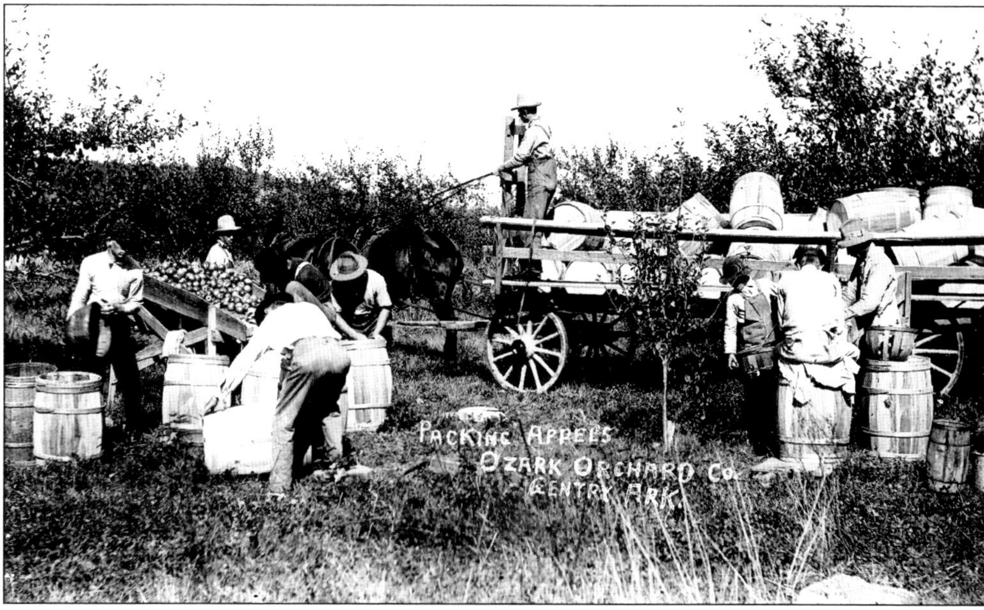

Like so much of Benton County, Gentry's economy was very much dependent on fruit, especially apples. In the photo above, men are seen loading apples into barrels for the Ozark Orchard Company's operation. The man standing while he drives a wagon is apparently delivering more barrels. Because of the dominant role of the apple crop, Gentry was briefly renamed "Orchard" for some three years in the late 1890s. In the photo below is seen the peach-packing operation at Wiberg's Orchards, which employed a number of women. The peaches had been delivered to the packing shed in the mule-drawn wagon behind the group. (c. 1912.)

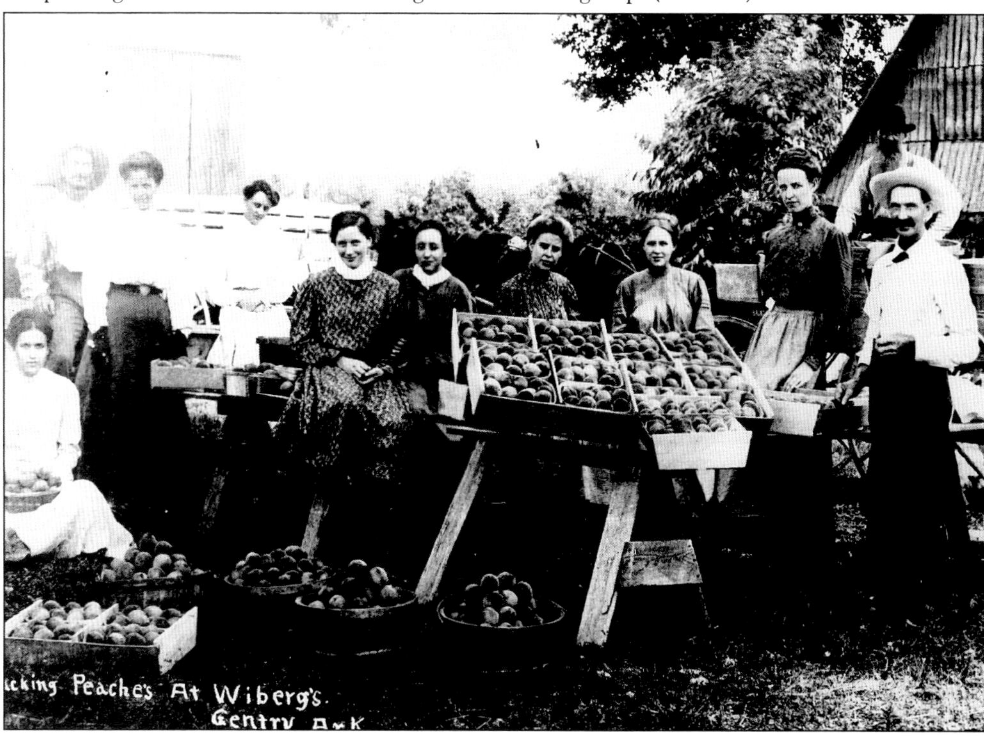

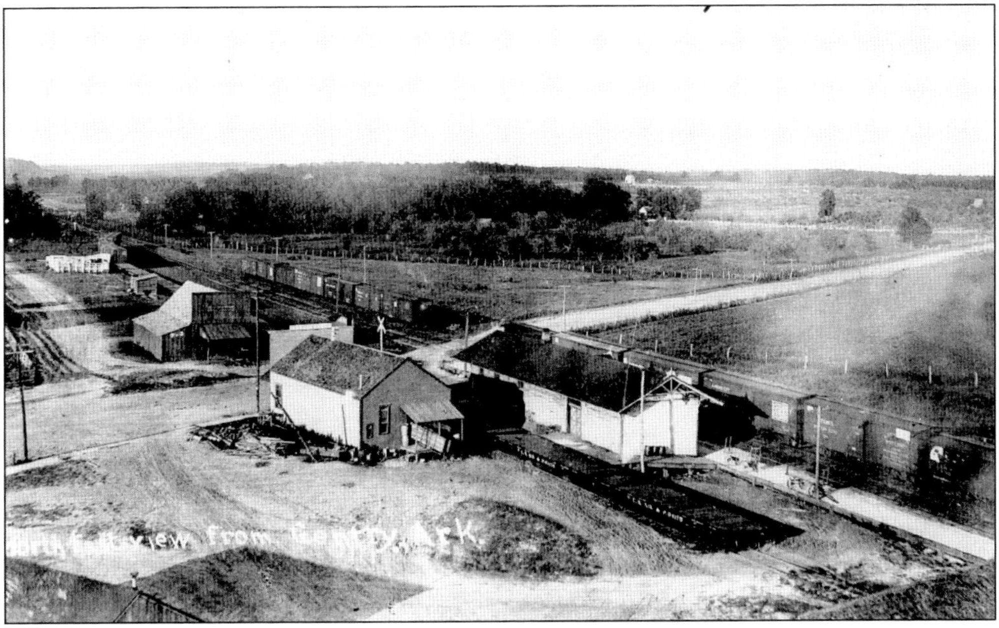

The photo for this postcard was almost assuredly taken from atop a water tower, giving an expansive view of the Gentry train depot and the surrounding farm and orchard lands. The dirt road coming in from the right would have carried wagons loaded with apples and peaches in barrels, along with crates to be loaded onto the long line of boxcars. The flatcars parked beside the depot probably transported railroad ties and lumber. (c. 1905.)

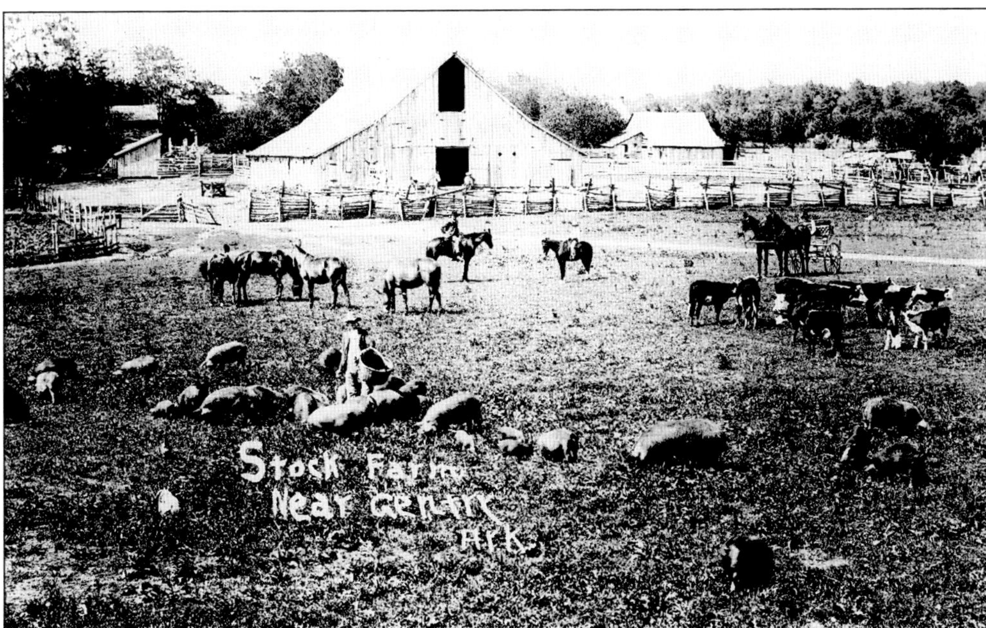

"Have been having such a good time on farm, didn't have time to come to town to mail cards," reads the penciled message on the card of a stock farm near Gentry. The prosperous farm had hogs, seen at feeding time courtesy of the young boy, along with cattle and sleek horses. Around the large barn runs a maze of rail-fenced corrals and various out-buildings.

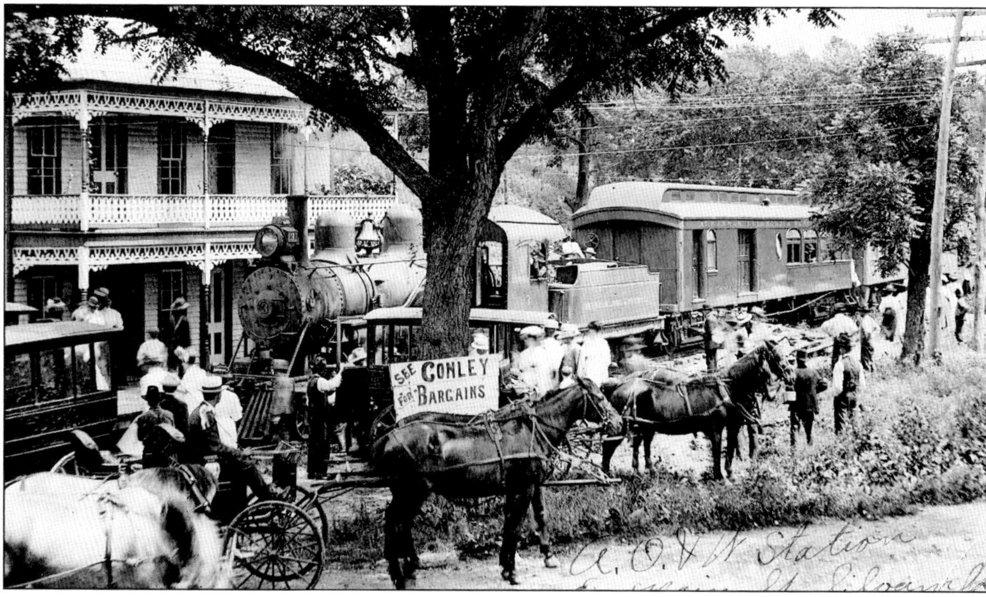

A pioneer settler named Simon Sager is believed to have been the first white man to settle around Siloam Springs, the two dozen springs ascribed with healthful properties; his cabin is a restored landmark. Originally the town was named Hico, but was changed to reflect the biblical spring of Siloam. In 1892 a lagging tourist economy was revived with the coming of the railroad. In this *c.* 1900 view, coaches and wagons have turned out to meet the arriving train. The back of the card reads, "It was 12 deg. below 0, much rain and snow. I would have sent this sooner but the weather and roads forbade."

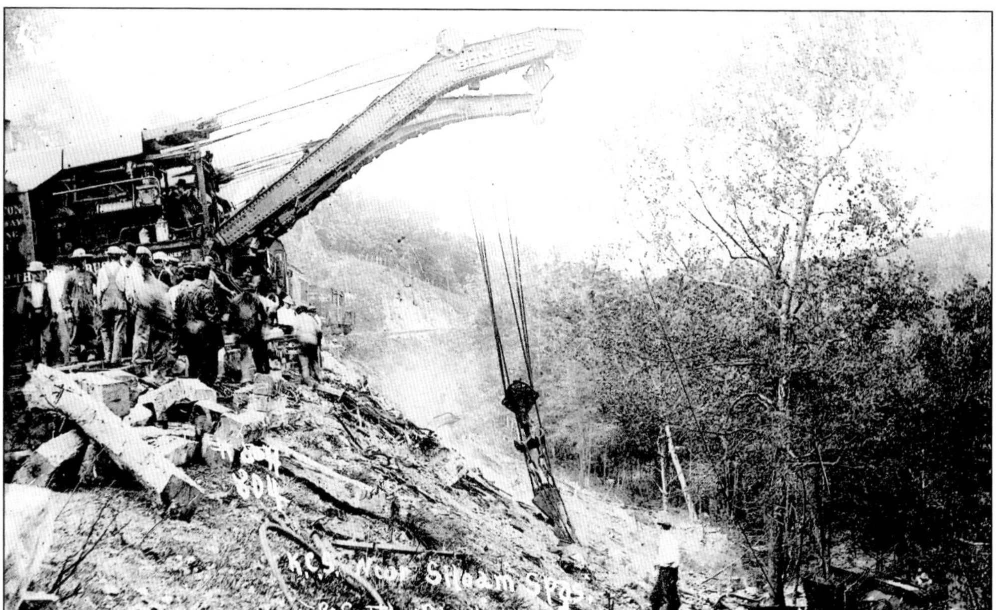

The train didn't always make it safely in and out of Siloam Springs. In this *c.* 1920 view the Kansas City Southern train had jumped the tracks and rolled into a ravine. The lettering on the side of the crane denotes it as a "400 Ton Railway Crane," which had been brought in on a flatcar in an attempt to pull the remains of the train up the steep hill.

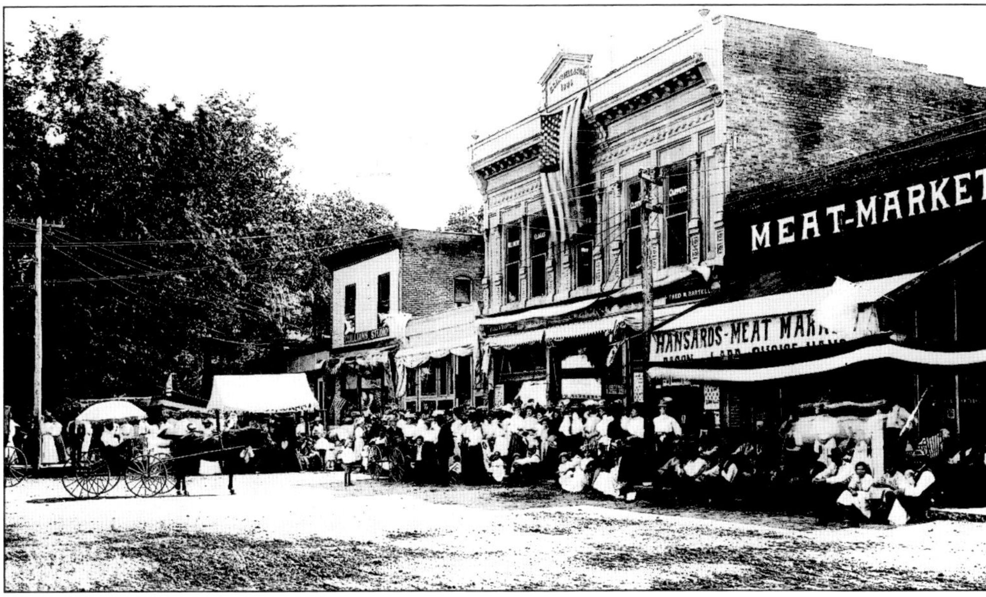

The crowd of townsfolk was dressed in their finest on this hot summer's day; the flags and bunting suggest an Independence Day celebration. Hansard's Meat Market advertised "bacon, lard and choice hams"; the business in the Chartwell and Sons building advertised "millinery, cloaks, carpets, and Butterick patterns." Note the buggy sheltered by a large umbrella, near C. Williams' Studio. A disastrous flood in 1970 destroyed the buildings seen here.

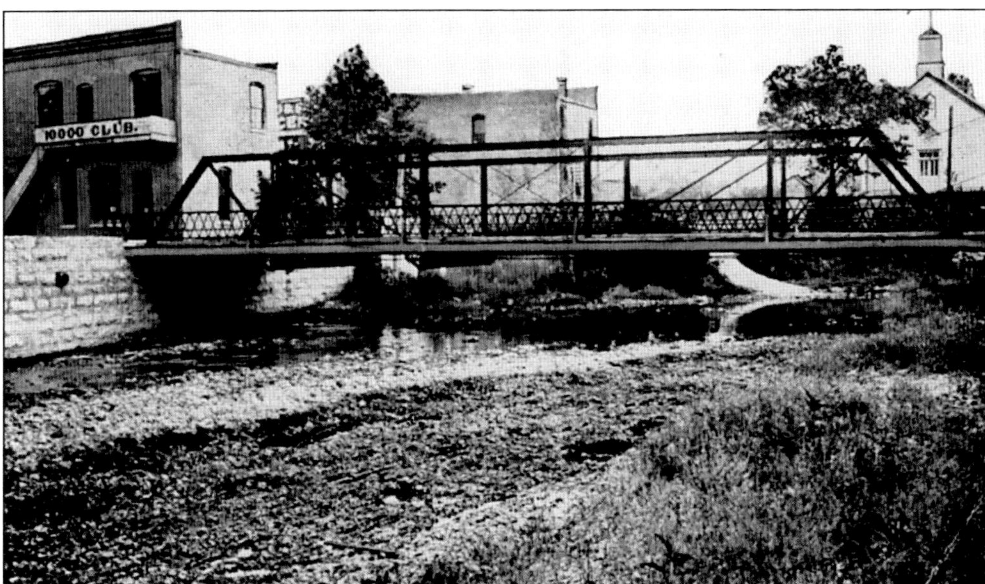

In the turn-of-the-century era before automobiles filled the streets, a wagon and foot bridge spanned Sager Creek, named for the first settler, Simon Sager. Of particular note is the building on the left bearing a sign reading "10,000 Club." The club was a group of civic boosters who promoted the goal of seeing the town's population grow to 10,000. That goal may be reached, but not in their lifetime—it is only today, almost a century later, that the goal is within sight, for the population has now passed the 9,000 mark. (*c.* 1905.)

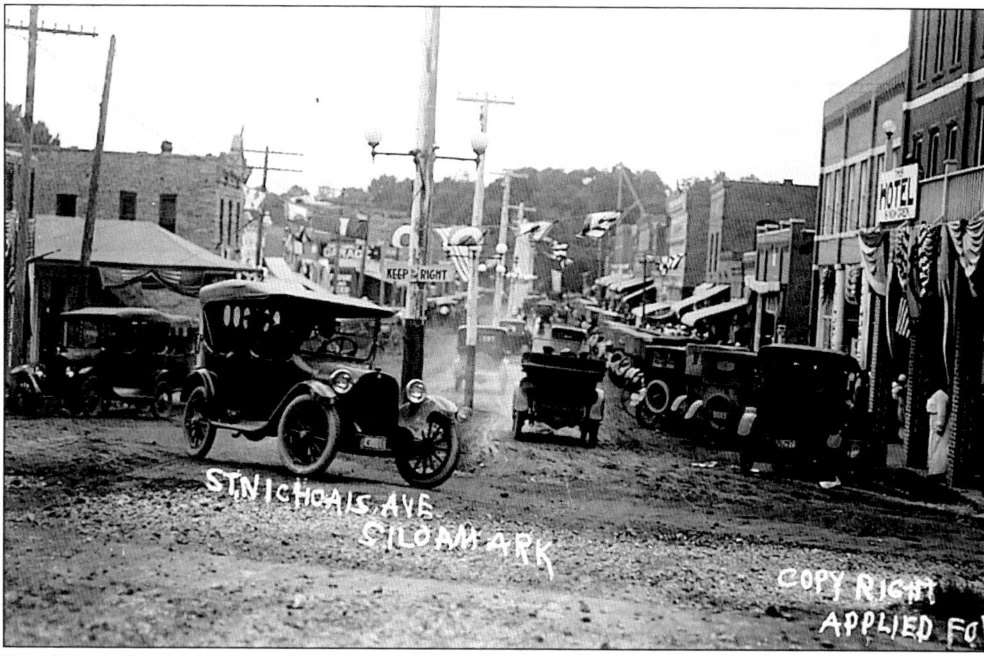

By 1920 St. Nicholas Avenue was not yet paved, but it was filled with automobiles. The street was divided into one-way traffic lanes by the row of utility poles; a sign nailed to the end pole cautions "keep to the right." A sign on the building in the foreground reads "This Hotel Now Open," an invitation to lodge at the Youree Hotel. The dozens of cars, the "Welcome" banner across the street, and the profusion of flags suggest a patriotic holiday.

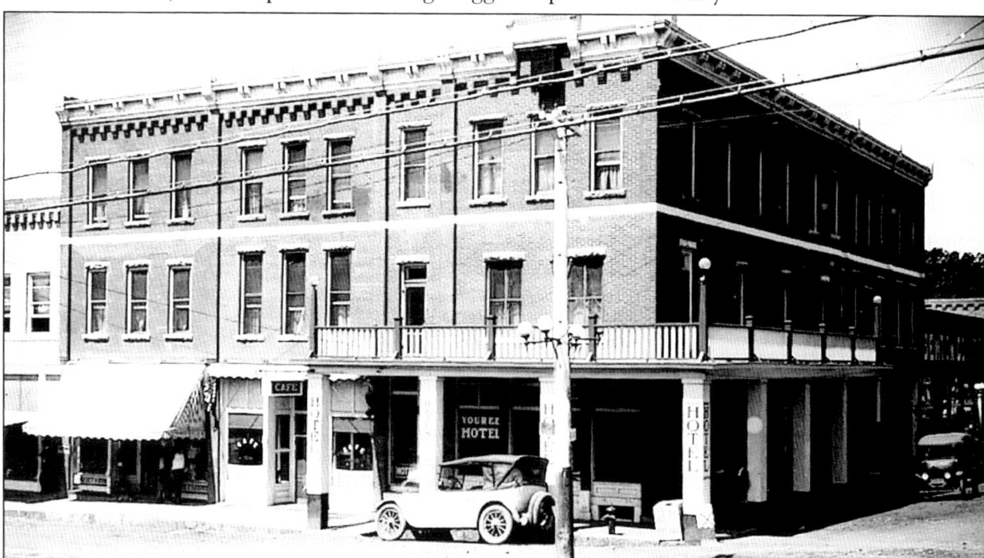

Snyder's Kodak shop in Siloam Springs produced a number of postcards of the area, including this c. 1920 view of the Youree Hotel on St. Nicholas Avenue. The hotel, which had been built as the Morris Hotel in 1898, housed a small cafe, along with the Bank of Siloam. The automobile bears the name of the hotel on its door, and might have been used to transport passengers to and from the train station. A fire destroyed the top floor of the hotel in 1970; today it houses only church and commercial ventures in the remaining two floors.

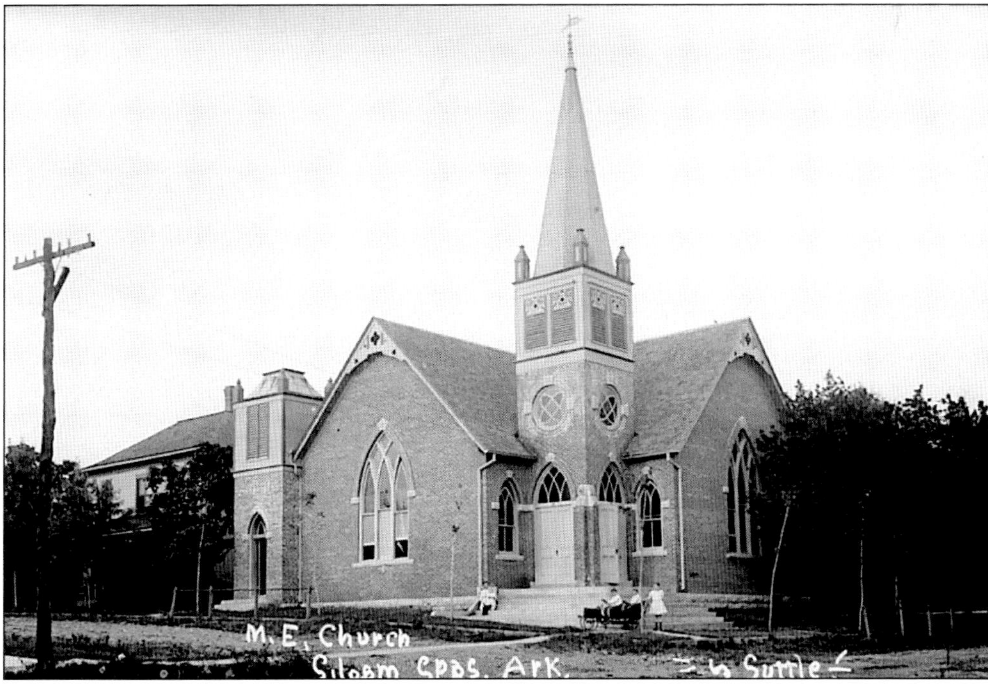

The steeple of the Methodist Episcopal church would have been visible from the hills around Siloam Springs. In this case it provided a backdrop for a group of children in a toy car parked at its steps. There is a plank walk crossing the dirt Maxwell Street to the left which would have kept mud off the feet and dress hems of worshippers attending the church. In the photo below is seen the interior of the same church, decorated around 1910 for "Old Folks Day." It is remarkable that "old folks" of that day would have all had vivid memories of the Civil War, and some would have been born before Arkansas entered the Union in 1836. Though the spire is gone, the church building still stands, and it has been converted to an apartment building.

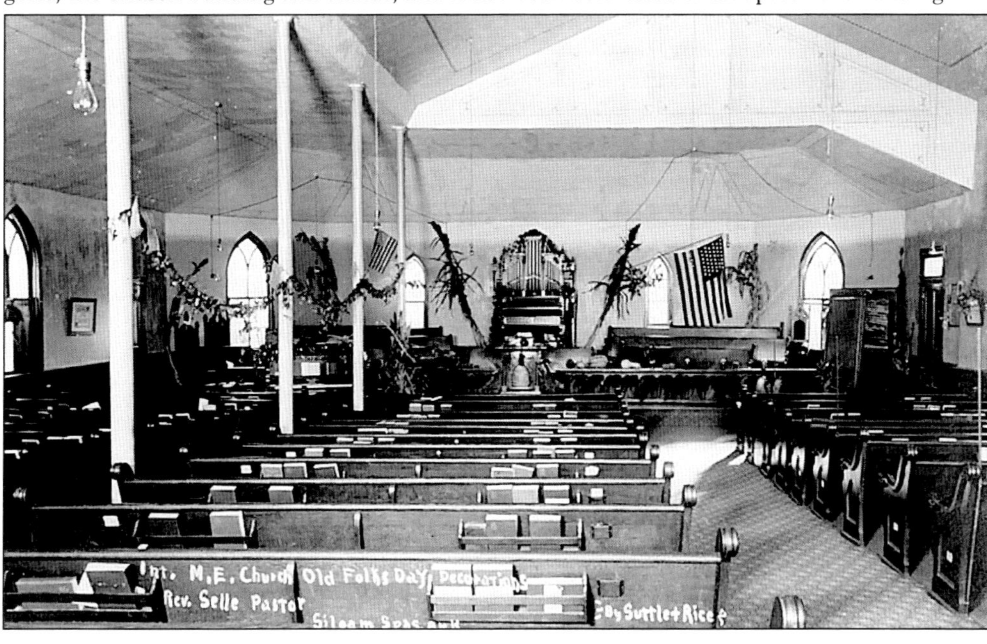

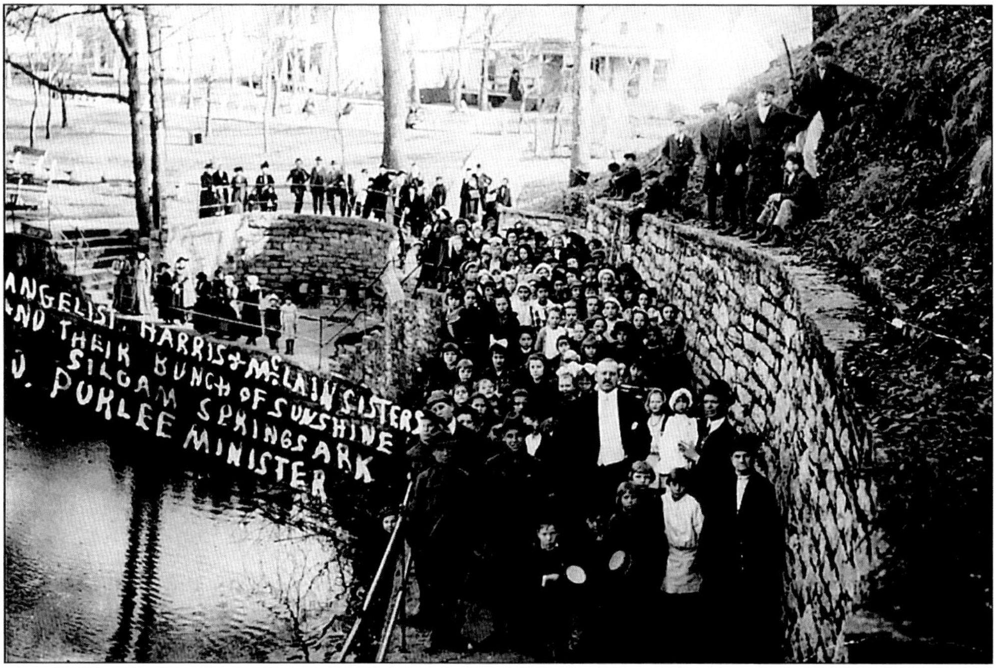

Bearing a photo taken at the largest of the city's springs, this *c.* 1915 card carried the message, "My wife conducts these bible drills after school. My! How they sing! I have a great 'Sunshine Chorus.' " The card had been mailed by W.L. Harris, the evangelist from Kansas seen standing in the midst of the children. Two older youths are wearing what appears to be Boy Scout uniforms; two of the youngest are carrying small drums. The spring and surrounding park remain an attraction today. In the card below is seen the fifth grade class of the local school, *c.* 1910. The faces of the youngsters are a study in the timeless nature of children that transcends generations.

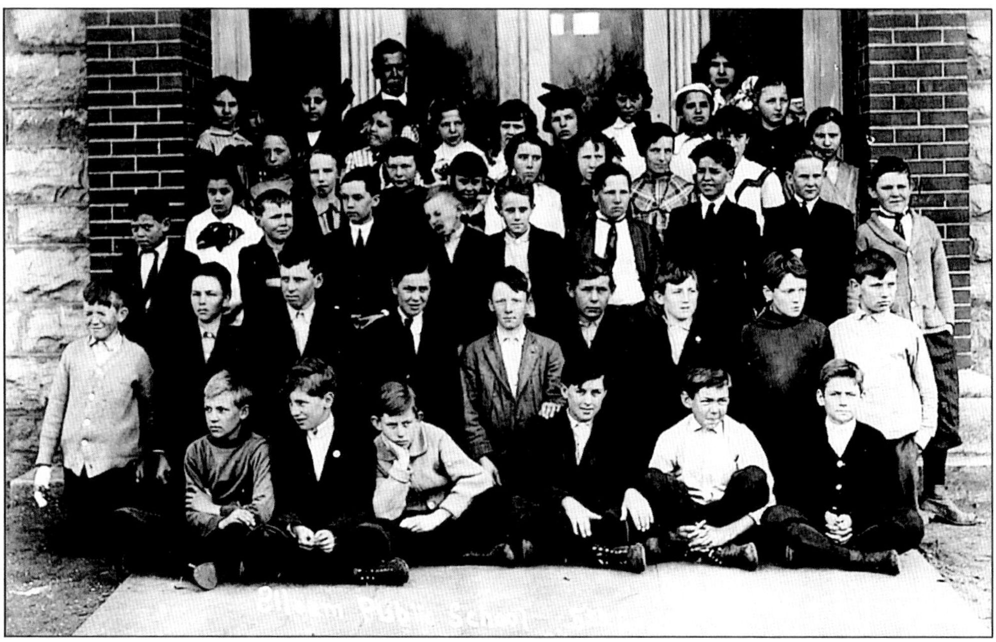

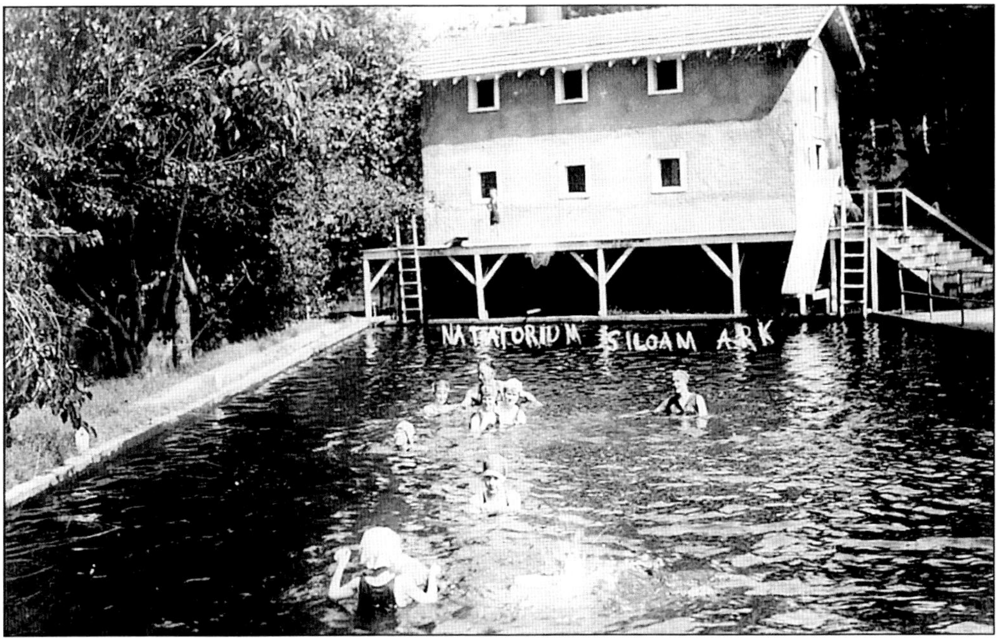

The springs of Siloam Springs were a recreational draw, but few were as well adapted as this one, which was used to provide water for the Natatorium, the term applied to this swimming pool which was located only a few feet from the spring. At the door to the bathhouse, to the right, a slide would have provided eager children a quick entrance into the cold spring water. The pool was closed in the 1920s and never reopened. (c. 1920.)

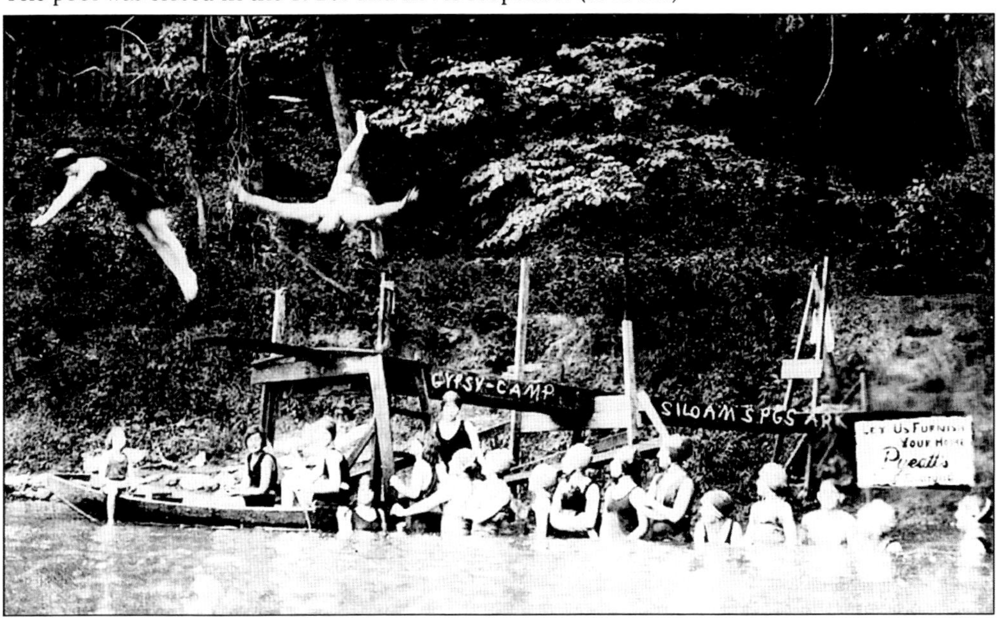

Swimming was a major attraction during the hot Arkansas summers in Siloam Springs. On the day this photo was made at Gypsy Camp, the diving board was an ideal place to perform for the camera. The photographer would have been very pleased to have caught the action of the two divers in mid-air. The girl's camp was begun by J.A. McAllister, a Tulsa lumber dealer, in the 1920s. (c. 1925.)

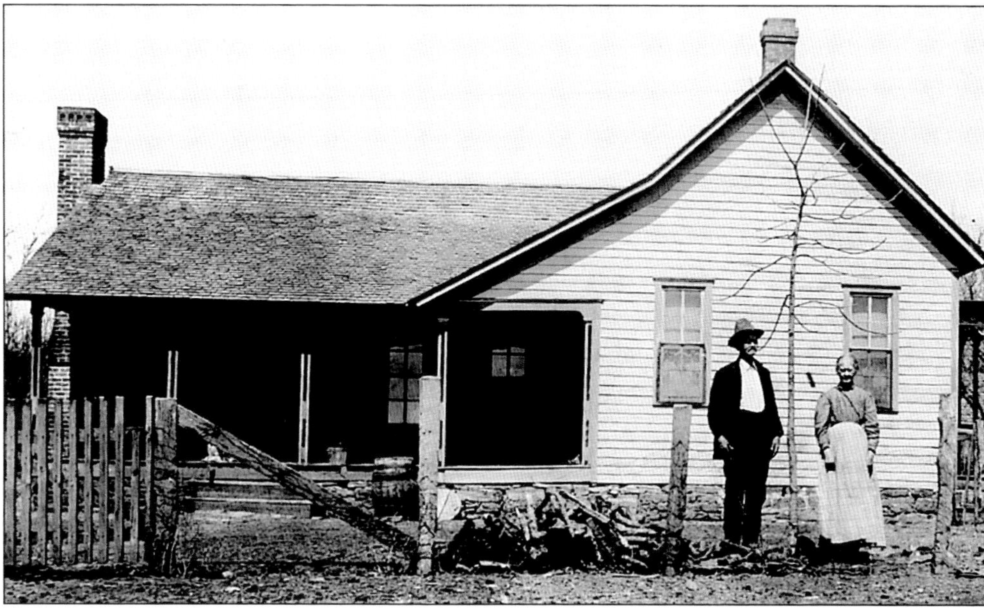

"August Caesar Sager and his sister Mrs. Mary Britt at her home near Silaom Springs"—the camera had captured descendants of the first settler in the area, Simon Sager. The home bore the classic touches of a rural, modest-income home. A woodpile is at the ready; a wire fence and gate would keep the animals out of the yard and Mrs. Britt's garden. A rain barrel sits by the porch, positioned to catch runoff from the roof. The home was heated by two fireplaces.

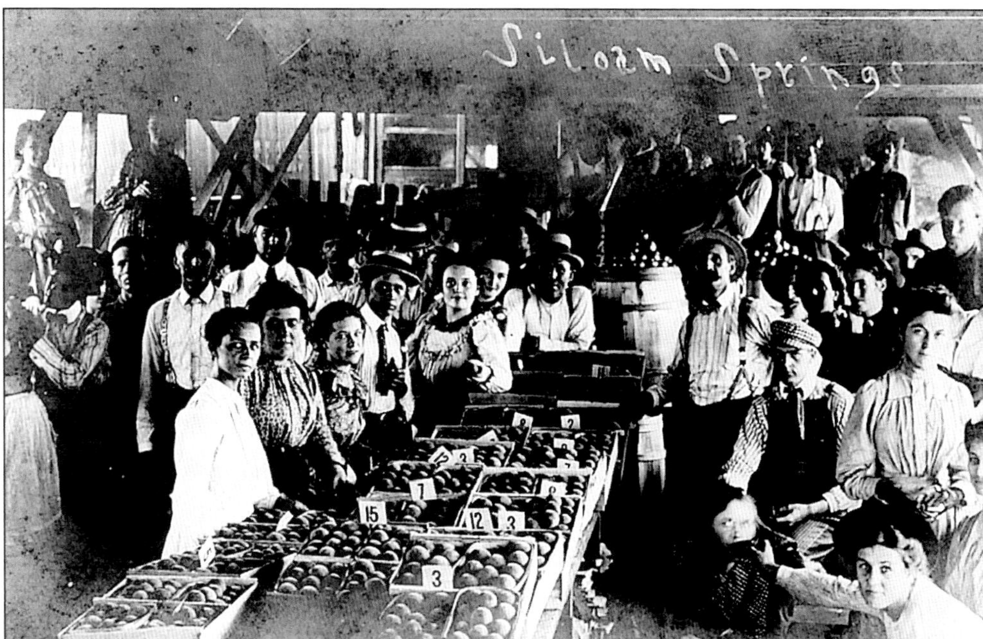

Though not as big a factor in the Siloam Springs economy as in much of Benton county, there were still those who earned a living with apples and peaches. This postcard's photograph was taken inside what was a packing shed. Large barrels of apples are in the background; the lady in the right foreground was stuffing an apple into her friend's mouth, playing to the camera.

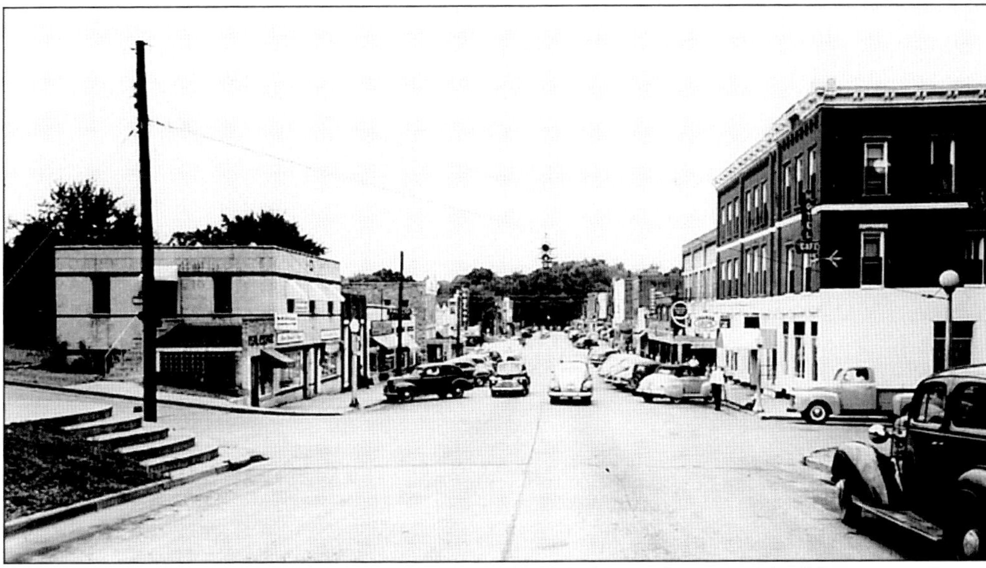

By the 1940s, St. Nicholas Avenue had been renamed Broadway and had been paved with concrete. The Youree Hotel and cafe, seen on page 110 some two decades before, was still operating at the time of this card. The Western Auto Store and the 5, 10, and 25 Cent Store, found on many small-town streets, are located down the block from the hotel. Compare this view with the two earlier ones of St. Nicholas Street, to see what changes the passing years had brought to the small town.

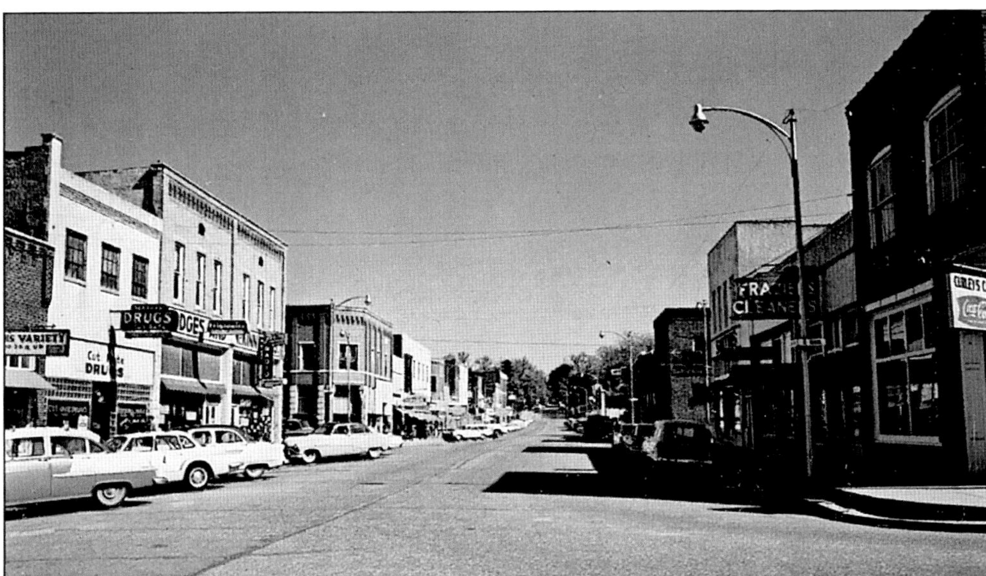

The mid-1950s found the small town of Siloam Springs with blacktopped streets; the Five & Dime store stands to the left, next to Cut Rate Drugs. Across the street is Frazier's Cleaners and Curley's Cafe. Today most of the stores have changed, but Siloam Springs can claim a number of remaining historic buildings that make for a pleasant stroll around the small town. (c. 1955.)

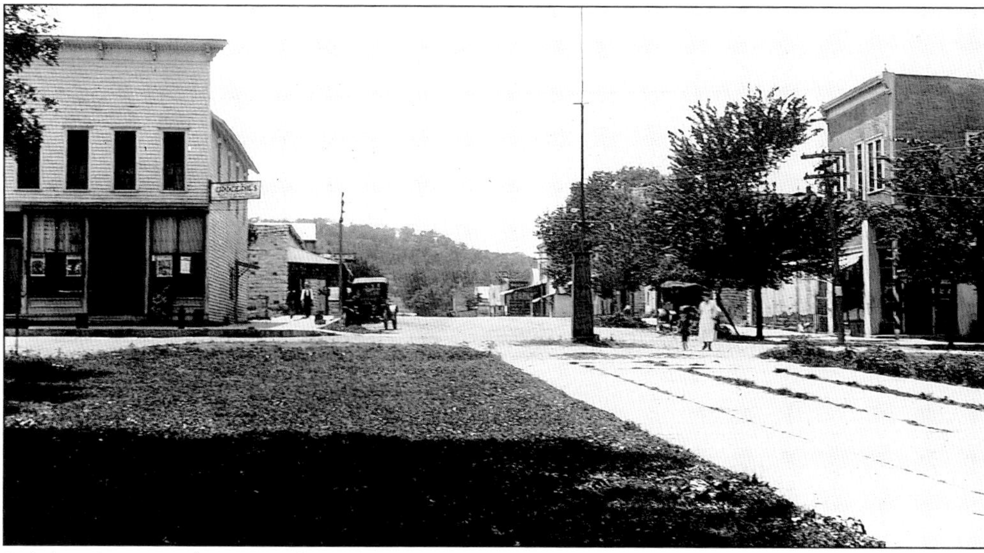

Sulphur Springs, almost touching the Missouri line on today's maps, was laid out in 1885 around four sulphur-bearing springs, and was billed as a resort for "invalids and pleasure seekers." Pictured on the left is a corner grocery store of the *c.* 1915 era; perhaps the Model-T at the curb belonged to a shopper.

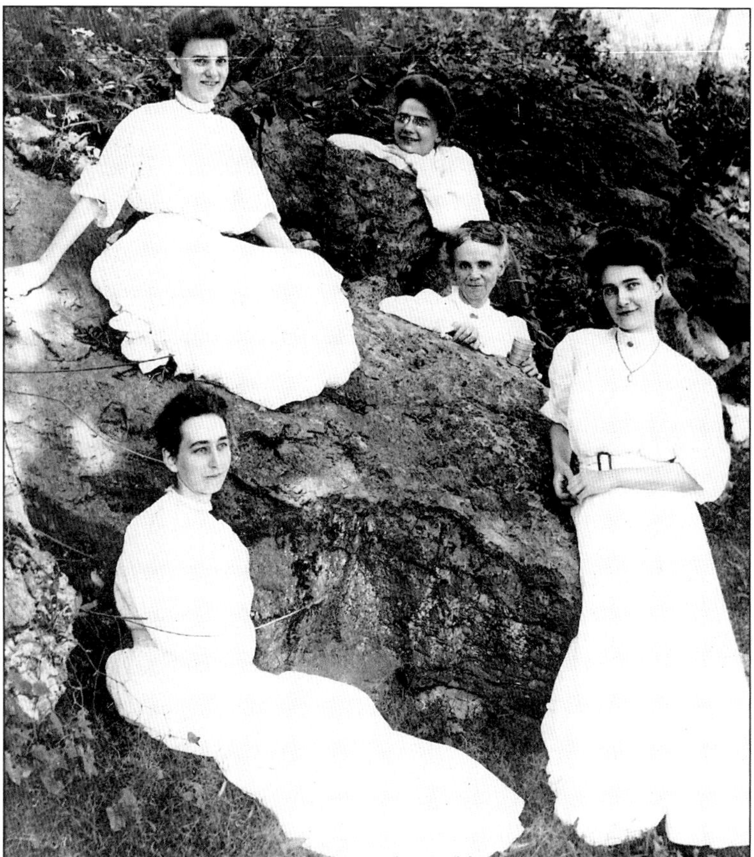

"We have sent ourselves on ahead and hope you are glad to see us" were Mary's words, penned on a card upon which she posed for a memento to send to her mother in Texarkana. Consider what a different world these women had been born into, in the late 19th century, and what issues might have been on their minds as they enjoyed a vacation in 1906 in the resort town of Sulphur Springs.

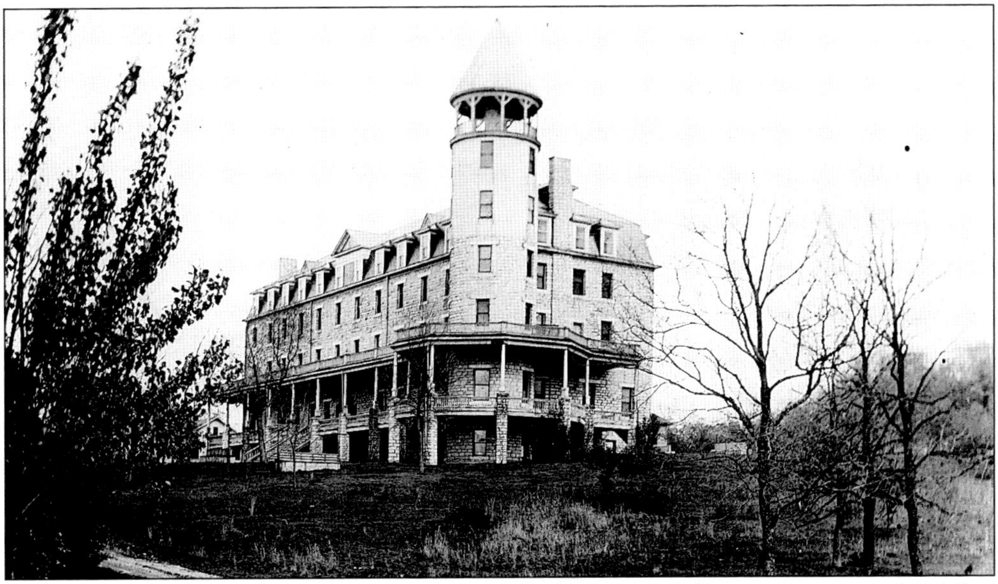

The Kihlberg Hotel was opened on May 9, 1909, high on a hill over the town of Sulphur Springs. For several years it was reportedly the largest hotel in northwest Arkansas. In later years the property was acquired by John Brown University; the upper level was removed after fire damage in the late 1930s. Today the single-story building, with basement, stands on the hill, with only a shell of its formerly imposing grandeur; the building houses a wholesale bakery operation. (c. 1915.)

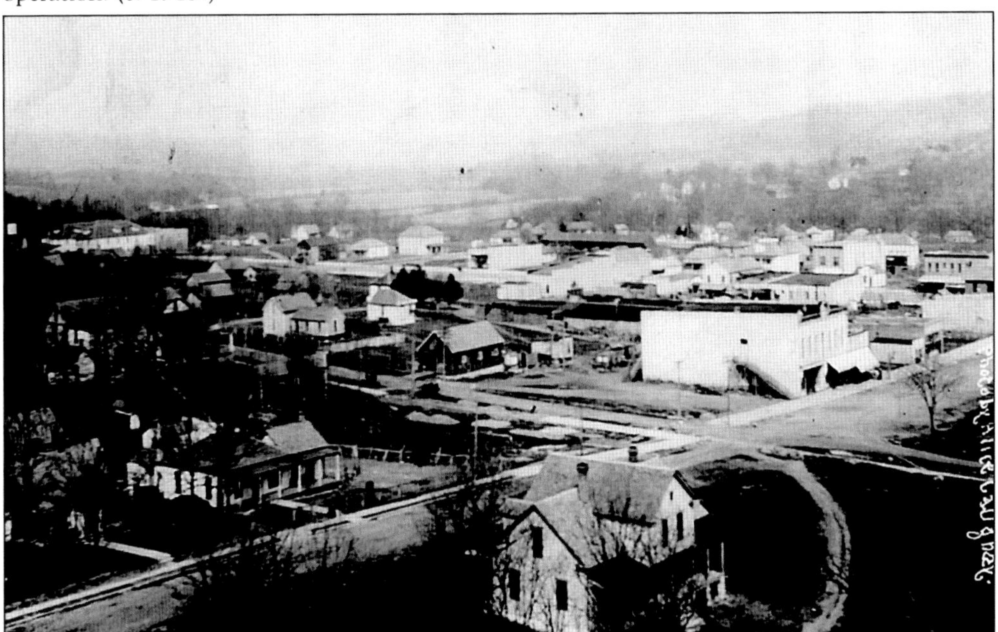

The view from the Kihlberg Hotel's tower was perhaps the most panoramic in Benton County. From the hotel's hilltop location, the entire town of Sulphur Springs was laid out. While the hotel guests gazed down, the residents of the town likely gazed up as they went about their daily chores, perhaps envying those with the means to summer in what looked like a storybook castle. The sender of the card wrote in 1910, "Sulphur is pretty dull."

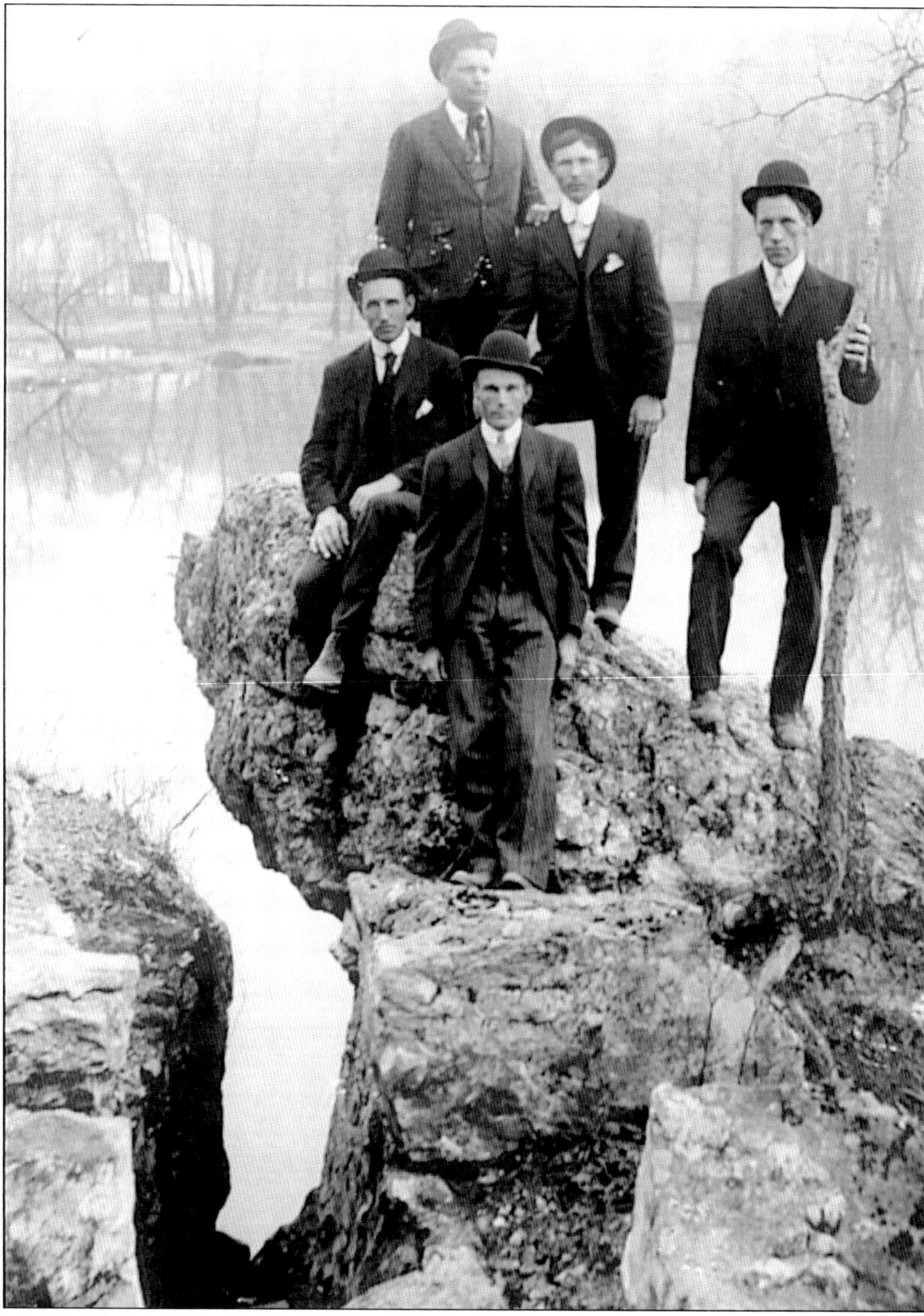

"Hello old Sop—what do you think of this bunch of Arkansawers?" was the 1910 greeting to a friend in Kansas. The photo was taken against one of the most popular backdrops in the Sulphur Springs area. The rock formation extending above one of the spring-fed lakes was a natural place for groups to pose. These well-dressed men had gathered on what seems to have been a misty day in winter of early spring.

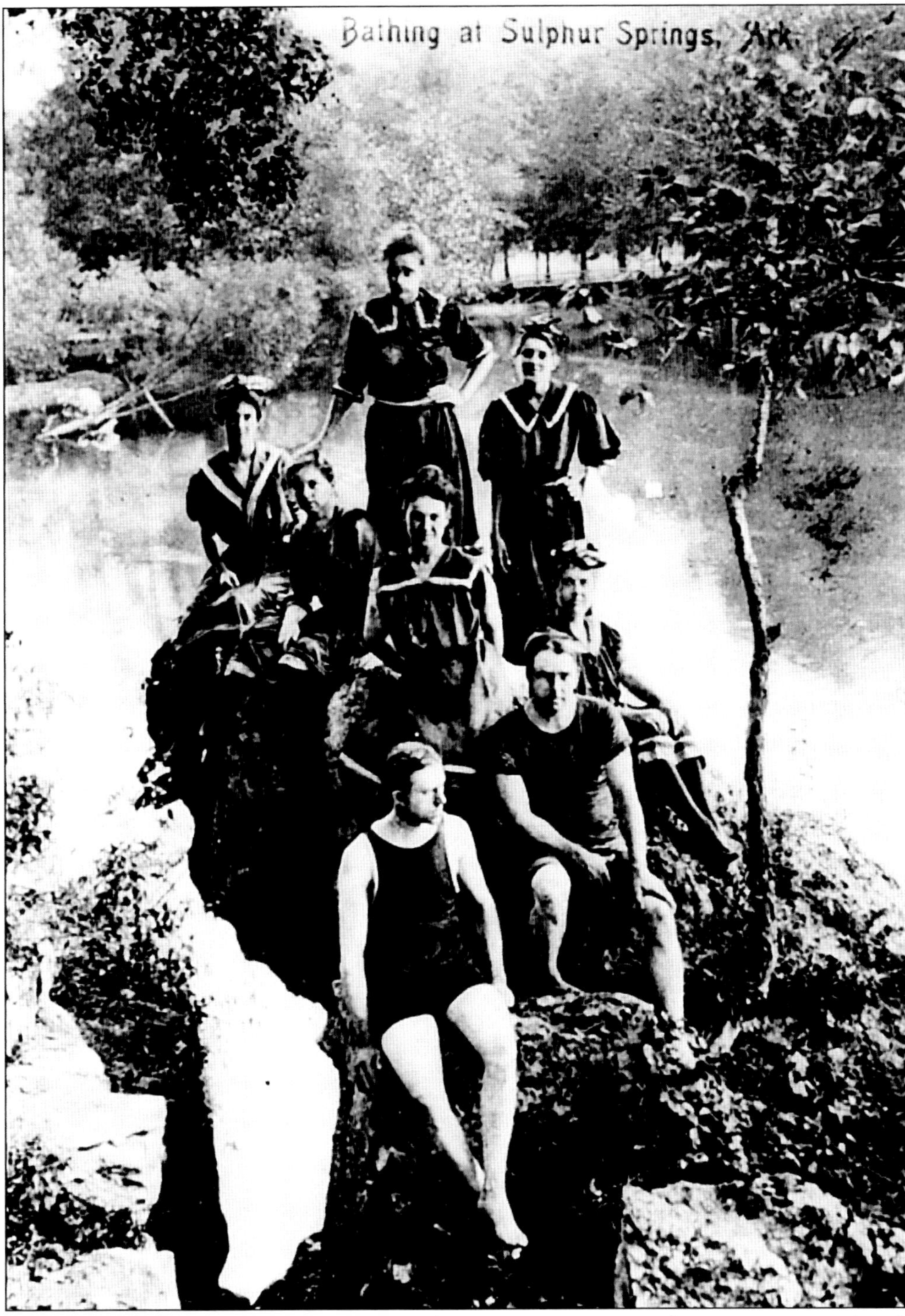

The same rock formation seen in winter on the opposite page is seen here in a summer view. It had drawn a group of visitors clad in bathing suits, taking a break from the water to pose on the landmark rock. The card offers ample evidence that bathing attire has changed greatly since the c. 1910 era of this postcard.

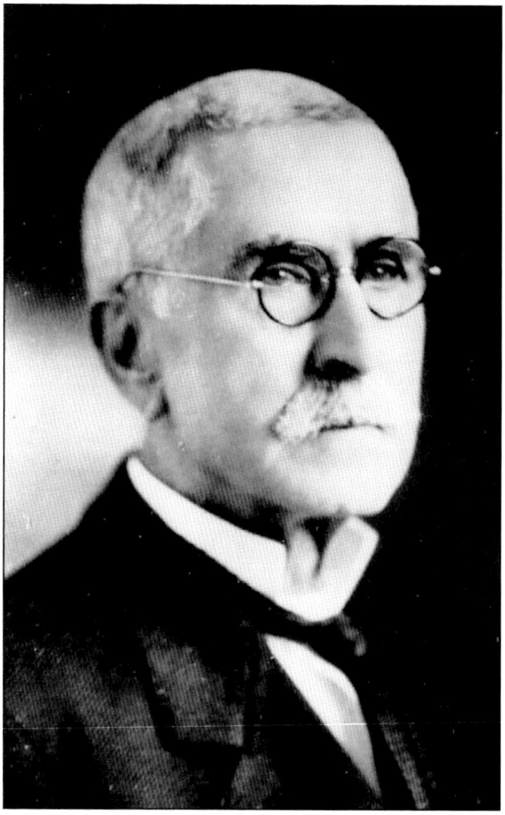

One of the most eccentric characters in Arkansas history was William Hope "Coin" Harvey, who moved to Benton County shortly before the turn of the century. Harvey's career up until that time gave evidence of a financial wizardry in publishing and mining, as well as talent in the law (he had passed the bar at age 19). This background gave Harvey the means to buy 320 acres, 5 miles outside of Rogers. Harvey had come to the hills of Arkansas to retire, a bitter man after having campaigned unsuccessfully to replace the nation's gold standard with silver. The nickname of "Coin" came from his writings on the subject, and it was by that name that he was most widely known. Harvey was convinced the banking system would collapse soon and ruin the world. He chose to retreat to Arkansas, and undertook the establishment of a resort called Monte Ne, which reportedly meant "mountain water." (Photo courtesy of the Arkansas History Commission.)

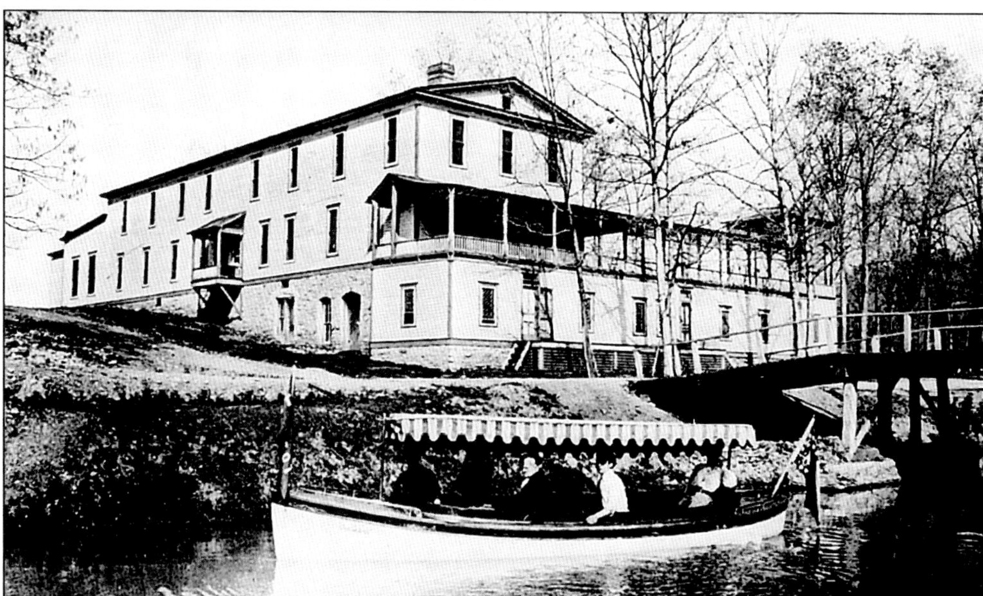

The people of nearby Rogers looked on at first with amusement and soon with amazement, as Coin Harvey's resort of Monte Ne began to take shape. By 1901, the first of several hotels had opened; soon lagoons were built to ferry guests around in launches like this one, seen below the Hotel Monte Ne, the first tourist accommodation to open at the resort.

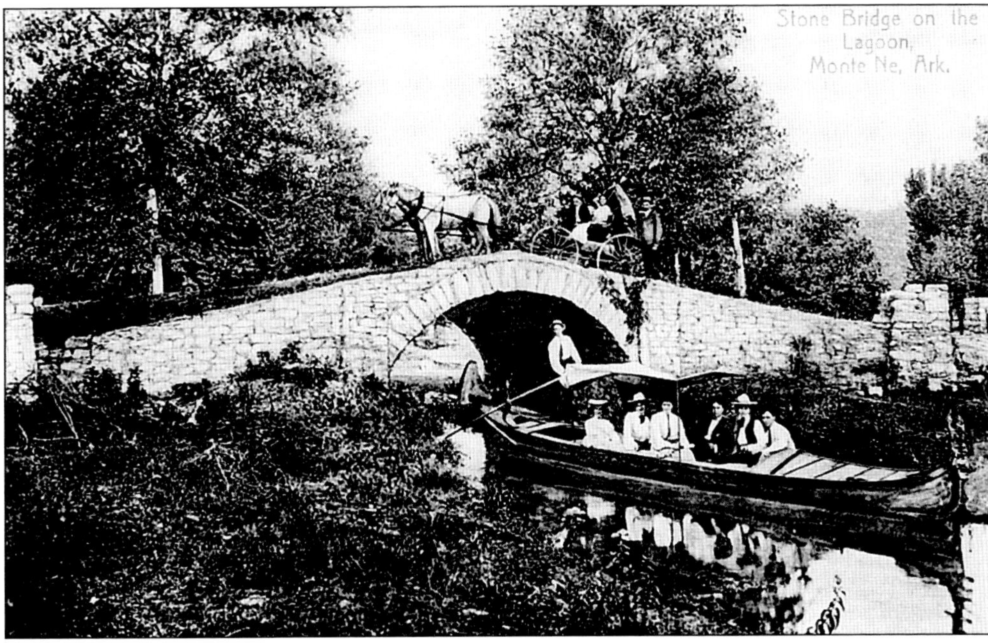

Harvey soon added to his fleet of watercraft several genuine gondolas imported from Italy, poled by men like the one standing at the rear of the boat. The arched stone bridge was one of several built to enhance the resort. The bridges and boats were frequent postcard subjects.

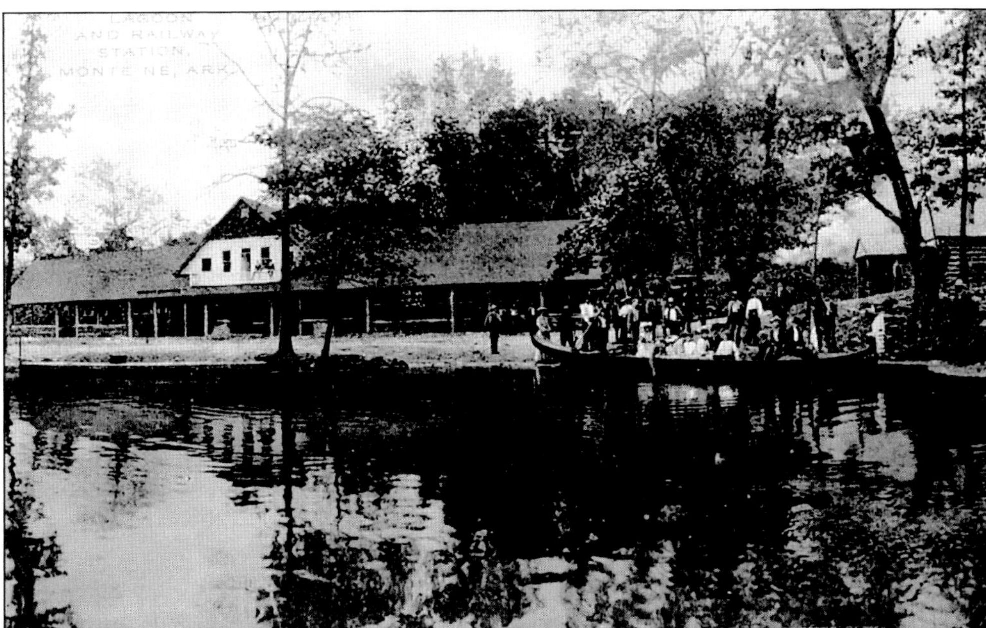

To further the development of his resort, Coin Harvey spent $25,000 to develop his own 5-mile long railroad; it led from the town of Lowell to a train station he erected beside this man-made lagoon at Monte Ne. The gondola docked to the right would often ferry guests across the lagoon, where they would register at one of the resort hotels. With Fayetteville and the University of Arkansas only 20 miles distant, Monte Ne proved a popular retreat for students on holiday.

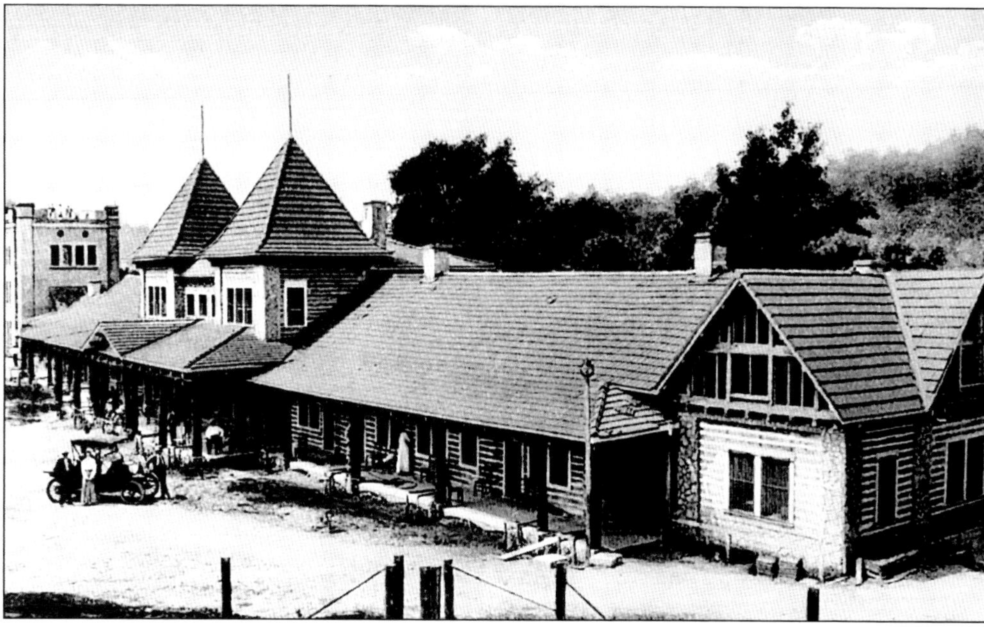

Coin Harvey continued to expand Monte Ne with a passion, especially by building hotels. Two of the best known were these log hotels, called "Rows." Each was 300 feet in length and had red tile roofs. On the back of the Oklahoma Row card (above), a college student wrote around 1910, "Had a real nice time, we had an extra seat in the auto, wish you had been here." Seen below, around 1907, is the companion hotel, Missouri Row, in a card that shows off both its length and a number of guests. Each of the hotels had 42 rooms, all with fireplaces. Servant quarters were located in the basement of each building. Harvey had plans for two more of the "rows," but these never came to pass.

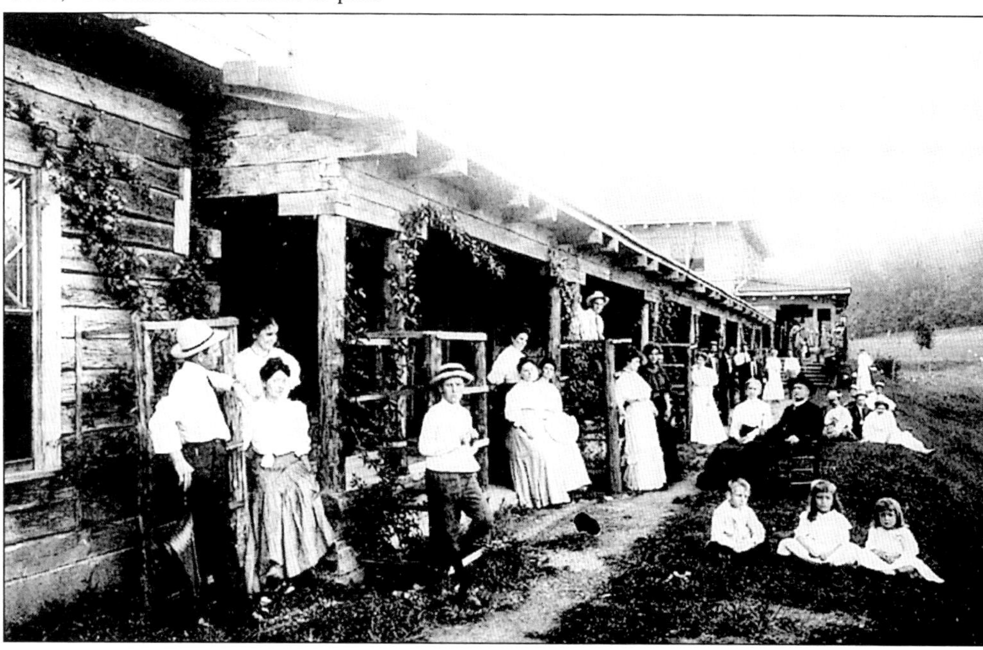

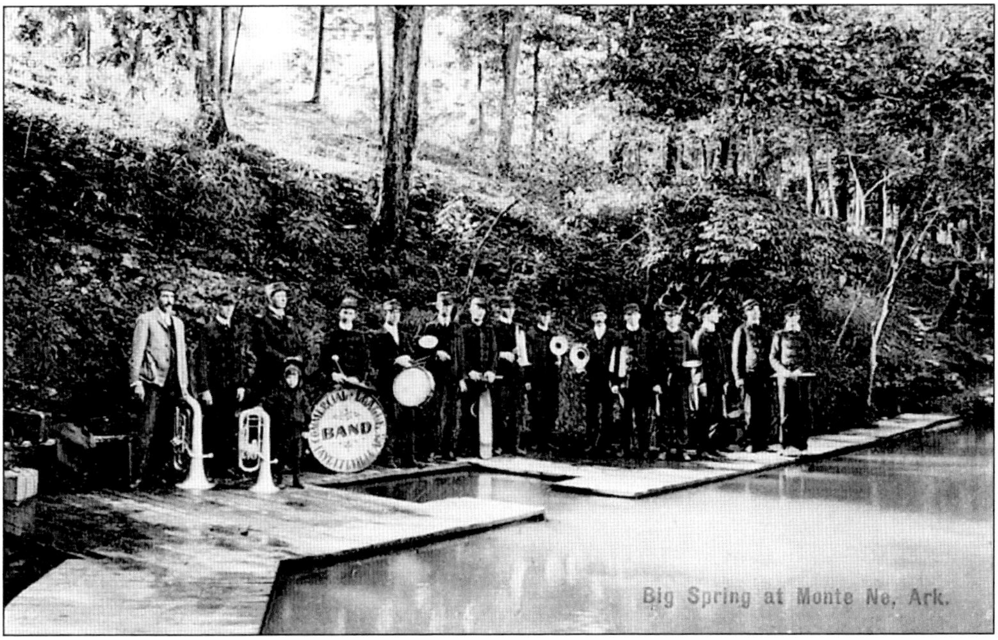

"This is quite a pleasant place. I have not heard this band but can imagine some things" were the 1910 words on a card picturing the visiting Commercial League Band from Fayetteville. The band had posed next to Big Spring, one of the natural features that added to the resort's appeal as guests watched ducks glide across its surface.

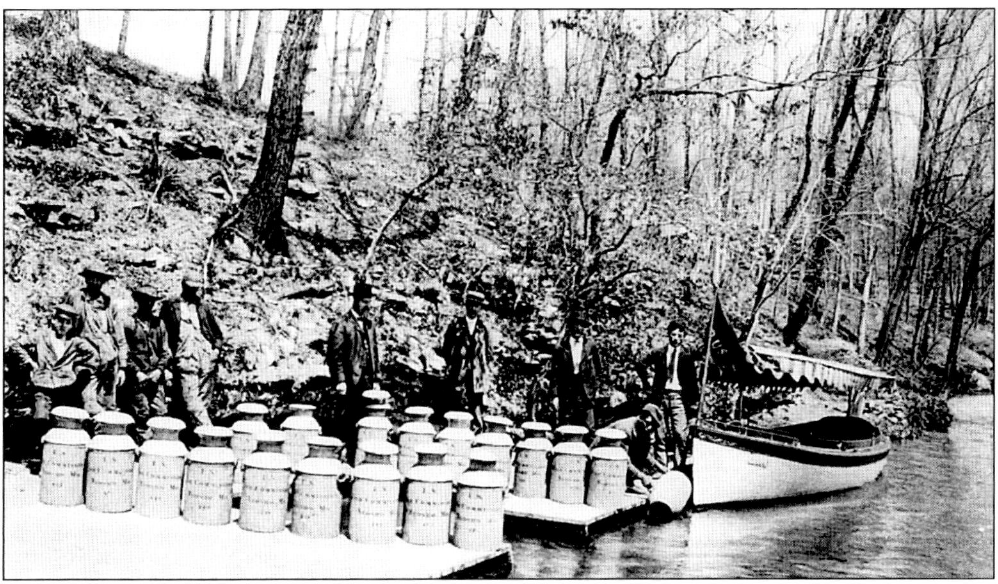

In his attempts to appeal to as many interests as possible, Coin Harvey arranged for the U.S. Fish Commission, an agency of the federal government, to stock rainbow trout in the cold spring waters of Monte Ne. The fish appear to have been transported by train, in cans from a hatchery in Neosho, Missouri. A man stoops near the boat, releasing fish into their new home.

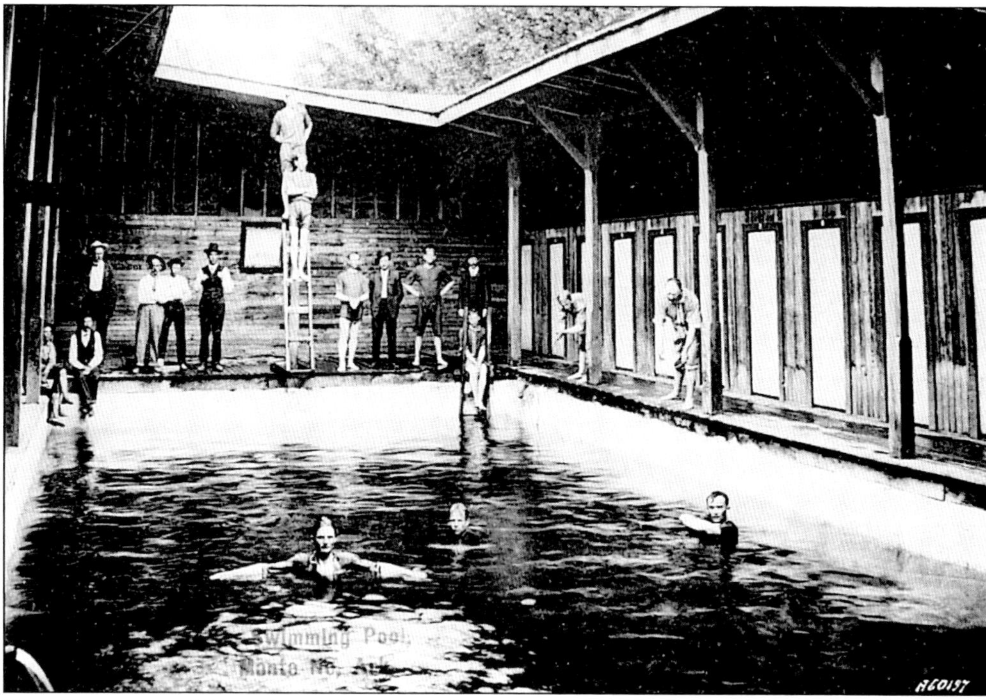

Coin Harvey would build a golf course at his resort, which was a novelty for the region and which certainly caught the attention of locals. However, it is likely that even more talk ensued when he built the first indoor swimming pool in the region, enclosed in walls but with the roof opened to the sky. Some of the locals, hearing tales of nightly swimming parties, reportedly expressed shock and disapproval when they heard that men and women actually swam together. In the view below is seen the bathhouse erected by Harvey, his attempt to capture some of the appeal of the bathhouses at Hot Springs—although Monte Ne had only cold water mineral springs. (Postcard at top *c.* 1909.)

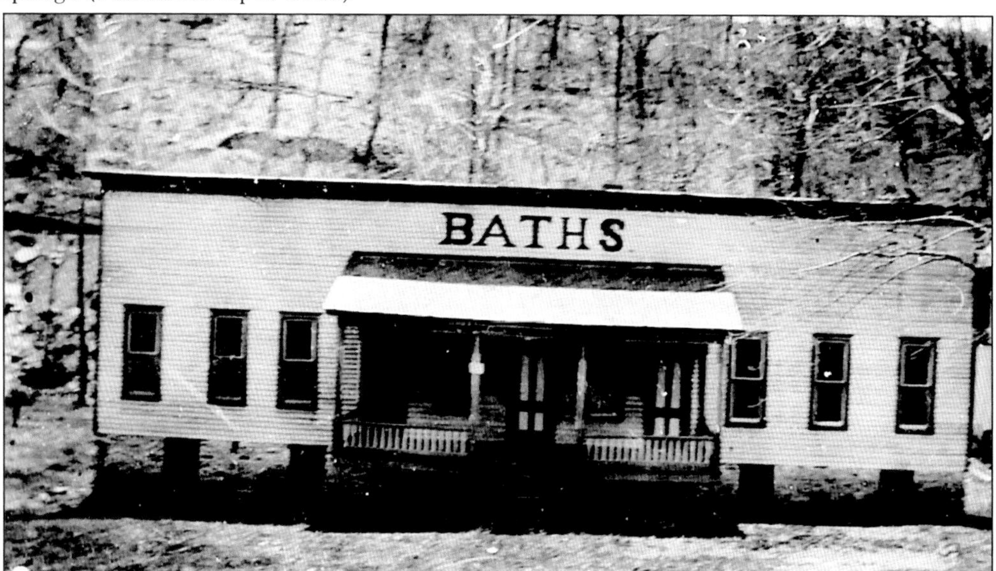

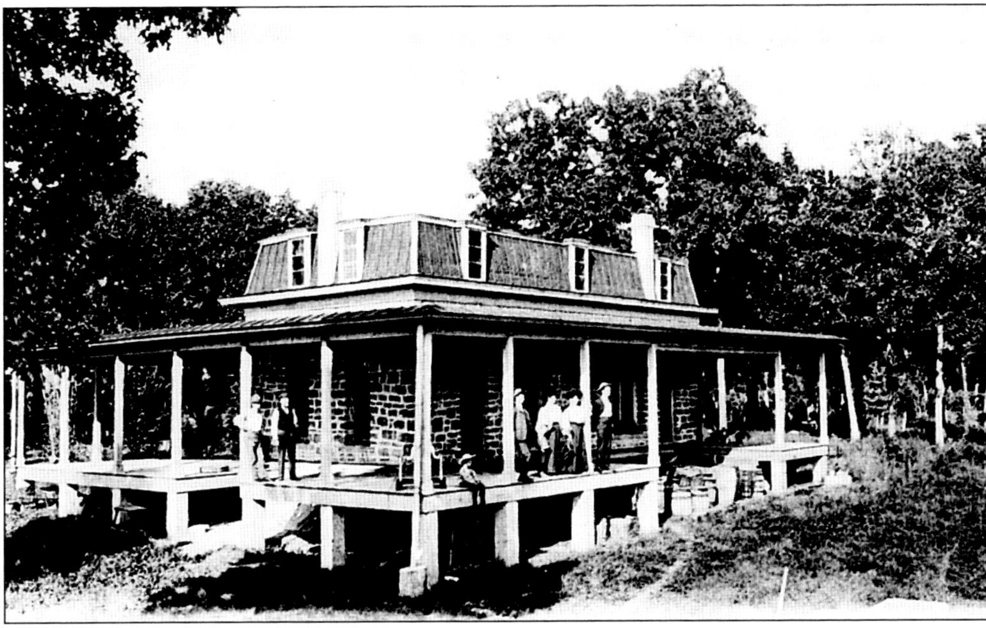

Fine meals were served at the resort of Monte Ne, especially in the grand dining room of the Oklahoma Row hotel, where dinner was often accompanied by music of a full orchestra. At the table, along with specially engraved Monte Ne-patterned silver, would have often been found wines from the Vinola Wine Ranche, located at the resort. The cellar beneath the building held barrels of wine and racks of bottles awaiting a special occasion. When Prohibition came to Arkansas in 1915, the local man who had cultivated the grapes lost interest, and the vineyards died out. (Both cards c. 1908.)

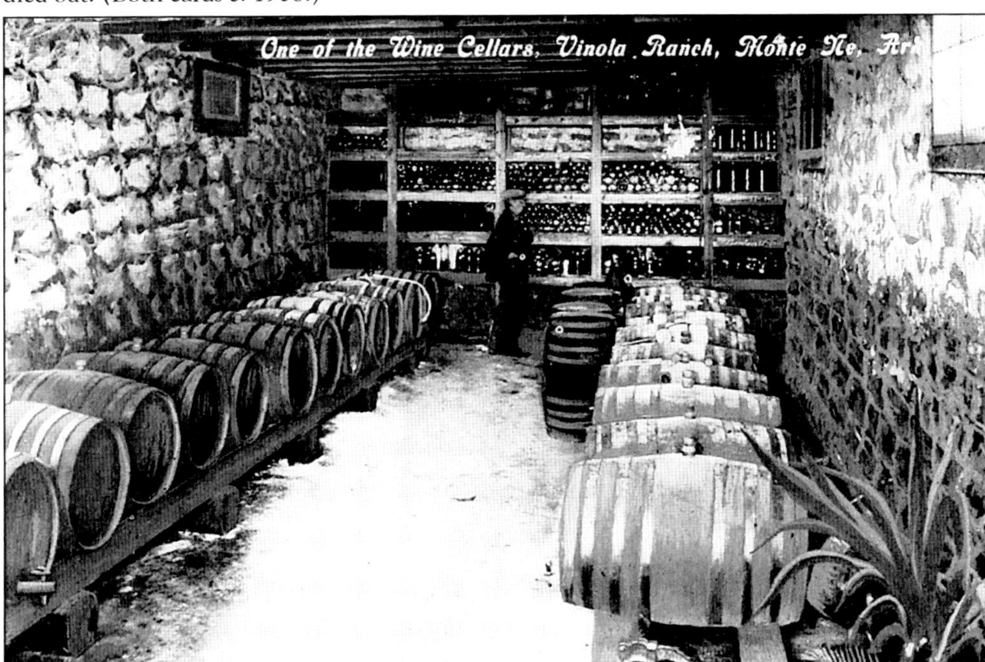

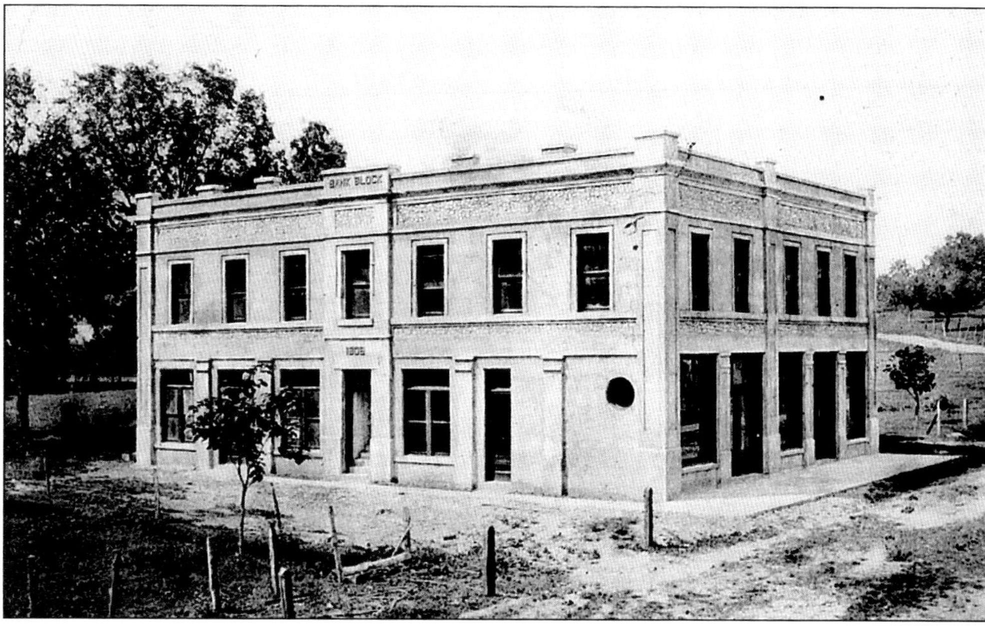

Coin Harvey railed with a fervent passion against banks, and he wrote much about the evils of the nation's financial and banking system; he even advocated closing all the banks. It is quite ironic, and some might say hypocritical, that Harvey built his own bank at Monte Ne that served not only his needs but those of the surrounding community. The bank closed in 1914 and the building later fell into ruin.

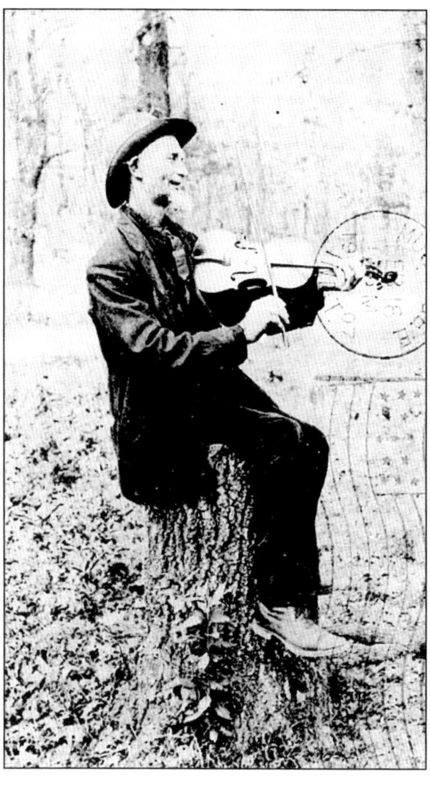

Coin Harvey once sponsored an Old Fiddlers' Contest for the amusement of his guests, and drew scores of mostly elderly men to compete in the contest. Tom Morgan, a writer, photographer, and producer of postcards, came from nearby Rogers to witness the event. Morgan spied a man whom he felt was the most photogenic of the group, George Wisely, who sported a long white beard. When it was discovered Wisely couldn't play a note of music, Morgan borrowed a fiddle and posed him anyway; the resulting photo became a very popular postcard. (c. 1908.)

Coin Harvey's fortunes and that of Monte Ne began a steady decline as the years went by. His marriage crumbled, his beloved son Hal was killed in a train wreck, and financial problems began to threaten his dream—but he didn't give up easily. Harvey saw, in 1915, how the automobile was going to change the recreational patterns of the region. He sought, with other parties, to form the Ozarks Trails Association, in order to link a system of roads in Arkansas, Missouri, Oklahoma, and Kansas that would promote tourist destinations in the four states. The road maps published by the group were reportedly the first highway maps ever printed. Along the roads, the "O.T." marking emblem was placed on telephone poles, rocks, and almost any flat surface. Harvey candidly admitted, "My personal interest in the Ozark Trails is that they all lead to Monte Ne."

Harvey continued to expound on his financial theories, particularly attacking the banking system, and wrote several books, including one on "character building," for which he donated thousands of copies to be used in the public schools. In 1917 his railroad link to Monte Ne was removed, and the resort became a lonely refuge for a troubled man. Harvey set out in the 1920s to build a great pyramid on the banks of the lagoon, with which he wanted to inscribe the words, "Go below and find the cause of the death of civilization." He intended to place in the pyramid's vault copies of his books that predicted the end of the world and its financial ruin. However, the work was halted before its completion, as Harvey's funds were depleted.

Coin Harvey had one last hurrah. He had been publishing a small paper called the *Liberty Bell* in 1930, which expounded his ideas for ending the Great Depression. From this effort came the Liberty Party, a political organization for which Harvey obtained the 1932 nomination for President of the United States. He had been nominated by 786 delegates from 25 states who converged on Monte Ne for the convention—remarkable among other reasons because Harvey was now 80 years old, a testament to his power to move people even in old age.

Harvey, of course, lost the election when FDR was elected to his first term, but the old gentleman did receive 53,425 votes, more than half coming from the state of Washington. He received just over 1,000 votes in Arkansas. Today his photo rests in the Smithsonian Institution, along with those of all other recorded candidates for President of the United States. Harvey had married his secretary in 1929, in a relationship that had been a source of local and national gossip for some time. After the election he returned to his beloved Monte Ne, where he died on a bitterly cold February day in 1936. He was buried in a concrete tomb, near his partially built pyramid, next to the Monte Ne lagoon.

The quiet Monte Ne valley and the remnants of Coin Harvey's resort remained a curiosity for many years. Missouri Row burned in the 1950s, and Oklahoma Row housed an art gallery for a time. The Joyzelle Girls' Camp was the most prominent feature in Monte Ne from 1923 to 1955. The camp taught girls art and modern dance, while allowing swimming and other outdoor activities. Harvey had been welcomed as an honored guest at the camp prior to his death. The 19 cabins and the many activities drew girls from a four-state area for some 30 years.

In the end, what might have been among Harvey's worst nightmares eventually came to pass—the civilization whose demise he once predicted came to destroy his beloved valley. The once-distant White River crept over Monte Ne with the rising waters of Beaver Lake in the 1960s, as the federal government worked tirelessly in a misguided effort to dam every free-flowing stream in Arkansas. Harvey's tomb was relocated to higher ground, and there he lies today, near the flooded dream he had poured his life into building. Over the years an occasional drought has exposed the partially completed pyramid and amphitheater, but then the rains come and the ghost of the complex, ever-driven man slips back beneath the watery gloom.

The saga of Coin Harvey and his beloved resort is but one of the many intriguing, romantic tales to be found in the beautiful northwestern part of the state of Arkansas. As life moves on and the area increases in population, economic diversification, and cultural diversity, new tales are being lived out among its people. May the old stories of the land and its people not be forgotten, even as the stories of a new generation and a new millennium are being written.

INDEX